Passions of the Cut Sleeve

Passions of the Cut Sleeve,

The Male Homosexual Tradition in China

BRET HINSCH

UNIVERSITY OF CALIFORNIA PRESS
Berkeley   Los Angeles   Oxford

*The woodblock prints that appear at the beginning of
each chapter are taken from a Qing-dynasty edition of*
Pinhua baojian.

University of California Press
Berkeley and Los Angeles, California

University of California Press, Ltd.
Oxford, England

First Paperback Printing 1992

Library of Congress Cataloging-in-Publication Data

Hinsch, Bret.
    Passions of the cut sleeve: the male homosexual tradition in China / Bret Hinsch.
        p.   cm.
    Includes bibliographical references.
    ISBN 0-520-06720-7 (alk. paper)
    ISBN 0-520-07869-1 (alk. paper–ppb.)
    1. Homosexuality, Male–China–History.   2. Lesbianism–China–
History.   I. Title.
HQ76.2.C5H56   1990
306.76'62'0951–dc20
                                                                89-49037
                                                                CIP

Printed in the United States of America
2   3   4   5   6   7   8   9

To my loving family

How violent are the seasons of love and hatred.
By observing the fate of Mizi Xia, we can guess
what will happen to favorites of later times. "Even
the future a hundred ages hence may be foretold."

Sima Qian

Contents

Note on Chinese Transliteration and Pronunciation

In this book, Chinese words are spelled according to a system known as *pinyin*, which was invented by the Chinese for the romanization of their language and is now used in mainland China. To this end, I have changed other romanizations to pinyin when quoting the translations of other scholars. For living Taiwan authors who write in English, I use their own preferred style in romanizing their names; for living or recent Taiwan authors whose works are in Chinese, I render their names according to pinyin but include the Wade-Giles equivalents.

For the convenience of readers familiar with the old Wade-Giles romanization rather than pinyin, the following chart may be helpful in converting between the two systems.

Pinyin	*Wade-Giles*	*Pinyin*	*Wade-Giles*
b	p	q	ch'
c	ts', tz'	r	j
ch	ch'	si	szu
d	t	t	t'
g	k	x	hs
ian	ien	yi	i
j	ch	you	yu
k	k'	z	ts
ong	ung	zh	ch
p	p'	zi	tzu

Moreover, because several pinyin values differ significantly from those of English, use of the following list should ensure that names, even if mispronounced, are at least pronounceable.

$$c = ts$$
$$q = ch$$
$$x = sh$$
$$z = dz$$
$$zh = j$$

Note, too, that throughout this book the term *sui* has been translated simply as "years old," even though actual ages might differ slightly between Chinese and Western reckoning.

Table of Chinese Dynasties

For convenience' sake, this book has been organized by chapter according to dynasty. The rise and fall of dynasties merely indicated political changes, with social, cultural, and intellectual changes occurring independently. Readers should therefore not see these divisions as descriptive of changes in the manifestations of homosexuality, which varied so according to factors such as geography and social class that any strict scheme of periodization must fail as overly simplistic. Periodization according to dynasty does, however, allow the state of homosexuality in a particular era to be more easily understood in relation to other events of the period.

Chinese Dynasties
Shang 1766?–1122? B.C.
Zhou 1122?–256 B.C.
    Western Zhou era 1122?–771 B.C.
    Eastern Zhou era 770–256 B.C.
        Spring and Autumn period 722–481 B.C.
        Warring States period 403–221 B.C.
Qin 221–207 B.C.
Western Han 206 B.C.–A.D. 9
Xin 9–23 A.D.
Eastern Han 25–220
Three Kingdoms 220–280

Six Dynasties 266–589
Sui 581–618
Tang 618–907
Five Dynasties 907–960
Northern Song 960–1127
Northern Conquest Dynasties 916–1234
Southern Song 1127–1279
Yuan 1264–1368
Ming 1368–1644
Qing 1644–1912

高品

Acknowledgments

Relatively little is understood about homosexuality outside the American and Western European contexts. In particular, homosexuality in China has been virtually ignored by both East and West. This paucity of reliable scholarly predecessors left me with as many problems as possibilities. Most fundamental was the basic form this study should take. Every person who has given me advice has had different expectations. The sinologist demands detailed footnotes crammed with scholarly minutiae. The historian looks for a comprehensive account of the subject through the dizzying sweep of Chinese history. The anthropologist expects comparisons that draw from the ethnographies of obscure cultures. The sex researcher hopes for a grand new explanation of the nature of human sexual behavior. And advocates for that most hapless of creatures, the general reader, plead for compassion in making the treacherous shoals of unpronounceable names and little-known dynasties more easily navigable.

With so many conflicting expectations, it is inevitable that this book should disappoint as much as it pleases. I have been constrained by finite space, the idiosyncratic nature of available sources, and my own scholarly limitations. My only hope is that this book will provide a shaky first step toward understanding a complex and important aspect of the Chinese past. Along the way, we might even learn something about ourselves.

This path has been made much easier by those many kind friends and colleagues who have shared their time and expertise. I see this book as the result of an ongoing dialogue. Without constant advice and encouragement, it would never have been written. Most important was the help I received on bibliography. Unlike many fields of Chinese history in which considerable prior groundwork has been accomplished by Chinese and Japanese scholars, I often found myself lacking the usual clues on where to find even basic sources. This study has been considerably enriched by the help of those who shared their knowledge of relevant books and articles. Among these I would like to extend my special thanks to David Woo, Kang-i Sun Chang, Paul Schalow, Ch'iu Sheng-wen, and Chao Jun-hai. Wayne Dynes and the Gay Academic Union of New York City deserve my gratitude for exceptionally useful and extensive bibliographic help and all manner of practical support.

William Skinner, Richard L. Davis, Rebecca Weiner, Gary Leupp, Joseph A. Marcus, Marc Pilven-Hall, and Rishona Zimring all made suggestions that greatly enhanced this book, enriching it in style as well as content. John Boswell and Louis Crompton both dispensed sage advice that has given me a deeper understanding of the importance as well as the potential perils of researching this controversial topic; I thank them for passing on the fruits of their experience.

My editor, Sheila Levine, and the University of California Press should also be recognized for their sensitive and professional handling of this book. The enormous care that was put into editing and production contributed greatly to the final version.

Finally, Allen Yu deserves beatification for the patience and good will he showed throughout the writing of this book. Lacking this, he will have to settle for my heartfelt thanks.

Introduction

When Western travelers first described Chinese society to their fellow Europeans they lavished ecstatic praise on many aspects of Chinese culture, including efficient government administration, awe-inspiring public works, and the opulent and sophisticated life-styles of the upper classes. Early European commentators even added Chinese moral values to their idealistic panegyric. But one aspect of Chinese society received strident condemnation and scorn from these first adventurers: homosexuality. For them, the popularity of "the abominable vice of sodomy" was an unforgivable flaw in an otherwise admirable society.[1] The sixteenth-century chronicler Galeote Pereira reported, "The greatest fault we do find [among the Chinese] is sodomy, a vice very common in the meaner sort, and nothing strange among the best."[2] The perceptive Jesuit missionary Matteo Ricci related his disgust at the sights he witnessed in Beijing: "There are public streets full of boys got up like prostitutes. And there are people who buy these boys and teach them to play music, sing and dance. And then, gallantly dressed and made up with rouge like women these miserable men are initiated into this terrible vice."[3] Friar Gaspar de Cruz was even more censorious, portraying China as a new Sodom. He composed an apocalyptic tract in which he described earthquakes, floods, and other natural disasters imposed on China by God in retribution for the tolerance shown by the Chinese toward "a filthy abomination, which is that they are so given to the accursed sin of unnatural vice, which is in no wise reproved among them."[4]

These disapproving Westerners were shocked by the perceived ubiquity and deep roots of homosexuality within Chinese culture. They were correct in sensing the existence of a historical tradition of homosexuality in China that dates back to at least the Bronze Age. It gave rise to highly developed expressions, including well-patronized meeting places and an accumulation of literature catering to homosexual tastes. Many times homosexuality acted as an integral part of society, complete with same-sex marriages for both men and women. It spanned a range of social classes, from famed emperors and aristocrats to impoverished laborers. In all of these circumstances, homosexuality serves as a convenient mirror for viewing an intimate area of human experience.

Unfortunately, we are left only tantalizing fragments recording the homosexual experience in China. From one century a poem may survive, while the next yields only a terse biography or legal case. In all periods lacunae outnumber surviving records, making systematic social history almost impossible. Nevertheless, this dearth does not condemn us to ignorance of Chinese homosexuality. Rather than study people, I have been forced to concentrate on the homosexual tradition itself. Because Chinese society has always held both literary pursuits and examples from the past in exceptionally high regard, it becomes possible to discern a homosexual tradition developing through time, with successive authors taking references from previous works and making them relevant to the collective experience of a writer's own time. Even the conceptions of "homosexuality" as a distinct realm of experience had roots in tradition. In general, homosexuality came to be described through reference to famous individuals of ancient times associated with same-sex love. The special nature of the Chinese experience and sources has therefore determined the approach I take to the subject. Rather than studying "homosexuals" or "homosexuality," this book concentrates on reconstructing the Chinese homosexual tradition.

Why should a modern Westerner be interested in understandting the sexual practices of a people far removed in both time and place? In Western-centric terms, this sort of investigation allows us to comprehend the sexual practices of our own culture by providing an alternate, sophisticated panorama of sexual behavior. Although contemporary Westerners are apt to regard our own sexual customs as normal and natural, in fact they often differ from the multitude of sexual views held by the bulk of humankind carelessly lumped together as "non-Western" peoples, as well as from many of the sexual practices considered normative in earlier periods of our history. By carefully examining the sexuality of a people divided from us by time and place, we can better understand and question the caprice implicit in our own social and sexual conventions. For a topic as controversial and misunderstood as homosexuality, this sort of cross-cultural comparison assumes particular importance.

The study of Chinese homosexuality also reveals striking new perspectives on the Chinese themselves. One stereotypical notion that this book should help to dispel is the conception that Chinese in dynastic times conformed to a narrow view of family-based sexuality. Because many scholars of China tend to emphasize the homogeneous aspects of the society, they often ignore the tolerance of diversity present among many peoples and in numerous places throughout Chinese history. The relative toleration of homosexuality by the upper classes, and perhaps among other less-documented social strata as well, stands as proof of this point.

The long duration of tolerance allowed the accumulation of a literature and sense of history that in turn enabled those with strong homosexual desires to arrive at a complex self-understanding. In many periods homosexuality was widely accepted and even respected, had its own formal history, and had a role in shaping Chinese political institutions, modifying social conventions, and spurring artistic creation. A sense of tradition lasted up until this century, when it fell victim to a growing sexual conservatism and the Westernization of morality.

Despite the denouement of the homosexual tradition in our own times, when viewed in a broad historical perspective the record is one of general tolerance toward homosexuality in China. We should note how the West has responded to this and similar examples of sexual tolerance. As Westerners made their way across Asia, they constantly found proof of their own moral excellence. The words of hostile Europeans such as Pereira and de Cruz reveal how travelers from the West were quick to divide the world into a morally virtuous Occident superior to what they saw as the exotic decadence of the Orient.[5] Europeans exalted their own hostilities as examples of moral purity while viewing tolerance of homosexuality as evidence of Oriental moral degeneracy. Thus homosexuality became a focal point for division between China and the West.[6]

Most importantly, homosexuality provides us with a convenient entrée into one of the most intimate, hence central, aspects of existence for the peoples of dynastic China. For example, the influence of family life on all aspects of society acquires new depth when seen from the standpoint of homosexuality. Likewise, homosexuality allows us to view a spectrum of personalities and institutions from a novel perspective. Yet precisely because homosexuality gives us access to the most intimate areas of the Chinese identity, we must take care not to project too much of ourselves onto our subject matter. As recent revisionist historiography has shown, the field of Chinese history in the West has all too often involved an imposition of our own priorities and intellectual frameworks onto a different culture.[7] This flawed approach has long been implicit in many Western studies of China, and occasionally even becomes explicit. For example, Max Weber, patron saint of social scientists, readily admitted that he undertook his monumental studies of Asian society according to a Western intellectual agenda: "These studies do not claim to be complete analyses of cultures, however brief. On the contrary, in every culture they quite deliberately emphasize the elements in which it differs from Western civilization. They are, hence, definitely oriented to the problems which seem important for the understanding of Western culture from *this* view-point."[8]

To avoid the methodological insensitivity of Weber and his intellectual heirs, we must deal carefully with our subject matter. For the topic of sexuality, which almost always evokes deeply held preconceptions while challenging even the most dispassionate reader's basic self-identity, culture-blind objectivity becomes a distant chimera. Nevertheless, we must strive for the difficult goal of understanding Chinese sexuality on its own terms if we are to understand it at all.

I have two main goals for this study: first, systematically to present translations of the most important original sources dealing with the history of the homosexual tradition in China; and second, to present an interpretive framework for understanding the Chinese homosexual tradition that is as free as possible from Western preconceptions. In structure, this book develops along both chronological and topical lines. Although I generally proceed chronologically, the nature of surviving records from each era determines the main points of focus for each period under discussion. Thus my description of ancient history, known primarily from a few official histories, deals with the sexual practices of the uppermost elite; the literature surviving from later periods provides insight into the lives of the literati; and late-imperial sources describe in detail the lives of young male prostitutes and their patrons. By combining these differing perspectives I hope to forge a broad survey of the homosexual tradition.

I do not intend to present all surviving evidence of Chinese homosexuality; such an undertaking would be needlessly vast for an introductory survey and would fill many volumes. Instead I will merely delineate the major forms of sexuality reflected in the evolving homosexual tradition. The continuity of these various practices and concepts, as seen in the variety of historiography and literature that describe them, constitutes the homosexual tradition of China.

Male homosexuality, like all other forms of sexuality in China, inspired few writings relative to other topics, such as the opposing concerns of court intrigue and ethics. In this respect the Chinese case contrasts starkly with the enormous literature on homosexuality from other cultures, such as Greece and Japan. While this relative dearth may seem puzzling in light of the repeated indications that homosexuality was quite open among the upper classes in many periods, the very nature of Chinese literature accounts for this lack. Chinese biography remained tightly tied to the narrow concerns of politics and failed to develop an independent epic tradition centered on the individual apart from society; prose fiction emerged late in imperial history and remained weak and despised compared to other literary traditions; and philosophers discussing questions of human nature and morality dealt only with the public face of virtue. Biography and philosophy therefore generally ignored the world of private experience, such as sex. By discouraging discussion of sex, this overall orientation of Chinese literature complicates the reconstruction of the homosexual past. Fortunately, though, despite these forces working against the recording of homosexual history, enough material remains for us to speak of a homosexual tradition in China.

Indeed, instead of a "homosexual tradition," it might be more accurate to speak of the "male homosexual tradition." Unlike modern Western society, which sees male homosexuality and lesbianism as related, the Chinese viewed them as completely separate forms of sexuality. A Chinese woman reading about the history of homosexual men would not have drawn a parallel with female sexuality. Consequently, what I say about the "homosexual" tradition in China applies only to men. Because Chinese literature was almost always written by men for men, very little documentation survives on lesbian life. I have gathered most of the scanty evidence I have found on the nature of lesbian relations into an appendix. I hope readers do not mistake my intentions in this "separate but unequal" treatment. This is not just a token section thrown in to appease a certain readership: it represents the results of my earnest efforts to uncover the Chinese lesbian past. I sincerely regret my limited success.

We must take care when discussing male homosexuality in the Chinese context, because classical Chinese lacked a medical or scientific term comparable to "homosexuality" or "homosexual." Instead, it was usually discussed using poetic metaphors referring to earlier men or incidents famed for association with homosexuality. Chinese terminology therefore did not emphasize an innate sexual essence, but concentrated rather on actions, tendencies, and preferences. In other words, instead of saying what someone "is," Chinese authors would usually say whom he "resembles" or what he "does" or "enjoys." Another popular way of describing homosexuality was in terms of social roles. Hence early records mentioning men who had sexual relationships with the emperors call them "favorites," a description of their political status, not of an innate sexual essence. Both abstract terminology and actual sexual practices differ between China and our own society, suggesting the need for great caution in dealing with the Chinese case.

Understanding the specific context of homosexuality in China requires us to decide on some specific theoretical tools. Most fundamental among the issues to be determined are the interrelated questions of what constitutes and "causes" homosexuality. On one side, "essentialists" like John Boswell argue that certain people have a predisposition to homosexual acts that transcends cultural conceptions of sexuality and therefore allows us to categorize them according to their sexual essence as homosexual. In the opposing camp, "social constructionists" like Michel Foucault see homosexuality as an artificial construct created by a limited number of cultures, like those of the contemporary West, and therefore lacking objective validity and indiscriminate cross-cultural applicability.

These positions have been portrayed as opposites, with a resulting polarization of studies regarding homosexuality. As a partial remedy to this split we should recall that anthropologists such as Claude Lévi-Strauss often note how human beings tend to divide the organic whole of reality into what sometimes seems like arbitrary polarities. Academic culture is not immune to this love of bifurcation. In fact, these "opposite" conceptions of homosexuality can be reconciled as simply different aspects of a complex phenomenon. The two groups disagree about the etiology of homosexuality because they see the phenomenon of homosexuality differently. Essentialists define homosexuality psychologically, according to inner thoughts, desires, and predispositions. Social constructionists prefer a behavioral definition, viewing homosexuality primarily as an action. Essentialists therefore emphasize factors of biology or psychology that condition individual tendencies, while social constructionists concentrate on how society shapes the expression of individual sexuality. Rather than mutual contradiction, both points of view have heuristic value for the investigation of sexuality on the level both of individuals and of society as a whole.

Next, we must decide on specific models and approaches that can help us understand the particular nature of homosexuality in China. On a physical level, surviving literature depicts anal intercourse as the preferred form of homosexual intercourse. Even in heterosexual contexts, references to anal intercourse appear in early sex manuals,[9] traditional sex jokes, erotic art, and vernacular literature. Among the references to homosexuality that mention explicit sexual positions, anal intercourse is most common by far; references to mutual masturbation, intercrural intercourse, fellatio, and other forms of intercourse are relatively rare.

Going beyond sexual intercourse, on examining social and sexual practices specific to China we can draw two basic sets of complementary roles: dominant/submissive and active/passive. It becomes easier for us to understand the Chinese case when we recall that a similar taxonomy also became the standard convention in both ancient Greece and Rome. The Greeks referred to the active male as *erastēs* and the passive male as *erōmenos*,[10] while the Latin language even contained separate words for male prostitutes, classifying them as active *exoleti* and passive *catamiti*.[11]

The first of these pairs, dominance and submission, was derived from the social standing of each partner. Chinese of dynastic times were acutely sensitized to disparities in social standing. This consciousness conditioned even mundane daily encounters among individuals, and in a matter as important as sexuality it was difficult to ignore. The three main factors determining dominance were gender, age, and status. It is difficult to generalize about gender, since female roles have undergone numerous transformations through the course of Chinese history. Even so, the patriarchal elements usually referred to as "Confucian" or "feudal" by modern scholars generally forced women into social submission; this social inferiority of women affected the condition of men who became identified with female gender. Age provided a more easily evident grounds for hierarchization, with a younger male yielding to an older. As for status, education, employment, family background, wealth, talent, and a multitude of other factors all contributed to the general perception of a man's overall social status, making the term somewhat nebulous. At times age, gender, and status could conflict, a clash of values that might lead a poor elderly peasant to kowtow to a young noblewoman. Despite such complications, age, gender identity, and status were important for apportioning dominant and submissive roles in many social and sexual encounters.

Separate from dominance and submission, but often related to them, is the second division: active and passive sexual roles. Like social dominance, sexual activeness was often based on a sense of hierarchy, with the active partner usually engaging in the penile penetration of the submissive partner. The majority of documentation concerning homosexual intercourse depicts partners taking distinct sexual roles. References to mutual anal penetration and other instances of flexible sexual roles are rare, though this lack of visibility might be due simply to the bias of the original sources.

These two hierarchies, sexual and social, are important to the study of Chinese homosexuality because in many cases they were related: the dominant male was also often the active male. Superior wealth, age, employment, or education could result in domination not only of social intercourse, but of sexual intercourse as well. The institutionalization of male prostitution by boys and low-status actors, among others, helped to solidify sexual roles. In later imperial history, certain types of feminizing clothing and cosmetics became associated with passive sexuality, and wearing them could depress social status. But despite all that this active/passive dichotomy can demonstrate about the influence of sexuality on society, it remains of limited use owing to the coy silence in most Chinese sources as to specific sexual acts. Only with the rise of vernacular literature catering to indelicate popular fancies do we find sufficient explicit evidence to apply this theoretical tool.

Moving from the sexual act to the individual, we find that men often manifested sexuality differently depending on their stage in life. Some men even progressed through a sexual life cycle. Chinese literature shows a tendency for boys and adolescents to take the passive sexual role and for grown men to take an active role. Thus a man's sexual role might change as he grew older. This acceptance of changing sexual roles gave a certain fluidity to the sexual development of an individual male while still allowing a sense of hierarchy within each relationship when hierarchy was desired.

The most clear-cut example of a transformation of sexual roles through a sexual life cycle is provided by the Sambia of Papua New Guinea. As part of initiation rituals into the men's cult that every boy undergoes, a prepubescent boy must regularly fellate boys from the adolescent age group. When this boy passes into the adolescent group, he ceases fellating his elders and is instead

fellated by his prepubescent juniors. Finally, on achieving manhood he marries and enters a heterosexual stage that lasts his entire
adult life.[12] Thus in Sambia society when we look at actions rather
than essence we cannot speak of "homosexual" but must instead
classify individuals according to their particular sexual role at a
particular time in their life cycle.

Many Chinese men experienced similar, though less rigid,
transformations in sexual roles. In addition to changes in
homosexual roles assumed at different stages of a man's life,
Chinese records also describe many men who experienced both
heterosexuality and homosexuality during their lives. Subsequent
chapters will explore the prevalence of bisexuality over exclusive
homosexuality in China. In part, this blindness to gender is attributable to religious, social, and economic factors. Some men un-
doubtedly had sexual intercourse with women because they were
expected to do so, not because they desired it. As with the Sambia,
society's expectations often determined the ways in which
Chinese men manifested their sexual desires.

The general social manifestations of homosexuality in China
can be illuminated through the typology popularized by David
Greenberg, who divides the social expressions of homosexuality
outside of the modern West into four categories: "trans-
generational homosexuality," "trans-genderal homosexuality,"
"class-structured homosexuality," and "egalitarian homosexuality."[13] All four of these paradigms are present to varying de-
grees in the Chinese tradition.

Trans-generational homosexuality, a common form of relationship in many periods of Chinese history, involves the deter-
mination of social and often sexual roles according to relative
age. In general, the older partner takes the active role, with the
younger acting in the passive role. Trans-generational homosexuality often occurs in ritual contexts as part of coming–of–age ceremonies, with the Sambia providing a prime example of this practice. Sexual relationships between men and boys also take place
outside of ritual contexts in many cultures, such as ancient Greece.
Rulers in several societies, among them the Mamlukes of medieval

Egypt and chiefs of the Big Namba, even included boys in their harems.[14] We see the similar appearance of boys kept for sexual purposes in the households of Chinese rulers and other wealthy men. Since dealings between boys and older men in China usually involved a gap in economic standing as well as age, prostitution often resulted. Consequently, we must consider many aspects of trans-generational homosexuality in China in terms of class-structured homosexual relations as well.

In trans-gendered homosexuality, one partner acts and even dresses as a woman, thereby allowing the relationship to be structured according to masculine/feminine roles. The best-known example of this practice is represented by the Native American *berdache*, a man who would dress as a woman and take on a female identity, usually as part of a shamanistic cult.[15] Most male *berdaches* limited themselves exclusively to passive homosexual intercourse, taking as partners men of a "masculine" gender identity rather than other "feminine" *berdaches*. Similar examples of trans-gendered homosexuality can be seen in other societies that include ritualized homosexuality as part of religion, from Mesopotamian male temple prostitutes to Paleo-Siberian shamans.[16]

Homosexuality in historic China was usually not ritualized or made a component of religion, as it was in many kinship-structured societies. Consequently, the Chinese lacked the basic impetus for institutionalized trans-gendered homosexuality, with only the stylized world of the theater promoting female identities for some men. As a result, trans-gendered homosexuality in China mainly occurred among some eunuchs who happened to favor other men, male actors who played female roles, and a small minority of men who simply preferred taking on a female gender identity.

Class-structured homosexuality is made possible by the division of society into unequal social classes, a condition that existed for most of Chinese history. Inequality of wealth allows members of one class to purchase the sexual services of another. Prostitution exemplifies class-structured homosexuality, and it functioned in China much as in the West. In addition, Chinese society experienced the rise of "favoritism," which resembled prostitution in that lower-status men accepted favors from those of higher status, and yet differed in that the favors were often more subtle in form than simple cash gifts. For example, many emperors lavished offices and titles on beloved courtiers.

The last category in this typology is egalitarian homosexuality. Under this form of sexual expression, active/passive roles do not exist, are unstable, or lack reference to social status. Egalitarian homosexuality is frequent among adolescents, as well as in societies with strict segregation based on gender or age. In other cases, sexual relationships among male equals are simply considered acceptable without any extraneous factors being necessary, such as among the Tapirape of Brazil and in the contemporary West.[17] In China, egalitarian homosexuality appears in the account of adolescent love in *Dream of the Red Chamber* (*Honglou meng*) and in some literati friendships. Rulers also often rewarded their favorites profusely with high office and large amounts of land and money, with the side effect of lessening the social gap between them.

Other forces at work within society could encourage egalitarianism as well. The Chinese language is relatively egalitarian, especially compared with other Asian languages such as Javanese and Japanese, in which inflections and the very lexicon are continually adjusted according to the relative social positions of the speaker and the person addressed. Group organizations and communities often emphasized the equality of members through ritual and ideology. And friendship itself has long been treasured in China, often allowing for a breakdown of social barriers whether the friends were refined literati or coarse laborers. Perhaps among the silent masses outside of this study—two peasants in the same village, fellow sailors on a grain barge drifting down the Yangzi, two apprentices in the same guild—their love might have been expressed as the love of comrades.

Having put forward all of these theoretical tools, we find ourselves with an impressive array of useful models: the sexual life cycle, division of roles as active/passive and dominant/

submissive, and a four-part typology of the forms of homosexuality as trans-generational, trans-genderal, class-structured, and egalitarian. Of course, these models lack absolute applicability or value and are intended only as general paradigms for helping to categorize and understand the Chinese homosexual tradition in all its complexity. But by attempting to comprehend the spectrum of Chinese sexuality on its own terms, rather than simply forcing our own practices and preconceptions upon it, we can begin to appreciate an important dimension of Chinese civilization.

In the end, I hope that the reader will gain an impression of the enormous diversity of the forms of homosexual life in China. Romance and lewdness, tolerance and violence, power and poverty—all were part of the intricate tapestry of human lives and passions that came together because of homosexuality. The area I cover, geographic and temporal, is vast, the amount of surviving information about this enormous expanse, minuscule. At best I hope to recreate a few fleeting glimpses of the human lives hiding behind the yellowed pages that remain our tenuous links to earlier times. The incalculable diversity of China frustrates this task: an emperor and peasant who both experienced love for another man would have had little else in common. But it is precisely because the homosexual tradition cut across all barriers that it presents us with an invaluable way to comprehend the complexity of the Chinese past.

颜仲清

1

Peaches, Pillows, and Politics

Zhou Dynasty (1122 to 256 B.C.)

Like so many aspects of Chinese culture, the origins of the homosexual tradition are both ancient and obscure. Mythology provides an aesthetically attractive if factually unreliable means of accounting for the genesis of homosexuality. Since ancient times scholars in need of a convenient etiology have "described the present and then traced back to the Yellow Emperor," the fountainhead of Chinese civilization[1]—a practice tantamount to denying true knowledge of actual beginnings of a phenomenon. It seems therefore almost inevitable that one tradition-minded scholar of the late imperial era referred to this old culture hero in explaining that "beautiful boys originated with the Yellow Emperor."[2]

More prosaically, our historical investigation begins with Zhou dynasty society (1122–256 B.C.), which seems to have been quite familiar with homosexuality. Since archeological evidence on this subject is virtually unobtainable, we must rely entirely on written documentation. Certain potential problems in this reliance on early texts should be recognized at the outset. In addition to the obvious interpretive questions of textual corruption and hermeneutics, most of these texts present a skewed perspective on ancient society. Because a small elite class controlled early literature, only the life of the uppermost strata of society is usually depicted. And with historical records focused on the courts, political interests determined what was included and how it was presented, limiting the scope of ancient literature. The entrancing glitter of court life thus blinds both ancient authors and ourselves to the mundane world of the average person.

The *Classic of Odes* (*Shi jing*), China's earliest surviving poetic anthology, presents a valuable exception to the general lack of information on life outside the courts. Reputedly taken largely from popular songs and poems, many of these verses date from long before their redaction sometime around the seventh century B.C. Unlike the stilted and stylized verses of many court poets, the poems of this anthology reflect the vital interests of the average farmer and soldier, concerns that included the threat of famine, the devastation of war, and, most important for us, the rhapsodies and laments of love.

The gender ambiguity inherent in classical Chinese nouns and pronouns complicates our search of early poems for homosexual content. For example, one often-used term, "beautiful person" (*mei ren*), usually refers to a woman. Yet the distinguished Qing dynasty literatus Zhao Yi pointed out that in many early texts this phrase refers to a handsome man.[3] Attentive scholars such as Hans Frankel have noted this ambiguity in their translations of the *Classic of Odes*. For one such vague lyric—

> There is a [*mei ren*],
> Clear, bright, and handsome.
> Unexpectedly we meet,
> Fitting my desire[4]

—although Frankel translates *mei ren* as "beautiful woman," he takes care to explain that the term could also mean "a good-looking fellow." The terse indefiniteness of the poem gives it several possible interpretations: a man meeting a woman, a woman meeting a man, or an encounter between lovers of the same sex.[5] This linguistic ambiguity makes it impossible to separate many potential references to homosexual love in China from the dominant heterosexual context, a problem that pervades the use of poetry throughout Chinese history.

Other poems from the *Classic of Odes* more directly record strong emotional bonds between men. For example, one selection describes the mutual admiration felt by two athletic noblemen:

> How splendid he was!
> Yes, he met me between the hills of Nao.
> Our chariots side by side we chased two boars.
> He bowed to me and said I was very nimble.
>
> How strong he was!
> Yes, he met me on the road at Nao.
> Side by side we chased two stags.
> He bowed to me and said "well done."
>
> How magnificent he was!
> Yes, he met me on the south slopes of Nao.
> Side by side we chased two wolves.
> He bowed to me and said "that was good."[6]

A similar poem expresses intimate camaraderie between two virile warriors:

> How can you say that you have no clothes?
> I will share mine with you;

The king raises his army, we put in order our
    dagger axes and *mao* lances;
I will have the same enemies as you.

How can you say that you have no clothes?
I will share my trousers with you;
The king raises his army, we put in order our *mao*
    lances and *ji* lances;
Together with you I will start (on the expedition).

How can you say that you have no clothes?
I will share my skirts with you;
The king raises his army;
We put in order our mail-coats and sharp weapons;
Together with you I will march.[7]

These and many other poems in the collection make clear that the
prevailing social conditions of the early Zhou favored the open
expression of affection between men. Such an atmosphere, in
which convention allowed men to admire their male peers openly,
effusively, and unabashedly, was certainly conducive to the pan-
sexual ethos that pervaded the royal courts of Zhou and Han.

In a sense, the sexual lives of the upper classes in ancient China
seem far removed from the rustic customs of everyday life. Sexual
etiquette at Zhou courts held the elite ranks to a more rigid sexual
ethic than pragmatic popular practices commanded, and marriage
ceremonies held greater significance. For the aristocracy, kinship
served a central role in perpetuating hereditary privilege. Yet for
the conquered peoples of the countryside as well as the growing
class of city dwellers, too, any political influence they had de-
pended on the preservation of kinship-based traditions of clan
rule.[8] Heterosexuality therefore allowed admittance into the central web of social and political ties that held ancient society
together. Beyond this realm of marriage and patrimony, however, the general sexual ethos seems to have been fairly fluid.
Homosexuality and extramarital heterosexuality both had an
accepted place in Zhou society.

Our information on Zhou homosexuality comes exclusively

from the upper classes, where marriage was subservient to kinship interests. Marriage was seen as the bonding of two lineage groups, not the romantic union of two individuals. With romance banished from marriage, a husband was free to look elsewhere for romantic love and satisfying sex. Even in the ancient period, we see men who maintained a heterosexual marriage and a homosexual romance without apparently seeing any contradiction between the two. Since this seeming sexual dichotomy between duty and pleasure resulted from the kinship-based tradition, it would survive for as long as kinship continued to provide the foundation for social structure. In most societies, as the economy becomes more complex, social organization gradually realigns according to occupation and social class rather than kinship. China, however, has maintained kinship as the fundamental social force down to the present day. With a kinship-structured society has come the sometimes problematic combination of heterosexual marriage and homosexual romance. What this social organization prevented, and still prevents, was the emergence of a self-identified homosexual life-style independent of marriage, as with gays of the contemporary West.

Political factors also influence social organization. The overall political organization of the Zhou dynasty was characterized by a gradually declining central kingship, matched by a commensurate increase in the autonomy of local nobles. By the second half of the dynasty, the Zhou monarch had become a mere figurehead as powerful regional lords strove for hegemony over the Chinese cultural region. The political and military turbulence that accompanied these continual transitions of power upset the existing social order, allowing commoners to play an increasingly important role in court life.[9] Because philosophers, military tacticians, and artisans all found their services in demand from competing states, they experienced a resulting increase in their social status.

It seems that another group also benefited from this breakdown of social stratification, for any man who could obtain the sexual favor of his lord could rise significantly in power and privilege. Although homosexuality may have existed among the royal courts of earlier eras (known to us only through extremely fragmentary evidence), these court favorites and their aristocratic lovers of the Eastern Zhou were the first identifiable practitioners of homosexuality in China. They established a pattern of class-structured homosexuality that continued down to the end of imperial history.

It seems fitting to begin a description of Zhou homosexuality with the fickle love of Duke Ling of Wei (534–493 B.C.) for Mizi Xia, the most famous representative of homosexual love from the period. His story, recorded in the ancient philosophic work *Han Fei Zi*, had an enormous influence on later generations, such that the name Mizi Xia became a catchword for homosexuality in general. The exceptional hold of this tale marks it as an important beginning of the homosexual tradition as well as a significant contributor to the way all literate Chinese conceived of homosexuality.[10]

> In ancient times Mizi Xia won favor [*chong*] with the ruler of Wei. According to the laws of the state of Wei, anyone who secretly made use of the ruler's carriage was punished by having his feet amputated. When Mizi Xia's mother fell ill, someone slipped into the palace at night to report this to Mizi Xia. Mizi Xia forged an order from the ruler, got into the ruler's carriage, and went off to see her, but when the ruler heard of it, he only praised him, saying, "How filial! For the sake of his mother he forgot all about the danger of having his feet cut off!" Another day Mizi Xia was strolling with the ruler in an orchard and, biting into a peach and finding it sweet, he stopped eating and gave the remaining half to the ruler to enjoy. "How sincere is your love for me!" exclaimed the ruler. "You forgot your own appetite and think only of giving me good things to eat!" Later, however, when Mizi Xia's looks had faded and the ruler's passion for him had cooled, he was accused of committing some crime against his lord. "After all," said the ruler, "he once stole my carriage, and another time he gave me a half-eaten peach to eat!" Mizi Xia was acting no differently from the way he always had; the fact that he was praised in the early days, and accused of a crime later on, was because the ruler's love had turned to hate.

If you gain the ruler's love, your wisdom will be appreciated and you will enjoy his favor as well; but if he hates you, not only will your wisdom be rejected, but you will be regarded as a criminal and thrust aside. . . . The beast called the dragon can be tamed and trained to the point where you may ride on its back. But on the underside of its throat it has scales a foot in diameter that curl back from the body, and anyone who chances to brush against them is sure to die. The ruler of men too has his bristling scales.[11]

The author of this passage, Han Fei, did not intend to explore social values or attack homosexual activities. As a Legalist thinker, he simply wanted to address the threat to a ruler's powers posed by institutional favoritism. The Legalist ideal strove for impersonal government by laws instead of men. Favorites threatened this order by gaining personal influence through love of the ruler.

Han Fei strikingly described Mizi Xia and the duke not according to sexual orientation, as in the contemporary West, but according to social relationship. Confucius set forth the primacy of human relationships when he defined the essence of wisdom as lying in earnest devotion to the duties due to people.[12] As a result of this stress on relationships rather than psychological essence, neither Han Fei nor any other Zhou source mentions any term equivalent to "homosexual." Instead the term *chong* is used, denoting a hierarchical relationship of regular patronage, or favor, bestowed by a superior on a man who happened to be a sexual partner. *Chong*, then, is not even remotely equivalent to "homosexuality": it could also refer to heterosexual or nonsexual relationships; indeed, ancient texts even use *chong* in portraying "respect" for the spirits.[13] This tendency to describe homosexual acts in terms of social relationships rather than erotic essence continued in China down to the twentieth century, when terminology derived from Western science gained predominance.

Han Fei's depiction of Mizi Xia in a sympathetic light emphasizes the story's generally favorable view of homosexuality. At first he risks horrible mutilation for the sake of filial piety, risking the duke's wrath by stealing the ducal chariot to see his ailing mother. Mizi Xia's actions in the peach orchard are seen as an expression of intimacy between two lovers. Throughout the narrative he is shown to be loving and unselfish. Only the duke's undependability leads to Mizi Xia's ruin. The morbid ending is merely characteristic of the historical literature of the period and does not in itself indicate a denigration of homosexuality. Even a conclusion of such abrupt violence does not cause the reader to forget the deep sense of love expressed earlier in the tale. In fact, the violent ending was probably what caused the narrative to be recorded at all. Han Fei does not comment on the presence of homosexuality as perverse or extraordinary, just as other ancient records mention it only in passing. He simply uses the tale as a particularly vivid example in a more general discussion of statecraft.

Description of homosexuality according to social relationships finds an extreme expression in the tale of Duke Jing of the powerful state of Qi, taken from the philosophic work *Spring and Autumn Annals of Master Yan* (*Yanzi chunqiu*).

> Duke Jing of the state of Qi was so exceptionally attractive that a minor official presumed to stare at his extravagant beauty. The duke said to his courtiers, "Ask him why he stares at me, overstepping his rightful place." The official replied, "If I speak I will die, but if I do not speak I will also die—I was stealing a glance at the beautiful duke!"
>
> The duke declared, "He lusted after me. Kill him!" Yanzi entered out of turn and said, "I hear that you are angry with an official." The duke said, "Correct. He lusted after me, so I will kill him."
>
> Yanzi replied, "I have heard that to resist desire is not in accordance with the Way, and to hate love is inauspicious. Although he was caused to lust after you, according to the law it is not fitting that he should be killed."[14]

Following Yanzi's sage advice, Duke Jing not only forgave the offending official, but promoted him to a position of greatest trust as a retainer in the ducal bath.

By staring suggestively at Duke Jing, the lowly official flagrantly violated accepted social conventions and acted as the dominant force in their relationship. The enormous disparity in social status between them demanded a penalty of the greatest magnitude, because for a lowly official to initiate sexual overtures challenged the duke's superior social standing.

Like Yanzi's story of Duke Jing, another tale surviving from ancient times describes the love felt by a shy official, Zhuang Xin, for his lord, Xiang Cheng of the powerful southern state of Chu. The account opens with a description of Xiang Cheng's noble appearance, resplendent in his magnificent robes and jade ornaments. Then it goes on to describe Zhuang Xin's daring courtship.

> The grandee official Zhuang Xin had an audience with Lord Xiang Cheng and asked, "May I hold your hand?" Xiang Cheng's expression changed, but he did not speak.
>
> Zhuang Xin edged backwards, then stepped up and said, "Has my lord ever heard of Lord E? He rode in an aquamarine boat carved with avian images and drew up azure coverlets. Men of Yue rowed to the sounds of bells and drums, singing:
>
>> "What a fine evening is this,
>>> that I've come to this islet midstream!
>> What a fine day is this,
>>> that I share a boat with you, my prince!
>> Unworthy that I'd be so desired,
>>> when have I ever felt such shame?
>> My heart's perplexed to no end,
>>> that I've come to know you, my prince!
>> There are trees in the mountain, and branches on trees.
>> I yearn to please you, and you do not know!"[15]
>
> Thereupon Lord E raised up the azure coverlets and responded to him." Lord Xiang Cheng also received Zhuang Xin's hand and promoted him. [16]

In this tale, Zhuang Xin found it awkward to make the first sexual overtures because of his submissive social status. When Lord Xiang Cheng seemed disconcerted by his underling's directness, in desperation Zhuang Xin related the tale of Lord E. Trying

to justify one's own actions through reference to a historical precedent is a standard method of persuasion in Chinese rhetoric.
According to Zhuang Xin's story, Lord E also had an official who
loved him. When Lord E learned of his retainer's love through
hearing the song of the oarsmen on his royal barge, he accepted
the affections of that unnamed courtier. In a parallel ending, after
hearing this story Lord Xiang Cheng was also moved to offer his
love to his admirer. These tales of Lord Xiang Cheng and Lord E
make quite a contrast to that of the official and Duke Jing.
Apparently in some cases love could lead even a ruler to overlook
the impropriety of a social inferior making sexual advances.

Another interesting suggestion emerges from the courtship of
Zhuang Xin and Xiang Cheng. Central to the structure of the
narrative is Zhuang Xin's quotation of a tale of unrequited love,
that of the retainer of Lord E. Zhuang Xin did not see his plight in
temporal isolation; instead he drew on a homosexual tradition that
could comfort him by allowing him to place his situation in a
broader social and historical context, and used a past example to
justify present actions. Reliance on the past to shape the present
marks one more beginning of a recorded, continuous homosexual
tradition in China.

Another remarkable story from the state of Chu glorifies the
love of Wang Zhongxian for a handsome and learned subject
named Pan Zhang—surely the most positive and romantic
account that survives from the Zhou period.

> When Pan Zhang was young he had a beautiful [*mei*] appearance
> and bearing, and so people of that time were exceedingly fond of
> him. Wang Zhongxian of the state of Chu heard of his reputation
> and came to request his writings. Thereafter Wang Zhongxian
> wanted to study together with him. They fell in love at first sight
> and were as affectionate as husband and wife, sharing the same
> coverlet and pillow with unbounded intimacy for one another.
>   Afterwards they died together and everyone mourned them.
> When they were buried together at Lofu Mountain, on the peak a
> tree with long branches and leafy twigs suddenly grew. All of these

embraced one another! At the time people considered this a miracle. It was called the "Shared Pillow Tree."[17]

In this passage we find perhaps the earliest analogy made between homosexual love and heterosexual marriage. The Yuan-dynasty edition from which a Ming compiler seems to have taken this story states quite straightforwardly, "They. . . were as affectionate as husband and wife." Unfortunately, because an ancient edition of this tale has not survived, we cannot be certain of the original wording; but the overall intent of the story seems indisputable—two men created a sexual and emotional bond so strong that it survived even death. If this story had ancient origins, as seems probable, it presents the earliest example of the sort of pair-bonding that later evolved into same-sex marriage rituals.

From this tale it also seems certain that the two lovers considered their homosexual desires to be the center of their emotional and erotic lives. Yet the text gives no labels such as "homosexual" to the pair; instead it stresses their relationship (like husband and wife) and their feelings. Once again we see the Chinese tendency to develop a sexual taxonomy derived from social and emotional bonds rather than attempting to bring forth an innate, essential sexual identity, as is often the case in the contemporary West.

One word that stands out in the passage is *mei* (beautiful), used to describe the good looks of Pan Zhang. Modern Chinese readers usually associate this term exclusively with female beauty, and its use for men seems somewhat affected. As seen earlier in the case of the *Classic of Odes*, however, to the ancients *mei* was applicable to the beauty and goodness of both sexes. Considering the surviving records of bisexuality from the Zhou and Han, the existence of a gender-free means of expressing attractiveness seems consistent. The Greeks, even better known for bisexuality, had a similar concept of unisex beauty in the term *kalos*. But the Greek term, unlike the Chinese, lacked the additional connotation of internal beauty and instead applied only to physical appearance, whether of men, women, animals, or objects.[18] Through the centuries, *mei* gradually lost its general applicability and came in the male case to be used mainly for effeminate and sexually passive men and boys.

The tale of Pan Zhang and Wang Zhongxian supplements the elegant simplicity of its literary power by invoking a standard convention of heterosexual romance: the intertwining branches of a tree. The famed Han-dynasty poem "The Peacock Southeast Flew" ("Kongque dongnan fei") uses a similar image of two trees embracing over the graves of a pair of lovers. In the heterosexual version, the lovers have committed suicide because of their forced separation; their families bury them together and plant two trees above their tomb.

> In the east and west they planted pine and cedar;
> On the left and right they planted firmiana and paulownia.
> Their branches covered one another;
> Their leaves intertwined with one another.

By using a common heterosexual motif, the unknown author relating the love of Pan Zhang and Wang Zhongxian demonstrates the convergence of homosexual and heterosexual romantic ideals in ancient times. In addition, the symbol of intertwining trees was a common auspicious omen in Han-dynasty pictorial art.[19] For it to be applied to a human relationship shows strong approval by supernatural forces.

While taking this tale into consideration, we must not exaggerate the extent of exclusive homosexuality in Zhou China. Most men of ancient times seem to have engaged in heterosexual intercourse, although whether out of desire or duty one cannot be sure. For the poor, procreation had vital economic significance. Without children to help in agricultural labor, the life of a peasant would have become increasingly difficult with old age. The thriving market for child slaves in early China attests to their high economic value.[20] Added to this economic incentive was the religious and social importance of continuing the family line—especially in royal courts, where children had particular value as dynastic heirs and for use in uniting families through marriage ties. The indispensability of children to rulers and peasants alike helps account for the prevalence of bisexuality over exclusive homosexuality among the men of ancient China. Only a privileged few would even have had the option of homosexual monogamy.

With bisexuality practiced in the highest circles of ancient courts, the relationship between politics and sex became increasingly perplexing. The example of Song Chao illustrates the potential for confusion. Early records note that he had "a beautiful appearance, and served the state of Wei as a grandee official. There he was favored by Duke Ling of Wei."[21] The mention of good looks and favored official position in tandem suggests the possibility of a link between the two. Antipathy to those who openly enjoyed homosexuality would no doubt have resulted in their exclusion from appointive office. Yet, as seen in numerous passages, some men not only held high official positions but also became sexual favorites of the rulers they served. Throughout ancient Chinese history the general attitude toward homosexual love seems to have been one of acceptance, which accounts for the portrayal of many such men as successful officials and rulers. The selfless love of King Wen of Chu for the Marquis Shen is one example of admirable virtue in a homosexual context. The dying king, who had favored Shen, ordered him to flee to the state of Zheng after the burial, where he was to find favor with that ruler as well. King Wen knew how vulnerable his favorite would be to jealous machinations after he was no longer under royal protection.[22] By handing over his beloved to another monarch King Wen hoped to insure Shen's continued worldly success. Even as he lay dying, he had concern only for his favorite.

The security of a male favorite at court rested entirely with the fate of his noble lover. As the example of Marquis Shen illustrates, the death or political ruin of a patron forced the beloved to seek the attentions of some other powerful aristocrat. Lord Anling, however, contemplated a more permanent attachment to his lover's fate.

Jiang Yi persuaded Lord Anling, "Your excellency has not one particle of accomplishment and no close kin occupying honored positions, yet you receive the greatest wealth and all the citizens of the state pull back their sleeves to bow to you and adjust their clothing to kneel to you. Why? Because the king gives too much to those who give him pleasure. Were this not so you would not have such a high estate.

"But," continued Jiang Yi, "those who have a relationship based on wealth find that when wealth is exhausted the relationship ceases. Those who have a relationship based on attractiveness find that when their beauty fades love changes—which is why the favored woman seldom wears out her sleeping mat and the favored minister seldom remains long enough to wear out his carriages."[23]

Jiang Yi's observations are borne out by the example of Mizi Xia. In this case, the only way to make the relationship permanent and thereby "be eternally honored in the state of Chu" was for Lord Anling to tell the king that he wished to share the royal grave with him. The same sentiments that led ancient rulers to include human sacrifice as a part of royal funerals determined Anling's decision. Rulers of the time were usually buried only with their consorts. Important officials might be interred nearby, but for a male favorite to share a ruler's grave would have been an extraordinary act, suggesting status comparable to that of a consort.

Lord Anling, with tears streaming down his face, came forward. "In the palace my mat lies beside the king's and abroad I share his chariot. A thousand autumns hence I intend to send my own body first to see the Yellow Springs [Hades] so that it may be a shield against the ants for my prince."[24]

As a gesture of appreciation for such devotion, the king took this occasion as a justification for first enfeoffing his beloved Anling.

These stories emphasize an important fact: for men as well as women of ancient China, the judicious use of sex could be a means for attaining upward political and social mobility. As noted previously, the later Zhou was an age of increasing social change.

Because hereditary privilege lost importance, talent and ability became increasingly prominent keys to social success. One such talent was in the erotic arts. For women, success as a sex partner was one of the only ways to obtain prestige within the household or court—a path to success that holds true throughout dynastic history. As for men, some tried to capitalize on their good looks to attain office. The sensual and even sexual roles of men cannot be ignored in understanding ancient political mobility.

A tale of voyeurism confirms the popular opinion that officials of Zhou China sometimes rose to power through use of sexual charms. In the seventh century B.C. when Chonger of Jin took refuge with the ruler of Cao, that duke had heard that Chonger had double ribs. Wishing to see this unique anatomical condition, the duke and his wife drilled a hole in the wall so they might spy on Chonger in his bath chamber. The bevy of voyeurs witnessed the unexpected sight of Chonger engaging in sexual intercourse with two male retainers, a scene that prompted a grandee's wife to remark drolly that Prince Chonger's retainers seemed capable of becoming ministers of state.[25] Although intended as a humorous jibe at the self-serving motives of many favorites, this remark could not have had a humorous effect unless it was known that officials did occasionally sleep their way into power.

By becoming a ruler's beloved, a favorite could be assured of high official position and generous emolument. But whereas the visibility of sexual favorites shows a general tolerance for homosexual acts, men who used sexual wiles for social advancement were censured and scorned. Criticism of the practice of basing official appointments on sexual abilities and good looks rather than political skill dates far back in Chinese political theory. A chapter found in the *Classic of Documents* (*Shu jing*) entitled "The Instructions of Yi" ("Yi lun") includes a series of severe instructions from a virtuous minister to the young Shang king. Although the text is widely considered inauthentic, it still dates from at least the late Zhou or early Han. In this passage, the wise adviser lists the many possible distractions facing an inexperienced ruler:

He warned those in authority, saying, "If you dare to have constant dancing in your palaces, and drunken singing in your chambers— that is called the way of shamans. If you dare to set your hearts on wealth and women, and abandon yourselves to wandering about or to hunting—that is called the way of dissipation. If you dare to despise sage words, to resist the loyal and upright, to put far from you the aged and virtuous, and to be familiar with shameless youths [*wan tong*]—that is called the way of disorder. Now if a high noble or officer is addicted to one of these ways with their ten evil vices, his family will surely come to ruin. If the prince of a country is addicted to these, his state will surely come to ruin.[26]

The term *wan tong* literally means "shameless youths." James Legge, an early translator of the classics, originally rendered the term into English as "procacious youths." Apparently he intended to write "proctacious," a Victorian circumlocution for "sodomitical."[27] As Legge suggested, this passage perhaps condemns the same practice of male favoritism that other authors examined in greater detail.

By the later Zhou the convergence of political and sexual favoritism had created such a threat to orderly government that philosophers felt compelled to speak out against the practice. Two political texts in the *Guanzi* anthology place favoritism first in a list of the most important threats to good government.[28] The sagacious Mozi repeats these warnings in greater detail:

Rulers employ their relatives, or men who happen to be rich and eminent or pleasant-featured and attractive. But just because a man happens to be rich and eminent or pleasant-featured and attractive, he will not necessarily turn out to be wise and alert when placed in office. If men such as these are given the task of ordering the state, then this is simply to entrust the state to men who are neither wise nor intelligent, and anyone knows that this will lead to ruin.

Moreover, the rulers and high officials trust a man's mental ability because they love his appearance, and love him without bothering to examine his knowledge. As a result a man who is incapable of taking charge of a hundred persons is assigned to a post in charge of a thousand, and a man who is incapable of taking charge of a thousand persons is assigned to a post in charge of ten thousand. Why do the rulers do this? Because if they assign a man they like to such a post, he will receive an exalted title and a generous stipend. Hence they employ the man simply because they love his appearance.[29]

Mozi's warnings indicate a general trend that allowed homosexual love to play a role in ancient Chinese politics. This custom was not confined to China: Islamic and Japanese rulers are also known to have considered male sexual favorites for government office.[30] In the case of China, Mozi seems to have been worried that practices such as these, as well as lesser forms of emolument based on good looks, threatened efficient government. In fact, homosexuality within ancient officialdom seems to have been prevalent enough that the Machiavellian Han-dynasty work *Intrigues of the Warring States* (*Zhanguo ce*), a collection of anecdotes recounting pre-Han political schemes, mentions Duke Xian of Jin using a favorite as a secret weapon for spreading disinformation among the enemy. The success of this plot speaks for the influence of male favorites in Zhou political life:

> Duke Xian wished to attack Yu but feared the presence of Gong Zhiqi. Xun Xi said, "*The Book of Zhou* [*Ji zhong Zhou shu*] says, 'A beautiful lad can ruin an older head.' Send the king a comely boy whom you have instructed to ruin Gong Zhiqi. The latter's admonitions will go unheeded and he will flee." Having done this, Duke Xian attacked Yu and took it.[31]

Xun Xi noted the common belief that "a beautiful lad can ruin an older head." This is not, however, a condemnation of homosexuality. The original quotation reads, "A beautiful lad can ruin an older head; a beautiful woman can tangle a tongue." The author of this saying compared two sexual partners, a beautiful woman and man, and remarked that each can blind men with lust and cause them to commit acts they normally would not consider doing. Sex in general is cautioned against as a disruptive force.

Historical writings support Mozi's and Xun Xi's abstract

moralizing: that favoring a beloved could cause a ruler to commit serious errors of judgment. An ancient incident relates the passion felt by Duke Huan of Song for the official Xiang Dui. The duke eventually upset the well-being of his court by favoring his beloved over his own son, a glaring breach of propriety. His decision led the state of Song to the brink of civil war.

> Xiang Dui was a grandee official of the state of Song. He had the favor of Duke Huan, who made him a military commander. At that time the duke's son, Tuo, had four white horses. Xiang Dui wanted them, so the duke took them, dyed their tails and manes vermillion, and gave them to him. The duke's son was furious and had his followers pursue Xiang Dui, who was afraid and wanted to flee. The duke closed the gates and wept for him until his eyes were bruised.[32]

Xiang Dui's thoughtless selfishness brought ruin to himself and his lover. This was the type of man feared by Mozi and Xun Xi.

A final example of homosexual love in the Zhou dynasty depicts altruism gone awry. The favorite Lord Long Yang made an elaborate demonstration of concern that he hoped would prove his devotion to the king of Wei:

> The king of Wei and Lord Long Yang shared a boat while fishing. Lord Long Yang began to cry, so the king asked why he wept. "Because I caught a fish." "But why does that make you cry?" the king asked.
>
> Lord Long Yang replied, "When I caught the fish, at first I was extremely pleased. But afterward I caught a larger fish, so I wanted to throw back the first fish I had caught. Because of this evil act I will be expelled from your bed!
>
> "There are innumerable beauties in the world. Upon hearing of my receiving your favor, surely they will lift up the hems of their robes so that they can hasten to you. I am also a previously caught fish! I will also be thrown back! How can I keep from crying?"
>
> Because of this incident the king of Wei announced to the world, "Anyone who dares to speak of other beauties will be executed along with his entire family."[33]

This tale dramatizes the extent of sexual opportunism in the Zhou court. Competition was intense among the many contenders for favor, and this constant struggle for the sexual attentions of the ruler made a favorite's position extremely precarious. As a sage observer noted to one good-looking favorite, "Your excellency serves the king with his beauty and Qi serves him with wisdom. Beauty fades with age but wisdom increases. If a daily increasing wisdom challenges an ever decreasing beauty you will be in difficulty."[34] The favorite who held power solely on account of appearance would inevitably find himself the target of court intrigues. Just as there were always more fish in the sea, there were also always more men and women eager to become the beloved of a powerful lord.[35] The wise and talented were a grave threat to those whose position rested only on sexual favor.

The tale of Lord Long Yang completes the historical evidence we have of Zhou homosexual practices. The available sources are extremely limited. Because same-sex love did not seem unusual to the litterateurs of the Zhou, they did not mention it except when it occurred in a greater context. Nevertheless, surviving accounts come from every region of early China and convey an impression of open homosexuality in court life. Only when political decisions came to be influenced by good looks did moralists bother to register complaints; otherwise homosexuality seems to have been considered simply part of the broad range of sexual expression. Still, with a body of information this minuscule, it would be foolhardy to attempt to generalize about the exact forms of homosexuality in ancient times. At this point it seems safe to draw just one important conclusion: homosexuality was at least tolerated, and seemingly accepted, by the political elite of Zhou China.

2

Cut Sleeves as the Height of Fashion
Han Dynasty (206 B.C. to A.D. 220)

Between the collapse of the Zhou and the founding of the Han dynasty in 206 B.C., China underwent political upheavals as painful as they were decisive. An onslaught of armies from the state of Qin finally swept away the decayed Zhou monarchy. For the first time, all under heaven bowed down before a single powerful ruler. But the Qin proved to be intolerable masters. Grandiose public works projects sent multitudes into forced labor, while those still at home chafed under a draconian code of law. Books were burned and wise men buried alive. The universal unpopularity of the Qin brought the dynasty down after just one generation. It took subsequent Han rulers decades to reunite and rebuild the devastated nation.

Although the traumatic change from Zhou to Han brought enormous political ferment, it does not seem to have significantly altered the patterns of sexual relations among the social elite. Throughout the dynasty, historical records speak openly of the bisexuality of numerous Han emperors. These inexhaustible monarchs retained large harems of wives and concubines while also indulging in regular trysts with male favorites. Although heterosexual intercourse was vital to the continuation of the dynasty, their homosexual liaisons were purely voluntary. The choice of the half-eaten peach by these emperors, together with the frank and straightforward manner in which contemporaneous sources recorded their loves, leaves no possible conclusion except that, like their Zhou predecessors, the social elite of the Han continued to include homosexuality as an accepted part of sexual life.

Like those of the Zhou, the vast majority of Han records concern the lives of rulers. Consequently, our view of homosexuality during the Han pertains almost exclusively to the male loves of the emperors. Just as Edward Gibbon observed that all but one of the first fourteen emperors of Rome were either bisexual or exclusively homosexual,[1] for two centuries at the height of the Han China was ruled by ten openly bisexual emperors.[2] We can better comprehend the extent of homosexuality at the Han court when we consider the emperors together with a few of their most important favorites.

Emperor	Reign	Male Favorite(s)
Gao	206–195 B.C.	Jiru
Hui	194–188 B.C.	Hongru
Wen	179–157 B.C.	Deng Tong, Zhao Tan, Beigong Bozi
Jing	156–141 B.C.	Zhou Ren
Wu	140–87 B.C.	Han Yan, Han Yue, Li Yannian
Zhao	86–74 B.C.	Jin Shang

Xuan	73–49 B.C.	Zhang Pengzu
Yuan	48–33 B.C.	Hong Gong, Shi Xian
Cheng	32–7 B.C.	Zhang Fang, Chunyu Zhang
Ai	6 B.C.–1 A.D.	Dong Xian

All of these attributions are made in the official histories of that period, the *Memoirs of the Historian* (*Shi ji*) by Sima Qian and the *Records of the Han* (*Han shu*) by Ban Gu, both respected works that include lengthy chapters describing in detail the biographies of the emperors' male favorites.[3]

These histories convey a detailed picture of an imperial court at which male favorites of the emperor had enormous prominence. In many ways, homosexuality became a central feature of early court life. Grand Historian Sima Qian attested to the power of imperial favorites in the introduction to his biographies of these influential men:

> Those who served the ruler and succeeded in delighting his ears and eyes, those who caught their lord's fancy and won his favor and intimacy, did so not only through the power of lust and love; each had certain abilities in which he excelled. Thus I made The Biographies of the Emperors' Male Favorites.
>
> The proverb says, "No amount of toiling in the fields can compare to a spell of good weather; no amount of faithful service can compare to being liked by your superiors." This is no idle saying. Yet it is not women alone who can use their looks to attract the eyes of the ruler; courtiers and eunuchs can play at that game as well. Many were the men of ancient times who gained favor this way.[4]

The first of the Han rulers was Emperor Gao, more commonly known as Gaozu. He and his heir, Emperor Hui, started the Han custom of emperors favoring officials willing to employ their sexual talents.

> When the Han arose, Emperor Gaozu, for all his coarseness and blunt manners, was won by the charms of a young boy named Ji, and Emperor Hui had a boy favorite named Hong. Neither Ji nor Hong had any particular talent or ability; both won prominence

simply by their looks and graces. Day and night they were by the ruler's side, and all the high ministers were obliged to apply to them when they wished to speak to the emperor.[5]

The men each ruler loved subsequently rose to lofty official ranks. These favorites accrued extraordinary privileges owing to their unique intimacy with the emperor and exercised even greater power by helping to determine who else could have access to the human hub of the Han cosmos.

One incident during the reign of Gaozu reflects the enormous power that came with a ruler's trust. When Gaozu became seriously ill he feared that autonomous nobles might use the opportunity to overthrow his unstable new dynasty; he therefore went into seclusion in the inner palace, where he was attended by just one faithful eunuch. Fan Kuai, a beloved of Gaozu, convinced the emperor to end his isolation, thereby bringing a serious political crisis to an end.

> Once when Emperor Gao was ill, he rested in the inner palace and ordered the gatekeepers to keep out the various officials. No one dared enter. After more than ten days of this, Fan Kuai arranged to enter the innermost chamber. All of the great officials followed him. Upon seeing the emperor lying alone on his pillow with only one eunuch there, Fan Kuai and the others burst into tears. He said, "Before, your majesty and I rose to prosperity and greatness together. What does your health matter? Now all under heaven has been put in order. What does exhaustion matter? Your majesty does not oversee the highest affairs alone!" Upon hearing this, the emperor laughed and got up.[6]

Fan Kuai and those like him were rewarded with love, wealth, and, as this incident shows, power. The sight of an imperial favorite rising rapidly from obscurity to attain the precarious status of powerful parvenu became less common during later dynasties as the bureaucracy developed a rational means for replenishing itself and a regular system of promotion and demotion. For Han officialdom, however, the ubiquity of patronage made favor and influence more important than skill. Nobles and high officials used influence on one another's behalf in return for similar favors. Such a system could easily be exploited by those willing to trade sex for office.

The life of Deng Tong demonstrates how catching the emperor's attention, whether intentionally or not, could earn even the uneducated an official position through imperial patronage. Deng Tong was promoted from the depths of base servitude to a lucrative position analogous to that of imperial concubine. While lengthy, his biography deserves to be read in full because it sums up all the possible phases in the life of a Han imperial favorite, from rags to riches to rags again. Although the lives of most favorites of Han rulers were far less eventful than that of Deng Tong, his shows the precariousness of these men's unexpected success.

> The gentlemen who enjoyed favor in the palace under Emperor Wen included a courtier named Deng Tong and the eunuchs Zhao Tan and Beigong Bozi. Beigong Bozi was a worthy and affectionate man, while Zhao Tan attracted the emperor's attention by his skill in observing the stars and exhalations in the sky; both of them customarily rode about in the same carriage with Emperor Wen. Deng Tong does not seem to have had any special talent.
>
> Deng Tong was a native of Nan'an in the province of Shu. Because he knew how to pole a boat he was made a yellow-capped boatman in the grounds of the imperial palace.
>
> Once Emperor Wen dreamed that he was trying to climb to Heaven but could not seem to make his way up. Just then a yellow-capped boatman boosted him from behind, and he was able to reach Heaven. When the emperor turned around to look at the man, he noticed that the seam of the boatman's robe was split in the back just below the sash.
>
> After the emperor awoke, he went to the Terrace of Lapping Water, which stood in the middle of the Azure Lake, and began to search furtively for the man who had boosted him up in his dream. There he saw Deng Tong, who happened to have a tear in the back of his robe exactly like that of the man in the dream. The emperor summoned him and asked his name, and when he learned that the man's family name was Deng (ascend) and his personal name was Tong (reach), the emperor was overjoyed. From this time on, the

emperor bestowed ever-increasing favor and honor upon Deng Tong.

Deng Tong for his part behaved with great honesty and circumspection in his new position. He cared nothing about mingling with people outside the palace and, though the emperor granted him holidays to return to his home, he was always reluctant to leave. As a result, the emperor showered him with gifts until his fortunes mounted to tens of billions of cash and he had been promoted to the post of superior lord. The emperor from time to time even paid visits to Deng Tong's home to amuse himself there.

Deng Tong, however, had no other talent than this of entertaining the emperor and was never able to do anything to advance others at court. Instead he bent all his efforts toward maintaining his own position and ingratiating himself with the emperor.

Once the emperor summoned a man who was skilled at physiognomizing and asked him to examine Deng Tong's face. "This man will become poor and die of starvation," the physiognomist announced. "But *I* am the one who has made him rich!" exclaimed the emperor. "How could he ever become poor?" With this, he presented Deng Tong with the rights to a range of copper-bearing mountains in the Yan region of Shu Province and allowed him to mint copper coins for himself until the so-called Deng family cash were circulating all over the empire. Such was the wealth which Deng Tong acquired.

Once Emperor Wen was troubled by a tumor, and Deng Tong made it his duty to keep it sucked clean of infection. The emperor was feeling depressed by his illness and, apropos of nothing in particular, asked Deng Tong, "In all the empire, who do you think loves me most?"

"Surely no one loves Your Majesty more than the heir apparent!" replied Deng Tong.

Later, when the heir apparent came to inquire how his father was, the emperor made him suck the tumor. The heir apparent managed to suck it clean, but it was obvious from his expression that he found the task distasteful. Afterward, when he learned that Deng Tong had been in the habit of sucking the tumor for the emperor, he was secretly filled with shame. From this time on he bore a grudge against Deng Tong.

After Emperor Wen passed away and the heir apparent, Emperor

Jing, came to the throne. Deng Tong retired from court and returned to his home. He had not been there any time, however,
when someone reported to the throne that he was guilty of smug-
gling cash which he had minted across the border to the barbarians.
He was handed over to the law officials for investigation and it was
found that the evidence for the most part supported the charges. In
the end he was condemned and all of his fortune was confiscated by
the government. Even so, it was claimed that his wealth was insuf-
ficient to cover the damages and that he still owed the government
several hundred million more cash. Emperor Jing's older sister
Princess Chang presented Deng Tong with a gift of money, but the
officials immediately seized this as well, until Deng Tong was not
left with so much as a pin to hold his cap on. After this Princess
Chang provided him with food and clothing in the form of a loan
so that it could not be confiscated. In the end Deng Tong did not
have a single copper cash to call his own, and he died as a dependent
in someone else's home.[7]

Deng Tong was just one in a long line of men who rose to high
position through the use of sexual wiles. A tradition of success[8] for
those willing to use homosexuality to their advantage had long
existed, and since others had succeeded in this career path, it became recognized as a viable means for political and social advancement. Through it one could go from a life as a lowly boatman to
that of a favored "male concubine" with enormous financial rewards. Although the gift of "tens of billions of cash" is probably
literary hyperbole, it gives us a glimmer of the magnitude of Deng
Tong's material rewards. To a typical peasant household spending
less than four thousand cash per year,[9] a net worth of even a frac-
tion of that attributed to Deng Tong would defy the imagination.
A grant to coin money would also have been an exceptionally
lucrative and honorable privilege, one normally jealously guarded
by the government.[10]
 The intense rivalry between Deng Tong and the heir apparent,
the future Emperor Jing, stands out as a remarkable episode, with
Deng Tong's lofty prestige allowing him to rival even the emperor's own heir. Deng was not the first to lick a superior's ulcers

out of loyalty, of course. Sometimes Han masters of medicine would exercise their miraculous powers to transform themselves into an ulcerated form and require an untested disciple to lick their pustules as proof of utter devotion.[11] But when the heir apparent had to perform this unsavory task on the emperor's diseased flesh out of competition with a common favorite, it was only a matter of time before he could exact harsh revenge for this distasteful indignity. Emperor Jing obviously did not disapprove of Deng Tong for his homosexuality; after all, he had his own beloved. Jing's hatred of Deng Tong stemmed from more personal antagonisms.

The life of Deng Tong highlights the source of a sexual favorite's power. By forming an emotional bond with the ruler, a favorite could reap huge rewards. The more flamboyant his devotion, the greater his influence. But with only the emperor's affections to shield him from harm, any sudden tremor in the volcanic world of Han court politics could place the vulnerable favorite in mortal danger. Once, for example, an imperial chancellor decided for political reasons to take revenge on Deng Tong. Charging Deng with lack of respect in his behavior toward the emperor, he ordered Deng beheaded. Only a timely message from the emperor kept the blade from Deng Tong's neck. Favorites such as Deng Tong, then, had to fear rivals not only in the imperial family, but also from within the government bureaucracy.

The passsages regarding Deng Tong and other favorites in *Memoirs of the Historian* and *Records of the Han* show the emergence of a more enriched vocabulary for describing homosexuality. The title of the sections regarding favorites in both of these works is "Ning xing." Originally *ning* referred to "artful flattery." As for *xing*, the ancient dictionary *Shuo wen* defines it as "auspiciousness and avoidance of calamity." *Xing* gradually gained a more specific meaning such that the Ming-dynasty dictionary *Zi hui* equates it with love and favor, a meaning similar to that of the earlier term *chong*. This definition seems to have been current during the Han. Thus these chapter headings translate literally as "[Those obtaining] favor [through] artful flattery"—an appellation that follows the Zhou tendency to describe sexuality through social relationships. In addition, the term *ai ren* also appears in Han texts. Literally this compound means "lover" or "beloved," and is currently used in China as an everyday term for one's spouse. The Zhou word *chong* continues to appear in Han texts as a synonym for *xing*.

Han works on the imperial favorites lack an etiology of homosexuality. Like most writers, those of the Han felt the need to account only for the extraordinary, not the ordinary. Since homosexuality was part of daily court life, we do not find hateful diatribes, impassioned defenses, or detailed explanations. Instead the historians Sima Qian and Ban Gu try to describe and understand the infamous practice of political appointments and emolument based on sexual favors. They show the continued existence of a sexual rationale for official appointments, a practice excoriated since the time of Mozi.

This method of government was followed not only by Wen, but by his son Jing as well. The most famous of Emperor Jing's favorites was Zhou Ren, whose talents at the "secret games" played in the imperial boudoir the emperor relished. As a result of sexual favor, Zhou Ren and his family found themselves showered with honors and presents from the emperor, aristocracy, and officialdom.[12] The advantages he gained were passed down to his progeny, enabling them to gain entry to the highest circles of government. As the careers of Zhou Ren and Deng Tong both show, the opportunity for favorites to pass on to their kin the advantages they gained allowed the entire family to benefit economically and socially from sexual favor. By maintaining the good will of his lover's successor, Zhou Ren was able to avoid the fate of Deng Tong and preserve a high social status for his posterity. Similar economic realities motivated less lofty favorites, all the way down to the common prostitutes seen in later literature.

One example of a favorite whose fate intertwined with that of another family member was Li Yannian, whose sister's rise to favor with Emperor Wu precipitated his own ascent.

Li Yannian was a native of Zhongshan. His mother and father, as well as he and his brothers and sisters, were all originally singers. Li Yannian, having been convicted of some crime and condemned to castration, was made a keeper of the dogs in the palace. Later, the princess of Pingyuan recommended his younger sister Lady Li to the emperor because of her skill in dancing. When the emperor saw her, he took a liking to her and had her installed in the women's quarters of the palace, at the same time summoning Li Yannian to an audience and appointing him to a higher post.

Li Yannian was a good singer and knew how to compose new tunes. At this time the emperor wanted some hymns set to music and arranged with string accompaniment to be used in the sacrifices to Heaven and Earth which he had initiated. Li Yannian accepted the task and performed it to the emperor's satisfaction, composing melodies and string accompaniments for the new words that had been written. Meanwhile his sister, Lady Li, bore the emperor a son.

Li Yannian by this time wore the seals of a two thousand picul official and bore the title of "Harmonizer of Tunes." Day and night he was by the emperor's side and his honor and favor equaled that which Han Yan had formerly enjoyed.

When some years had passed, his younger brother Li Ji began carrying on an affair with one of the palace ladies and becoming more and more arrogant and careless in his behavior. After the death of Lady Li, the emperor's affection for the Li brothers waned, and he ended by having them arrested and executed.[13]

Once again a handsome young man of humble origins obtained imperial favor and the commensurate perquisites. At first Li Yannian shared in Lady Li's good fortune; but he was easily replaced by the subsequently favored official Wei Qing, and so shared Mizi Xia's fate.

Li Yannian, like several other favorites, was a eunuch. The stereotype of Han eunuchs derives from the effeminate behavior of such men as Zhao Zhong, who referred to himself as Emperor Ling's "mother" and often identified himself as a woman. Yet the behavior and reported attractiveness of favored eunuchs contradicts this grotesque caricature of castrated men as obese androgynes. The use of eunuchs as sexual partners by men of high status may have been preferred because their sexual passivity was assured and they fit a clearly defined sexual role.

Since during most periods eunuchs came from the lowest social realms of Chinese society and from less developed tribal neighbors, most eunuchs would probably have repelled refined emperors with their coarse visages and unsophisticated bearing. Only in eras of eunuch ascendency at court would these men receive the polish and learning that someone brought up in genteel surroundings might admire. During certain times in Han history, eunuchs such as Li Yannian acquired the graces that helped endear them to their rulers.

Both eunuchs and noncastrated favorites reaped enormous rewards. The celebrated love of the Han Emperor Ai for his beloved Dong Xian exemplified the privileges a devoted imperial patron could bestow, as well as the political ramifications this kind of relationship could entail. The following passage summarizes the account of his life in *Records of the Han.*

> Dong Xian's father, a respected censor, appointed Dong Xian to be a retainer to the Emperor Ai. He was a person whose beauty incited admiration. Emperor Ai gazed at him and spoke of Dong Xian's deportment and appearance. The emperor asked, "What about this retainer Dong Xian?" Because of this Dong Xian spoke with the emperor. Thus began his favor.
>
> Dong Xian's favor and love increased daily. He held high office and each year was granted ten thousand piculs of grain. His honors alarmed the court.
>
> Dong Xian's nature was always gentle, affable, and flattering. He was good at seducing by holding fast. Every time he was granted a leave of absence he turned it down. Instead he remained constantly at the palace studying medicine. The emperor found it difficult to make Dong Xian return home. He summoned Dong Xian's wife, and, like an official, she took up residence in a government estate. The emperor also summoned Dong Xian's sons and daughters, finding them to be bright and well mannered.

The emperor ennobled Dong Xian's father as the marquis of Guannei, with an attendant fief. Dong Xian became the marquis of Gao'an. These fiefs were each worth two thousand piculs of grain annually. Everyone in Dong Xian's household, down to his slaves, received grants from the emperor. The prime minister repeatedly remonstrated that because of Dong Xian the regulations of the state were in chaos.[14]

Dong Xian's powers and privileges were extraordinary. Their sheer numbers and repetitiveness make it needless to recount them all here. His biography enumerates the highest offices and titles attainable, the greatest of which he received by the age of twenty-two. He was even entrusted with the construction of the emperor's tomb, a duty of the greatest ritual importance and solemnity. Dong Xian's power was such that he was even able to help block one of the most important land reform proposals of the Han, since any such restrictions would have had most effect on the wealthiest subjects of the realm, such as himself.[15]

During a feast, a visiting chieftain from the northern nomads remarked on the incongruous youth of such a mighty official. The emperor explained that Dong Xian was a sage, which accounted for his early attainments. At this, the chieftain rose and bowed to the youthful prodigy, congratulating his hosts on the good fortune of having a flesh-and-blood sage in their midst. Of course, the real reason for Dong Xian's rank was just the opposite of sagacity. Sexual favor together with a privileged background better explain how someone might attain the pinnacle of worldly success at an age so young that it would even warrant comment from foreign visitors.

Dong Xian's family also received exceptional benefits from his favor. Father, father-in-law, brother, and grandson all received office and privilege. We should not be surprised at the emperor's willingness to reward the family of a beloved. This practice directly parallels the custom of choosing important officials from the families of imperial consorts.[16] Treating a favorite's family with the same esteem accorded the families of favored concubines further indicates the similarities between male homosexuality and heterosexual concubinage in early China.

Before his death, Emperor Ai openly suggested handing over his empire to Dong Xian. The imperial counselors quickly dismissed this possibility.[17] Even so, on his deathbed, lacking both sons and a designated heir, Ai handed over the imperial seals to Dong Xian and declared him emperor. In doing so he appealed to the ancient precedent of the mythical Yao's abdication in favor of Shun instead of handing the throne over to his son. Such a tenuous pretense to legitimacy did not impress Dong Xian's many political enemies. He was forced to commit suicide, and the usurper Wang Mang placed a child on the throne, through whom he ruled. Eventually Wang Mang did away with the child emperor and ruled in his own right.[18] Since Ai was the last adult emperor of the Western Han, his failed attempt to hand over his title to his male lover doomed the dynasty. The bond between emperor and favorite was strong, but not strong enough to overcome the traditions of succession. With no successful opponent to counter Wang Mang, the Western Han dynasty came to an end.

The love of Emperor Ai for Dong Xian, with its cataclysmic political consequences, stands out as the most decisive involvement of favoritism in Han government. But awareness of the immense rewards awaiting any gentleman who could catch the emperor's eye altered court life in more subtle ways. As the following excerpt from *Records of the Han* describes, the prospect of becoming a sexual partner of the emperor led Dong Xian and others to dress strikingly. This trend turned the Han court into a showcase for flamboyant dandyism.

> The courtiers competed to ornament themselves as seductive beauties and used artful speech to captivate. In contrast, Dong Xian wore a simple garment of misty plain silk. It draped upon him like cicada wings. The emperor would enter the Martin's Breath Quarters and order Dong Xian to change into a light short-sleeved garment. Dong Xian did not use an extravagant belt or long skirt. The people of the palace were all apprehensive and alarmed about their sleeping together.[19]

A similarly heightened concern with male fashion transformed the sartorial styles of the court of the Han Emperor Hui. As Sima Qian notes, "All the palace attendants at the court of Emperor Hui took to wearing caps with gaudy feathers and sashes of seashells and to painting their faces."[20] This image of sumptuously attired courtiers arming themselves with ornate baubles and exquisite fabrics to sally forth on the field of beauty captured the fancy of later generations, as this line crops up again in the Tang-dynasty "Poetical Essay on Supreme Joy" discovered in the Dunhuang caves.[21] What must have struck these Tang readers, as it strikes us today, is how a man of the Han could ensure his future prosperity by attracting the emperor's attention. This situation led to a sophistication in dress and adornment that may appear effete to present sensibilities. Significantly, this sort of behavior prevailed at a time noted for the openness of homosexual love. In subsequent dynasties male cosmetics came to be associated with passive homosexuality, acting, and prostitution. But during the Han these affectations were probably seen as manifestations of dandyism rather than effeminacy. Similar flamboyance in dress characterized the court of Louis XIV, where it was seen by elegant aristocrats not as effeminate but as merely genteel. At the Han court, awareness that sexual favor could lead to honor and riches fueled the concern with appearances present at all royal courts.

Han authors did not portray favorites as stereotypically effete or effeminate, despite the attention men at court gave to outward ornamentation. Emperor Wu and Han Yan equally typify Han ideas of ruler and favorite.

> Han Yan was an illegitimate grandson of Han Tuidang, the Marquis of Gonggao. When the present emperor was still king of Jiaodong, he and Yan studied writing together and the two grew very fond of each other. Later, after the emperor was appointed heir apparent, he became more and more friendly with Yan. Yan was skillful at riding and archery and was also very good at ingratiating himself with the emperor. He was well versed in the fighting techniques of the barbarians and therefore, after the emperor came to the throne and began making plans to open attacks on the Xiongnu, he treated

Yan with even greater respect and honor. Yan had soon advanced to the rank of superior lord and received as many gifts from the ruler as Deng Tong had in his days of honor.

At this time Yan was constantly by the emperor's side, both day and night. Once the emperor's younger brother Liu Fei, the king of Jiangdu, who had come to court to pay his respects, received permission from the emperor to accompany him on a hunt in the Shanglin Park. The order had already been given to clear the roads for the imperial carriage, but the emperor was not yet ready to depart, and so he sent Yan ahead in one of the attendant carriages, accompanied by fifty or a hundred riders, to gallop through the park and observe the game. The king of Jiangdu, seeing the party approaching in the distance, supposed it was the emperor and ordered his own attendants off the road while he himself knelt down by the side of the road to greet the emperor. Yan, however, raced by without even noticing him, and after he had passed, when the king of Jiangdu realized his error, he was enraged and went to the empress dowager in tears. "I beg to return the kingdom which has been granted to me and become a bodyguard in the palace," he said. "Perhaps then I may be accorded as much honor as Han Yan!" From this time on the empress dowager bore a grudge against Yan.

Because he attended the emperor, Han Yan was allowed to come and go in the women's quarters of the palace and did not have to observe the customary prohibitions against entering them. Some time later, it was reported to the empress dowager that Yan had had an illicit affair with one of the women there. She was furious and immediately sent a messenger ordering him to take his life. Although the emperor attempted to make apologies for him, he was able to do nothing to change the order, and in the end Yan was forced to die.[22]

Traditional historians regarded Emperor Wu as a quintessentially masculine emperor. His name itself means "martial," and he spent his long reign subjugating the surrounding non-Chinese peoples. Wu garnered fame as both a warrior and a hunter. His beloved shared these interests. In addition to being literate and intelligent, Han Yan enjoyed stereotypically masculine pursuits, including riding, archery, and warfare. In this sense he epitomized the masculine virtues valued by the aristocracy since the Shang dynasty. Although many court officials pursued vain stylishness in their attempts to attract favor, Han Yan and Emperor Wu's intimacy conformed to the earlier Zhou-dynasty conception of close friends and even lovers as not different from other men in their behavior.

Together with this homosexual ethos came the necessity of heterosexual marriage. Two anecdotes demonstrate the mechanics of bisexual behavior, which ranged beyond the imperial court. The first involved the slave Qin Gong, who was the young and handsome beloved of the general Liang Ji. Not only was the general married, but his wife also had sexual designs on her husband's favorite.[23] Liang Ji openly maintained both a wife and a male favorite, a dual relationship that the social conventions of the time regarding marriage and slavery would have made acceptable. Because Qin Gong was a slave, epitomizing class-structured homosexual roles, his master owned him much as a man could own a concubine. Just as Chinese wives were expected to tolerate a husband's affection for a female concubine, Liang Ji's wife tolerated her husband's dalliances with a male slave. The intermingling of bisexuality, slavery, and marriage adds a complex dimension to this instance of early Chinese social relations.

Nor was this example an isolated case. An earlier instance of bisexuality in marriage provoked similar results:

> General Huo Guang oversaw the exceptionally attractive slave master Feng Zidu. Huo Guang loved and favored him, and often planned his actions together with him. Feng Zidu was extremely content—he had enough power to overthrow even the capital. Later men said, "In times of old there was a slave master of Huo Guang named Feng Zidu who was favored and trusted with a general's power. This provoked laughter in the wineshops of foreigners. . . ." After Huo Guang died, his widow, named Xian Guang, roamed playfully throughout the house together with Feng Zidu.[24]

Huo Guang (d. 68 B.C.) was the paramount political figure of his time. Despite the fact that his beloved was a mere slave master, Feng was more than tolerated by Huo Guang's wife. After Huo's death, his "male concubine" and wife completed a period of mourning and then engaged in a passionate affair of their own. Later generations, and perhaps even their contemporaries, saw the involvement of such a high-status woman as Xian Guang with someone so humble as an act of the greatest wickedness. Ideally a widow of her social rank would be expected to confine her choice of partners for postmarital sexual encounters to the upper classes, as exemplified much later in the Tang short story *Dwelling of the Playful Goddess* (*You xian ku*). After the Tang dynasty, of course, a widow would ideally have been expected to remain celibate for the rest of her life.

For the Chinese man, however, the substitution of male and female passive partners was free of obloquy. In a society that regarded heterosexuality and homosexuality as analogous, men were free to live out their full range of sexual desires. The most complete study of male homosexuality ever conducted in any culture, that of Alfred Kinsey done in the United States in the 1940s, concluded that even in a culture vehemently hostile toward homosexuality, over one-third of the American adult male population had engaged in a homosexual act.[25] In a society such as early China, which accepted and even honored same-sex relationships yet still mandated heterosexual marriage, it seems plausible that bisexuality would be at least as popular as pure homosexuality or perhaps even strict heterosexuality. Unfortunately, the paucity of data that survives makes it impossible to determine the precise extent of homosexuality among the upper classes, much less in early Chinese society as a whole.

In these accounts we also see clues to the origins of practices that later developed into same-sex marriages. The first such custom was that of male pair-bonding, an integral part of Zhou and Han homosexuality, which celebrated male couples for their deep affections. Another precursor to same-sex marriage was the practice of de facto male concubinage. We would be completely distorting the Chinese conception of marriage by viewing it in the distinctive terms of the modern West. From ancient times, wealthy men in China could supplement their regular wives with concubines purchased as an addition to the household. Because these women were often bought from their families, such procurement in fact resembled the purchase of slaves. Yet a concubine differed from a slave in that by gaining her master's sexual attentions she also gained a special social and legal status.

The acquisition of men and boys by the wealthy of early China seems similar in many respects to concubinage. For example, in one famous incident a male beloved killed another of Emperor Wu's favorites; the emperor flew into a rage, and was assuaged only when he found out the reason for the murder: the dead man had seduced one of the female imperial concubines. Male favorites had access to the imperial seraglio, since both female and male sexual partners were allowed into the heavily guarded depths of the inner palace for the emperor's pleasure. Later dynasties restricted access to the inner palace even more carefully, so that a favorite's privileged entry became an increasingly extraordinary prerogative. This similarity between the physical access of male and female concubines to the emperor further heightens the congruence between the social roles of these sexual counterparts.[26] Even the language used to describe the relationships resembled the terminology of concubinage.[27]

Within the general framework of Han society, homosexuality had several advantages over heterosexuality. For example, the friendships formed through loving other men could be continued as a complementary emotional outlet to married life. Choosing the right lover could even benefit the social climber. And in an era prior to dependable contraception, homosexuality left no possibility of unwed mothers, a group that would have had a precarious position in a society acutely conscious of kinship and ancestry.

When heterosexual marriage finally did occur, it was arranged entirely by the male head of the household—the parties immediately involved did not even need to be consulted. Marriage was primarily a union of two households, with individual interests subsumed in favor of the interests of the household as a whole. Consequently, many couples must have found themselves emotionally or sexually incompatible. For the wife, expected to remain faithful to her husband, there was no honorable recourse. But men could escape an unpleasant marital situation in several ways. A wealthy man could simply purchase concubines or female slaves to fulfill his sexual demands. Other men could form extramarital heterosexual affairs with women outside the household, but such opportunities were limited. Homosexuality, which included neither shame nor potential for pregnancy, became an attractive option for those seeking sexual gratification outside the household.

Within marriage, the husband held supreme authority. Prior to the Han, a man could even legally kill his own son,[28] and traces of this life-and-death authority remained even during the Han. A woman would not dare to question her husband on the vital question of his sexuality or object when her husband sought others, such as concubines, for sexual companionship. In fact, jealousy was one of the seven reasons for which a husband could divorce a wife.[29] This recognition of polygamy as an unquestioned Han custom sanctioned male promiscuity. Wives were legally required to acquiesce to their husbands' demands for alternate sexual partners, among whom were other men. By denying wives any say in their sex lives, married men could favor the half-eaten peach at will. The government did not interfere with the sexual status quo because it left most moral questions regarding the household to be solved within the household itself—which in a patriarchal society meant that decisions regarding sexual morality inevitably favored male interests. The very organization of the Han household therefore facilitated the acceptance of male homosexuality.

This atmosphere of openness allowed further development of an emerging sense of homosexual tradition, taking many of its most moving accounts from Han historical literature. The Han tradition finds its greatest exemplar in the famous tale of the Emperor Ai and his favorite Dong Xian. As Ban Gu succinctly observed, "By nature Emperor Ai did not care for women,"[30] and

the genuine tenderness he felt for his beloved Dong Xian capti-
vated the popular imagination. This short passage describing his
love is the most influential in the Chinese homosexual tradition:

> Emperor Ai was sleeping in the daytime with Dong Xian stretched
> out across his sleeve. When the emperor wanted to get up, Dong
> Xian was still asleep. Because he did not want to disturb him, the
> emperor cut off his own sleeve and got up. His love and thought-
> fulness went this far![31]

Just as Mizi Xia gave a homosexual connotation to the term "eating peaches," so did the image of a cut sleeve come to signify the
devotion of Emperor Ai to Dong Xian and, broadly, male
homosexual love. All of Ai's courtiers "imitated the cut sleeve,
also calling it the chopped sleeve," as a tribute to the love shared
by their emperor and Dong.[32] The tender power of this image—
an array of opulent courtiers fastidiously dressed in colorful silk
tunics, each missing a single sleeve—guaranteed that the moment
would continue to burn in the imaginations of readers for almost
twenty centuries.

The terse account of the cut sleeve became absorbed into a tradition of recorded homosexuality that must have seemed ancient
even to Emperor Ai. Men of dynastic history did not feel alone in
having affectionate feelings for other men. The complete integra-
tion of homosexuality into early Chinese court life, as reported in
Memoirs of the Historian and *Records of the Han*, was alluded to repeatedly in later literature and gave men of subsequent ages a
means for situating their own desires within an ancient tradition.
By seeing their feelings as passions of the "cut sleeve," they gained
a consciousness of the place of male love in the history of their
society.

The dramatic ascendency of Dong Xian almost to the imperial
throne marks a high point in the Chinese homosexual tradition
and in the influence of homosexuality over Chinese society. Not
only was male love accepted, but it permeated the fabric of upper-
class life. From the vital concerns of politics to the frivolous world
of men's fashion, homosexuality played an important role. This

sway over elite society was most pronounced at the height of the Western Han, when homosexuality occupied an esteemed and powerful place in court life. Still, the patterns and images of homosexuality formed during the Zhou and brought to fruition during the Han became even more elaborated under subsequent dynasties.

杜琴官

3

Powdered Jade

Three Kingdoms and Six Dynasties (220 to 581)

After four hundred years of national unity, the fall of the Han dynasty in A.D. 220 plunged China into another period of division and chaos. Internicine warfare, weak emperors, strong generals, and transcendental philosophies marked the age. A quick succession of rulers and dynasties continued for another four centuries until the founding of the illustrious Tang dynasty in the seventh century. As in previous periods, homosexuality continued as a part of the sex lives of the social elite. Famed emperors, poets, and philosophers openly professed their attachments to other men. The enthusiasm with which the ruling elites of the minor dynasties following the Han embraced male love led authors to remark on the popularity of half-eaten peaches and cut sleeves at the royal courts. The official records of the short-lived Liu Song dynasty go even further in describing the extent of homosexuality among the upper classes:

> From the Xianning and Taikang reign periods (275–290) of the Western Jin dynasty onward, male favoritism flourished considerably and was as extensive as attraction to women. All of the gentlemen and officials esteemed it. All men in the realm followed this fashion to the extent that husbands and wives were estranged. Resentful unmarried women became jealous.[1]

In a more specific case, a poem by Liu Xiaozhuo (481–539) describes one woman's anxiety over whether the man she loves will ignore her in favor of a boy. It concludes, "She dawdles, not daring to move closer, / Afraid he might compare her with leftover peach."[2] We will never be sure whether this admiration for male love actually led to a decrease in heterosexual marriage and consternation among unmarried women. It is possible that, as these authors' observations suggest, bachelors who preferred men delayed taking a wife for as long as possible. And records of the period mention ardent gynaphobes who would flee at the sight of a woman.[3]

Even allowing for the hyperbole to which early historians were prone, these passages attest to the continued visibility of homosexuality after the fall of the Han. R. H. Van Gulik, a scholar of Chinese sexual history, even singled out the late third century as a high point in the openness of male homosexuality.[4] Moreover, the expanding variety of sources from this period gives us a broader range of views of male homosexuality than we find in earlier periods. Official histories continue to provide detailed information on the lives and loves of the ruling elite. In addition, less formal works include descriptions of officials, writers, and men of less exalted status. These new sources include sufficient information to begin probing enigmas such as the patterns of homosexual relationships and ideals of male beauty.

As for terminology, many of the words appearing in Han records continue to be used after the dynasty's demise. Use of the terms *chong* and *xing*, which appear frequently in histories of the period, shows a continuation of the earlier tendency to describe sexuality in terms of social roles rather than sexual essence. A less objective term also comes into use: *xie xia*.[5] *Xie* means both "nude" and "dirty," linking the carnal aspects of sex with a negative value judgment; *xia* means "intimacy" or "intimate" and sometimes appears alone as well. The compound therefore means something like "undue familiarity" and was used by censorious historians to express their disapproval at the improper influence that favorites exercised in court life.

Records of the Wei (*Wei shu*) gives an early example of the use of another new term to describe homosexual attraction to men: "*nanfeng,*" literally meaning "male wind," though a more accurate translation would be "male custom" or "male practice." This term marks an important development in Chinese sexual terminology, for whereas previous terms described only social relationships, this compound describes the male homosexual act itself. *Nanfeng* became a popular word, and remains in use today as a literary expression for male homosexuality.

The official history of the Northern Qi dynasty (550–577) added to this expanding vocabulary. That work speaks of men's delight in *nanse*, with *se* denoting sexual attraction, passion, or lust. Thus this term might be translated as "male eroticism," further reflecting the new trend of defining sexuality according to sexual act rather than social role. During this period, then, we see that Chinese developed a vocabulary for describing homosexuality that endured until the introduction of Western scientific terminology, with its implicit Western classifications of sexuality, during the late nineteenth century.

Most of the official dynastic histories describing the period date from the early Tang dynasty, and consequently often reflect the concerns of the age in which their authors lived, the Tang, as much as the earlier periods they purport to describe. These histories include sections detailing the lives of male favorites of the emperors. The names of these sections remain linked to Han precedents, though with modifications. For example, while *Records of the Wei* adopted the Han practice of synthesizing biographies of imperial favorites into one chapter for the official history of a dynasty, the Wei title for this chapter is "En xing," which differs in connotation from similar chapter headings in *Memoirs of the Historian* and *Records of the Han*. With meanings such as "favor" and "imperial grace," *en* lacks the negative associations of the Han term *ning* (artful flattery). This chapter in *Records of the Wei* can consequently be literally translated as "Favorites." *Records of the Liu Song (Song shu)* explains the etymology of this particular title: "*Records of the Han* has the 'Tables of Favored Nobles' ('Enzhe hou biao') and the 'Biographies of Those Obtaining Favor Through Artful Flattery' ('Ning xing zhuan'). Now I have drawn on these names, rearranging them as the 'Article on Favorites' ('En xing pian')."[6] As *History of the North (Bei shi)* recognizes, subsequent histories followed the example of *Records of the Wei* in including a chapter on favorites.[7] Only *Records of the Southern Qi (Nan Qi shu)* differs in its terminology for this chapter, calling it "Favored Officials" ("Xing chen"), a title similar in connotation to others of the period.

Many of these historians, apparently finding the subjects of sex and political favoritism distasteful to their Confucian sensibilities, felt the need to justify inclusion of a chapter on imperial favorites. These statements provide a rare glimpse of early attitudes toward one particular form of homosexuality, and are among the few abstract musings that survive from Chinese literature on this topic. Most straightforward among the reasons given for including information on favorites is precedent: several historians state that they wrote these biographies because previous chronicles, such as *Records of the Han*, had such a chapter. Other reasons, however, provide a perspective on how scholars of the period viewed male favoritism at court.

Records of the Northern Qi sees sexual patronage as a part of the larger natural order. "When there are celestial portents, there will

certainly be people acting accordingly. When there is the star of
favored officials, they will be arrayed beside the imperial throne."[8]
Cosmological necessity creates imperial favorites, and so the
historian's duty lies in recording the influence of these men on
government.

Other historians preferred to take a more severe tone, setting
forth the lives of these favorites as a warning to future rulers on
the dangers of allowing loved ones too much power. *Records of the
Liu Song* opens with a moralistic parallel, stating that the distinction between talented officials and favorites is like that between the
superior man (*junzi*) and lesser men (*xiaoren*) spoken of by
Confucius.[9] These historians do not fault favorites for their sexual
practices, but only for the pernicious effects of their political
opportunism. The ornate *History of the South* (*Nan shi*) makes the
point more poetically: "Among the actions people take are those
as stinking as abalones and as fragrant as orchids. People of ordinary character can become either inferior or superior."[10] *Records of
the Liu Song* lists historical examples that prove this point, discussing favoritism as disruptive to good government and as a catalyst
to factionalism. Eventually, the historian concludes, favoritism
contributes to the speedy fall of a dynasty.[11]

This moral didacticism using historical examples of favorites
finds its most eloquent exposition in the *History of the North*. Here
the author points to favorites as an example of the forces that
"harm the worthy and injure good government," and blames
favoritism as a cause for the corruption and fall of previous dynasties such as the Yin, better known as the Shang. He therefore
calls these examples of unbridled favoritism a "Yin Mirror,"
reflecting the mistakes of the past in order to teach the present.[12]

In taking a historical perspective on favorites, these scholars
evince a concrete sense of the literary and historical homosexual
tradition. *History of the North* finds favoritism as far back as the Xia
and Shang.[13] *Records of the Southern Qi* emphasizes the numerous
accounts of favoritism from the Zhou and Han.[14] And *History of
the South* notes the continuation of such practices, drawing a link

between past and present: "In the Liang and Chen dynasties, this custom did not change. Since the four dynasties suffered from these favorites, I am now setting forth this chapter in continuation of the works of previous historians."[15] Literature of the period also shows the tendency to refer to the past as a way of understanding the present. Taken together, historical writing and literature from this age display a distinct awareness of the male homosexual tradition.

Beyond tradition, these dynastic histories speak about more contemporary matters as well, bluntly acknowledging the extent of homosexuality in court life. One historian laments, "How widespread favoritism was at the end of the Qi!"[16] As *Records of the Southern Qi* observes, "Everyone at the court desired intimacy."[17] The sheer number of biographies surviving from these dynastic histories describing the period of disunity following the Han attests the extent of favoritism. *History of the North* alone contains forty biographies of favorites. The full translation and explanation of these records would require a book in itself. Since the lives of these favorites often repeat themes explored in detail in the previous chapter, here I will try simply to extract some general trends exemplified by this period.

One perennial theme, dating back to the unhappy story of Mizi Xia, concerns the fickleness of the ruler's affections. A world-weary historian muses, "The old ones were not the original old ones because the new had become the old. The intimates were not the previous intimates, because the distant had become the intimate."[18] A favorite's position was generally insecure. Given the added instability inherent in the chaos of the period, capturing a ruler's affections did not necessarily lead to permanent power or prosperity. The sheer number of imperial favorites during this period demonstrates their ephemerality.

These favorites are often shown in the larger context of imperial sensuality—their inherent undesirability stems from their tendency to distract the ruler from serious matters of state. One historian uses the rococo prose style of the period to create a sense of the temptations an emperor faced:

With gates like those of a jade hall of state and a home like a golden
grotto; concubines and serving women; the music of Yan, Qin,
Cai, and Zheng; pearly pools with jade bridges; frolicking fish, dra-
gons, peacocks, and horses; flowery halls stuffed full of delights
whose sparkling rays penetrate even the azure clouds—these harm
good government and injure people. Intimates are also among
these distractions. And so with accounts of youthful rulers and
widespread chaos, I have recorded how flatterers and evildoers can
prevail.[19]

This historian does not identify favorites as a singular menace to
good government, but puts them in the context of the myriad
distractions that could corrupt an undisciplined monarch. And yet
the danger presented by favorites could not be avoided. One chapter of biographies ends with a summary of the long list of famous
imperial favorites, at the end of which the despairing historian
rhetorically asks how something so ubiquitous could possibly be
avoided.[20]

As for the favorites themselves, looking through the accounts
of their lives we do not find a stereotyped formula repeated for
each person, as often happens in Chinese biography. Because
favorites advanced through irregular channels, their lives show a
wide range of backgrounds, skills, accomplishments, and fates.
Many came from well-connected families, which is understand-
able since the children of officials and nobles would have had the
greatest access to their rulers. Wang Zhongxing, for example, was
born the son of an official and eventually became the beloved of
the fourth-century Emperor Wei Gaozu.[21] In contrast, Wang
Zhongxing's rival for Gaozu's affections, Wang Rui, had an impoverished father who made his living as an astrologer and
fortune-teller.[22] Zhou Shizhen came from even lowlier origins as a
servant.[23] Several favorites came from minor merchant families.
Dai Faxing, for instance, began life helping his father sell coarse
hemp cloth in the marketplace.[24] Even a variety of ethnic backgrounds appears in these biographies. The importance of Central
Asian peoples to China at this time is shown by the rise of Gao'a
Nagong, of nomadic origins, and the Sogdian dancing boys of the

Northern Qi rulers.[25] Whatever the origins of an imperial favorite, it was certain that he would be able to achieve wealth and even exalted office. David Johnson even singles out this route as one of the only ways available during this period for the plebeian upstart to rise to high status.[26]

Imperial favorites came to a ruler's attention in many different ways during this time. Some arrived at court as clerks and officials in the bureaucracy—Liu Xizong, for example.[27] The violent chaos of the age gave military men close contact with emperors, and several favorites, such as Xu Yuan, made their mark while on military expeditions.[28] And of course these histories also include the occasional tale of the supernatural, such as Ji Sengzhen's rise to favor after repeating an auspicious dream to his imperial lover.[29]

Many favorites receive mention for their special skills. Some were quite scholarly; Xu He, for instance, authored several books and enjoyed debating metaphysical subtleties with Buddhist monks.[30] Others gain praise for skill and craftiness in battle, as did Ji Sengzhen. One historian also singles out Ji for his eloquence, good looks, and stylishness, combining martial valor with a rakish bearing. Mu Tipo became well known for his erotic skills—which, the historian assures us, equaled those of his mother, who found a place at court in a similar manner.[31] And some men came to their emperor's attention for possessing unusual talents: Li Xian, for one, impressed his imperial lover with his horsemanship, while He Shikai soothed the ruler with beautiful lute music.[32]

The favor these men received translated into numerous practical benefits. For the politically ambitious, such as Ru Hao, imperial favor could lead to rank and enormous power.[33] Some even achieved noble rank—Wang Rui, for example, rose from the obscurity of poverty eventually to become enfeoffed as a king. Such men inevitably received great wealth as well. Lacking words to convey the splendors of the riches given to Wang Rui, the author of *Records of the Wei* declares: "The amount of baubles and cloth granted him is unimaginable."[34] Special privileges awaited the favorite too. Some were able to drop the awkward formalities that normally existed between the emperor and his courtiers. He Shikai and his imperial lover "did not follow the ceremonies of ruler and subject."[35] Perhaps because he realized the unique position his relationship with the emperor gave him, He Shikai called personal service to the emperor the most important office of all.[36]

Some favorites were able to gain permanent upward mobility for their families, and in this way they resembled the families of male favorites and female consorts during the Han. The biography of Wang Rui includes pages of descriptions of the honors lavished on his family. His mother was posthumously honored, while his father and brothers received high rank and office. In addition, many of his sons achieved office and considerable prominence. Even members of the families of his brothers received high office.[37] The privileges won by favorites such as Guo Xiu allowed them to educate their sons in the classics, giving their children a chance to enter the bureaucracy.[38] Other favorites, among them Hou Gang, increased their children's chances of success by marrying them off to scions of other wealthy families.

These favorites ended their lives in a variety of ways. Some lived to a happy old age—Liu Xizong, for example, died at age seventy-seven. Some even received a state funeral, the death of Wang Rui being met with an outpouring of grief and elaborate funeral arrangements. Others were less fortunate. Zhao Xiu abused his considerable power, alienating important rivals; eventually they denounced him and he was killed.[39] A favorite's disgrace usually devolved on his family as well. When Ru Hao was killed because of his involvement in court intrigue, his son suffered the same fate. The forces that could be harnessed for power and wealth also contained the seeds of dishonor and even death.

The choice of eunuchs as the sexual favorites of emperors from the Han to the Qing also deserves comment, since many of the men portrayed in these biographies had been castrated.[40] To understand this preference, we must remember that eunuchs were a major fixture of a Chinese emperor's environment, and it would therefore not seem inappropriate for him to view them sexually. The easy access of eunuchs to the imperial bed made their involvement in the emperor's sexual activities almost inevitable.

Fortunately, beginning in this period we are no longer limited to discussing only the imperial sex life. Whereas Zhou and Han writings deal mainly with the affairs of rulers and their intimates, records from periods following the collapse of the Han give a detailed sampling of the lives of a wider range of public figures. For the first time, these sources indicate that homosexuality could be found not just at court but throughout the upper strata of society. This new literary genre are exemplified by Liu Yiqing's (403–444) *A New Account of Tales of the World* (*Shishuo xinyu*), a collection of notable anecdotes and conversations, a lively and witty potpourri of famous remarks and interesting gossip about the greatest figures of the preceeding three centuries. The work is conveniently divided into sections according to subject, such as "Affairs of State" and "Letters and Scholarship"; one section deals specifically with renowned male beauties of the day.

The inclusion of a separate chapter concerning "Appearance and Behavior" of distinguished men shows a high regard for handsome men that mirrored the admiration popular prior to the fall of the Han. From this chapter it seems that men of the fifth century regularly discussed and admired male beauty. This appreciation often included sexual overtones, as in the friendship between the poet Pan Yue (247–300) and Xiahou Zhan (243–291). One account described them as "sworn brothers" who "consequently liked to wander about together."[41] According to *Tales of the World*, "Pan Yue and Xiahou Zhan both had handsome faces and enjoyed going about together. Contemporaries called them the 'linked jade disks.'"[42] This motif of linked jade disks reappears centuries later in a section devoted to homosexuality in the "Poetical Essay on the Supreme Joy"; thus Tang readers evidently considered the two men's relationship sexual.

The description of Pan Yue and Xiahou Zhan's love is not the only passage of *Tales of the World* with homosexual connotations. Huan Wen (312–373), a powerful grand marshal at the Eastern Jin court, asked his subordinate Wang Xun for his opinion as to the Chancellor-Prince Sima Yu's appearance. (Sima Yu was famous for his handsome and dignified presence.) Wang Xun replied, "The chancellor-prince has been taking responsibility for the government and is naturally majestic like a divine ruler. But Your Excellency, too, is the object of all men's gaze. Otherwise how could the vice-president of the Court Secretariat have subordinated himself to you?"[43] This passage shows how a subordinate could flatter his superior by remarking that his looks, like those of a ruler noted for his beauty, could attract the attention of other men.[44] A striking appearance could even help win the cooperation of other government officials.

Men throughout this period therefore valued good looks, and some attempted to improve them by artificial means. One early-fifth-century source even criticized Zuo Si (d. 306) because "he had no use for fine manners or ornaments."[45] According to the aesthetic of the day, a man could improve his appearance by applying white powder; one common saying asserted that the esteem for white skin even went beyond the easily visible portions of the body. "Oiled hair, powdered face, and small gleaming buttocks" described the ideal man.[46] The use of facial powder by men dates back at least to the Han. In the mid–second century, one official scandalized the courtiers by arriving at an imperial funeral with a powdered face. This practice seems to have originated among the non-Chinese peoples, as indicated by the Chinese name "barbarian powder." By the fall of the Han the use of "barbarian powder" to lighten facial complexion had gained such popularity among both men and women that the state of Wei during the Three Kingdoms period even made trade in powder a state monopoly—a sure sign of high profits.[47]

Records from the period following the fall of the Han are filled with references to men's use of powder. He Yan was described as "by nature egocentric, and whether active or at rest was never without a powder puff in his hand. When he walked anywhere he looked back at his own shadow."[48] From this account a sixth-century commentary to *Tales of the World* tartly concludes, "[He

Yan's] seductive beauty was basically dependent on external ornament."[49] *Tales of the World* itself relates an incident in which the emperor doubted that He Yan's visage could be so white naturally. He therefore concocted a scheme to detect whether or not He Yan used cosmetics.

> He Yan was handsome in appearance and demeanor, and his face
> was extremely white. Emperor Wen of Wei [r. 220–226] suspected
> that he used powder. At the peak of the summer months he offered
> him some hot soup and dumplings. After [He Yan] had eaten it he
> broke into a profuse sweat and with his scarlet robe was wiping his
> face, but his complexion became whiter than ever.[50]

Fortunately for He Yan, he had not powdered his face that day.

Light skin has long been a mark of beauty in China. Indeed, in most agricultural societies a fair complexion distinguishes rich landlords from poor peasants. Only with the rise of the middle class, as in the United States, has the tan come to represent rare leisure time and the price of a plane ticket to some distant vacation spot.

Because men of early China considered a pale countenance attractive, they often praised a pallid complexion as the perfect contrast to gleaming black eyes. When the calligraphic master Wang Xizhi (309–ca. 365) saw the capital intendant Du Yi (d. before 335), "he sighed in admiration, saying, 'His face is like congealed ointment and his eyes like dotted lacquer; this is a man from among the gods and immortals.'"[51] Du Yi's looks were so renowned that even after his death when men would praise the appearance of someone other than Du Yi his former acquaintances would remark, "It's a pity you never saw [Du Yi], that's all."[52] The admiration of white-skinned men is rendered in striking terms in another passage from *Tales of the World*, which compares the skin of the high official Wang Yan to the white handle of a ceremonial fly whisk: "Wang Yan's face and appearance were symmetrical and beautiful. . . . He constantly gripped a sambartail chowry with a white jade handle which was completely indistinguishable from his hand."[53]

This passage brings up another stock metaphor for lauding male appearance: comparison to jade. The "man of jade" was the paragon of male physical beauty, as exemplified by a scholar-official of the third century, Pei Kai (237–291):

Pei Kai possessed outstanding beauty and manners. Even after removing his official cap, with coarse clothing and undressed hair, he was always attractive. Contemporaries felt him to be a man of jade. One who saw him remarked, "Looking at Pei Kai is like walking on top of a jade mountain with the light reflected back at you."[54]

References to the man of jade and jade mountains linked male beauty with what ancient Chinese considered the most beautiful precious substance. In contrast to the gaudy brilliance of gold, the icy beauty of jade represented elegant understatement. This metaphor appears again in another account of a powerful general who further praised Wang Yan. Perhaps attempting to find a more flattering simile than that of a fly whisk, he stated: "When he's in a crowd of other men, he's like a pearl or jade in the midst of tiles and stones."[55]

The flamboyant tropes with which men of the age could describe male beauty often employed imagery from nature. Perhaps this tendency represents the hold that nature-oriented Neo-Taoism exercised over all aspects of intellectual and literary life of the period. A fourth-century work reports that one young man, on seeing Chancellor Wang Dao of the Eastern Jin, felt "as if a refreshing breeze had come to caress me."[56] *Tales of the World* quotes one contemporary exclaiming of Wang Meng, "How light and airy his graceful soaring!"[57] An admirer of Sima Yu's handsome features explained that when he entered the imperial court for the morning audience, "all became radiantly light, like dawn clouds rising."[58] The official Wang Gong (d. 398) was called "sleek and shining as the willow in the months of spring."[59] And Wang Shao (fl. ca. 350) was so famed for his appearance that one powerful admirer said of him, "[He] surely and unmistakably has the plumes of a phoenix."[60]

From the broader selection of available sources of the period we see for the first time evidence of homosexuality among military men, great artists, and philosophers. For example, the honored poet Pan Yue and the grand master of calligraphy Wang Xizhi both fervently admired male beauty. Significantly, the greatest intellectual force of his age, Xi Kang (223–262), had as a lover the gifted poet Ruan Ji, author of a beautiful encomium to male lovers of the Zhou and Han. Even surviving incised stone portraits from the period show these two lovers sitting side by side.[61]

As the most outstanding member of the "Seven Worthies of the Bamboo Grove," a literary and philosophic society of talented bohemians, Xi Kang is remembered both for his sublime poetry and his personal adherence to Neo-Taoist principles that shocked establishment scholars. During his own lifetime, however, Xi Kang was as renowned for his appearance as for his talents and intellect. His biography records this striking presence: "Kang was seven [Chinese] feet, eight inches tall, with an imposing facial expression. He treated his bodily frame like so much earth or wood and never added any adornment or polish, yet had the grace of a dragon and the beauty of a phoenix."[62] Some contemporaries described him as "like the wind beneath the pines, high and gently blowing," while one admirer said, "As a person Xi Kang is majestically towering, like a solitary pine tree standing alone. But when he's drunk he leans crazily like a jade mountain about to collapse."[63] From the profuse praise of his contemporaries it seems clear that Xi Kang possessed an extraordinary appearance, with the stereotypical Taoist metaphor of the pine tree representing his transcendental character, while jade and the phoenix related his beauty.

One tale of Xi Kang parallels that of the wife of the Zhou-dynasty Duke Gong of Cao, who gazed through a peephole at a noble guest having sexual intercourse with his male retainers. In this variation on an ancient theme, the wife of Shan Tao covertly observed the nocturnal activities of Xi Kang and his lover, Ruan Ji. Apparently impressed by the sexual talents of Xi Kang and Ruan Ji relative to those of her husband, she told Shan Tao that he could compare to them only on an intellectual level.

The first time Shan Tao met Xi Kang and Ruan Ji he became united with them in a friendship "stronger than metal and fragrant as orchids." Shan's wife, Lady Han, realized that her husband's relationship with the two men was different from ordinary friendships, and asked him about it. Shan replied, "It's only these two gentlemen whom I may consider the friends of my mature years."

His wife said, "In antiquity Xi Fuji's wife also personally observed Hu Yan and Zhao Cui. I'd like to peep at these friends of yours. Is it all right?"

On another day the two men came, and his wife urged Shan to detain them overnight. After preparing wine and meat, that night she made a hole through the wall, and it was dawn before she remembered to return to her room.

When Shan came in he asked her, "What did you think of the two men?" His wife replied, "Your own ability is in no way comparable to theirs. It's only on the basis of your knowledge of men and your judgment that you should be their friend."[64]

In this tale of comic voyeurism we find affirmation that leading literati openly discussed and practiced homosexuality. Not only was Shan Tao's wife aware of the homosexual tradition, as indicated by her reference to a famous Zhou account of homosexual voyeurism, but she even praised Xi Kang and Ruan Ji for their sexual prowess.

In contrast to these sorts of egalitarian friendships, the unusual relationship of Yu Xin (513–581), author of the famous "Lament for Jiangnan," and Wang Shao brings up the question of how class-structured and trans-generational relationships could change when the partners' social statuses and ages changed.

When Wang Shao was young he was beautiful, and Yu Xin opened up his home to him and loved him. They had the joy of the cut sleeve. Wang Shao relied on Yu Xin for clothing and food, and Yu Xin gave him everything. Wang Shao received guests and was also Yu Xin's wine server.

Later Wang Shao became the censor of Yingzhou. When Yu Xin went west to Jiangling he passed through Jiangxia. Wang Shao greeted Yu Xin very weakly. Sitting together, Wang Shao's affec-

tion for him decreased. He had Yu Xin enter the feast and seated
him beside his couch. Yu Xin looked like a widower.

Yu Xin could bear this no longer. Having drunk too freely, he
jumped directly onto Wang Shao's couch and repeatedly trampled
and kicked his food. Looking directly at Wang Shao he said, "Today your appearance seems very strange compared to your former
one!" Guests filled the hall. Wang Shao was extremely embarrassed.[65]

Although Wang Shao's later rise to officialdom indicates that he
was probably not a common prostitute, he did rely on the illustrious poet Yu Xin for patronage during his youth. In return for
entertaining guests, acting as a cup bearer, and rendering sexual
services, he received clothing, food, and lodging. Despite the fact
that highly literate men commonly served as retainers to the rich,
this former servitude made Wang Shao uncomfortable in the presence of his former patron. In any event, Wang's early service did
not interfere with his official career; he eventually rose to a powerful post, indicating that society still did not view sexual subservience among important men harshly.

The complexity of homosexual relationships inevitably led to
the creation of poetic works immortalizing conflicting sentiments.
Ruan Ji (210–263), lover of Xi Kang, was one of the most famous
poets to apply his brush to a homosexual theme. This work, one
of several dealing with homosexuality from the "Jade Terrace"
collection of love poetry, beautifully illustrates the stock imagery
on which men of his time could draw in conceptualizing and
describing love for another man.

> In days of old there were many blossom boys—
>   An Ling and Long Yang.
> Young peach and plum blossoms,
>   Dazzling with glorious brightness.
> Joyful as nine springtimes;
>   Pliant as if bowed by autumn frost.
>
> Roving glances gave rise to beautiful seductions;
>   Speech and laughter expelled fragrance.

> Hand in hand they shared love's rapture,
> Sharing coverlets and bedclothes.

> Couples of birds in flight,
> Paired wings soaring.
> Cinnabar and green pigments record a vow:
> "I'll never forget you for all eternity."[66]

The poem begins by reference to the past, a standard poetic convention. This technique emphasizes the sense of tradition holding together all of these events, a device seen fleetingly in earlier homosexual literature. Invoking the revered notion of antiquity automatically lent an air of dignity and importance to an author's writings. Ruan Ji continues with the names of two famous favorites of the Zhou: Lords An Ling and Long Yang. These men, together with Mizi Xia and Dong Xian, formed the core of a pantheon of figures seen by later generations as symbols of male love. Literate Chinese throughout dynastic history looked to these ancient icons of homosexuality much as medieval Europeans did to Ganymede. The poem then ends in a descriptive paean to the devotion expressed by these early figures.

The Jin-dynasty (265–420) poet Zhang Hanbian wrote another early poem praising male love, a tribute to Zhou Xiaoshi that described the boy's charms in glowing terms:

> The actor Zhou elegantly wanders,
> the youthful boy is young and delicate,
> fifteen years old.
> Like the eastern sun,
> fragrant skin, vermillion cosmetics,
> simple disposition mixes with notariety.
> Your head turns—I kiss you,
> lotus and hibiscus.

> Your appearance is already pure,
> your clothing is new.
> The chariot follows the wind,
> flying after fog and currents of mist.

> Inclined toward extravagance and festiveness,
>   gazing around at the leisurely and beautiful.
> A pleasant expression delights in laughter,
>   a handsome mouth delights in talking.[67]

Zhang's beloved Zhou Xiaoshi was in fact a male prostitute. The poem specifies his age as fifteen. It is impossible to know the extent of prostitution among boys during the Jin dynasty, but the existence of a network of patronage and even outright prostitution is hinted at here. While male prostitution probably existed in earlier periods as well, at this time a genre of literature emerged that openly discussed sexual themes, providing eloquent testimony to the practice of male prostitution. This poem also provides an early link between the professions of acting and prostitution, an association that became more visible during later dynasties. Zhou Xiaoshi was young but still applied cosmetics to enhance his appearance. Perhaps it was the conspicuous use of cosmetics by male prostitutes and actors that led to the gradual disappearance of powder from the toiletries of most upper-class men. Not only did cosmetics become associated with sexual passivity, but they took on class connotations as well. In later periods, the powdered man gradually became relegated to the lowest classes of social subservience. Yet despite Zhou Xiaoshi's need to sell his own body for a living, the poet portrays his life as one of carefree ease. The Zhou Xiaoshi of Zhang Hanbian's poem inhabits a world of fragrant flowers, beautiful clothing, sybaritic leisure, and festive vivaciousness. Of course, this interpretation is made from the point of view of his client: the boy himself might have had quite a different sense of the indignity and uncertainty of his own life.

Subsequent readers must also have detected the biased viewpoint of this poem. The Liang-dynasty poet Liu Zun (d. 535) attempted to present a more balanced view in his poem "Multitudinous Blossoms," commissioned by the Crown Prince Xiao Gang.

> How pitiful the young boy Zhou is!
> Barely smiling, he plucks orchids professionally.

Fresh skin paler than powdered whiteness,
Mouth and face like pink peach blossoms.
He hugs his catapult near Diaoling,
And casts his rod east of Lotusleaves.
Wrists whirl through fragrant musk,
Light clothes at the mercy of the wind.

Lucky to be chosen to brush off a pillow,
Serving in flowery halls.
Gilt screens enclose his kingfisher quilt,
Indigo cloth drapes his incense clothes-frame.
From an early age he knew the pain of scorn,
Withholding words; ashamed to speak.
Favors of the cut sleeve are generous,
Love of the half-eaten peach never dies.
Moth eyebrows—What's the use of envy?
New faces stream steadily through the palace.[68]

This poem presents a far less glamorous perspective on the life of a young male favorite. While the earlier work compares Zhou Xiaoshi's sexual encounters to "lotus and hibiscus," here he "plucks orchids professionally" and "casts his rod" to lure customers. "Flowery halls" are just a place of business. His humiliation and degradation have left him psychologically scarred, unable to communicate self-confidently. Nevertheless, this poem also portrays Zhou as extraordinarily attractive. His pale skin and rosy complexion evoke ideals of female beauty that apparently transferred to sexually passive men.

The poet then ties his work to the homosexual tradition by reference to the "cut sleeve." Liu states that love between men is not all frivolity; there is a pathetic side to the lives of male favorites. He also cites the case of Mizi Xia by reference to "love of the half-eaten peach." Ironically, he declares that the love between socially dominant and submissive men is eternal—yet Mizi Xia came to an unfortunate end after his lover tired of him. This is also the probable fate of the young favorite. As his looks fade, so do the passions he aroused. His later life promises to be uncertain. The poem ends with the arrival of a bevy of new moth eyebrows—a synecdoche for young beauties—which will cause him to be forgotten.

The jaundiced view of a favorite's life presented by Liu Zun does not indicate that the Liang-dynasty poet rejected homosexuality in general. He merely criticized the social conditions under which male favorites were forced to exist. Others were no less critical of the background to the colorful facade of sexual relations between older and younger men. The most famous poem of the age written on a homosexual theme was by Emperor Jianwen (r. 550–551) of the Liang. A masterful poet, Jianwen is best remembered for his lyrics describing plum blossoms and female beauty. Yet one of his greatest works is a short encomium to his boy beloved.

> Charming boy—You look so handsome!
> You surpass Dong Xian and Mizi Xia.
>
> Our feather curtains are filled with morning fragrance,
> Within pearl blinds I hear the distant drips of an evening
>   water clock.
> Kingfisher quilts bear the hues of mandarin ducks,
> Our curtained bed is inlaid with ivory.
>
> You are as youthful as Zhou Xiaoshi,
> Your face is more beautiful than rosy red dawn clouds.
> Sleeves made of regal jade brocade,
> Tunic of delicate flowery cloth.
>
> When you touch your pants, I lightly blush.
> As you tilt your head, two curls fall out of place.
> Your coy glances now and then cause me to smile.
> Jade-like hands grasp flowers.
>
> Deep in your heart you probably suspect you're not my
>   latest catch,
> But your intimate love for me is still like that of the
>   "former carriage."
> You're enough to make the girls of Yan envious,
> And cause even Zheng women to sigh.[69]

Like Liu Zun's poetic description of Zhou Xiaoshi, this poem also invokes the homosexual tradition of Zhou and Han. Jianwen's greatest tribute to his favorite's beauty is that it surpasses even that of Dong Xian and Mizi Xia. The poet then hints at their intimacy by describing the sights, smells, and sounds of their bedchamber. A portrayal of the unnamed boy's looks and clothing progresses to examples of the effects these attributes have in arousing the poet's passions. To close the poem there are again references to the famed male lovers of ancient times. The "latest catch" refers to the conversation between the king of Wei and Lord Long Yang comparing the love of a ruler to catching fish; and "former carriage" harks back to Mizi Xia's improper use of his lord's vehicle to visit his sick mother. These allusions reinforce both the beautiful and pathetic aspects of male love. But not only does Jianwen's boy surpass famous youths of antiquity; he even incites jealousy among the most beautiful women of the day.

In general, literature from this period shows a regard for homosexuality that extended beyond the tiny circle of the court and down to at least the literati. Sometimes the passions of the cut sleeve appear as an ardor of burning intensity, as in a poem by the sixth-century writer Liu Hong.

> So pretty he stands out easily from the crowd,
> Fair, fair, most exquisite.
> Elegant eyebrows arch smooth over twin eyes,
> Mellifluous flows his murmuring voice.[70]

The terseness of this short love lyric leaves much to the imagination. We cannot tell anything about the respective social classes of lover and beloved, or even whether this was an example of comradely love or favoritism. All that we can see is a love so intense that it spilled over into verse, immortalizing an instant of private passion.

Other examples are more easily understood. The acclaimed poetic innovator Wu Jun (469–520) describes how the love of handsome boys could be bought by anyone willing to pay the price.

> Dong Sheng smiles with true charm,
> Zi Du has such lovely eyes.
> A million pays for one word,
> A thousand in cash buys surrender.
>
> Don't mention hide-and-seek mallow!
> Who cares about virtue meek and mild?
> I want you to bring your broidered quilt,
> Come lie with your man of Yue![71]

This poem shows another aspect of the many passions of the cut sleeve. Whereas Liu Hong described his love in the beautifully ornamented terms of idealized physical manifestations, Wu Jun focuses on the more mundane subject of boys for sale. Both poems point to a society in which homosexuality stepped beyond the isolated confines of the imperial court to be taken up by members of the scholarly elite and officialdom as well. One speaks of genuine love, the other of commercialized lust. Taken together they allows us to view homosexuality as a Janus, from dual perspectives, and to see the passions of the cut sleeve in all their contradictory variety.

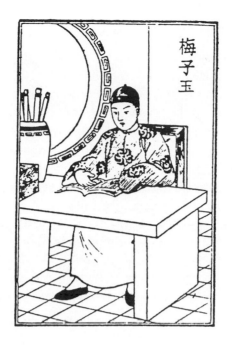

梅
子
玉

4

Men of the Misty Moon
Tang and Song Dynasties (618 to 1279)

The founding of the Tang dynasty in 618 turned out to be more than just the rise of yet another petty kingdom. Taking the unity thrust upon China by the short-lived Sui dynasty, the Tang rulers solidified their hold over both north and south, forging a lasting empire. For the first time since the fall of the Han, all under heaven was once again a single realm. The Tang rulers, still heavily influenced by the martial nomads of Central Asia, melded native Chinese arts and customs with the best they found from the Western regions. This mingling of cultures produced a society of profound sophistication. With this cultural brilliance came a high regard for sensuality, reflected in many poems of the age as well as in records of homosexuality.

Official histories of the Tang have few references to homosexuality compared with the sexual cornucopia of earlier dynastic histories. Perhaps male favorites found themselves more removed from positions of power, which would explain their absence from the records of Tang politics. Or maybe male love was out of favor among the Tang elite relative to the rulers of earlier dynasties. After all, emperors would certainly still have had opportunities to meet potential favorites: eunuchs continued to populate the imperial household, and the emperor's gardens, such as the "Eternal Spring Garden" of Xuanzong (r. 712–756), were filled with handsome young singing boys.

One of the few accounts of a male favorite at court deals with the beginning of the dynasty, when the boy Chengxin became enmeshed in the succession struggle of two heirs of Emperor Taizong (r. 627–650). The heir apparent, Li Chengqian, favored the young entertainer, who was little more than ten years old at the time. Chengqian's jealous younger brother Li Tai reported this relationship to the emperor, who had Chengxin killed for unclear reasons. Chengqian went into extravagant mourning over his slain beloved and had a statue of the youth constructed in his palace, to which he tearfully sacrificed. When he found out that Tai was responsible for the boy's execution, Chengqian plotted violent revenge. Realizing the danger of Chengqian's wrath, Tai accused Chengqian of plotting to overthrow Taizong and establish himself as emperor. The mercurial Taizong reacted to this news by demoting Chengqian to commoner status and exiling him to the frontiers, where he died.[1]

Another memorable mention of a Tang favorite comes from an account describing in vivid terms a bizarre incident that led to the death of the Tang Emperor Xizong (r. 874–889), who reigned during the final years of the crumbling dynasty. The passage begins by stating how Xizong "favored the inner-garden boy Zhang Langgou, and could not sleep peacefully without him"—thus confirming suspicions that male entertainers from the imperial gardens may also have served a sexual function. The narrative describes how the emperor purchased a fine horse for Zhang. While Zhang was showing off his spirited steed to the emperor and courtiers, the horse suddenly reared up and trampled the emperor's left arm. In shock the emperor fell down and passed out. The frightened Zhang tried to revive the ruler and finally in desperation urinated into a silver goblet and forced the emperor to drink it. After a long time the emperor revived; he never completely recovered from this accident, however, but gradually worsened and died.[2]

This strange incident can hardly be considered typical of anything, and probably only the unusual turn of events caused it to be recorded at all. From the passages regarding Xizong and Li Chengqian we can ascertain a few facts about homosexuality among the Tang elite. The somewhat subdued treatment of Tang favorites in surviving records suggests that they lacked the significant power of earlier favorites. Instead, the influence of steppe peoples enabled powerful women to monopolize the niche in court life held earlier by male favorites. Many of these Tang favorites were probably only entertainers and never received the office and emoluments that would have made them a political force. Both Li Chengqian and Xizong, moreover, had boy favorites, perhaps showing a trend toward trans-generational homosexuality at the imperial court.

Literature, especially the poetry for which the Tang is so rightly famous, provides a more comprehensive window on Tang homosexuality. Unfortunately, the gender ambiguity of so much Chinese poetry often prevents us from determining the gender of a poet's beloved. Added to this ambiguity are the poetic conceits of the period, which allowed a man to write poems from the point of view of a love-struck woman. Taken together, this scrambling of pronouns and genders makes much of this potentially rich source material useless for the investigation of homosexuality.

Despite these problems, some clues to the nature of homosexuality can still be extracted from poetry of the period. Tang poetry collections overflow with verses passionately extolling the ideal of friendship. Many poets seem to have looked to their male friends for the emotional sustenance and intellectual companionship denied them by arranged marriages with illiterate women or fleeting liaisons with facile courtesans. Cultivated litterateurs exchanged poetry of romantic intensity. Poems tearfully proclaiming deep love for friends, an ideal first seen among aristocrats in the ancient *Classic of Odes* (*Shi jing*) and adopted by men of letters such as Xi Kang and Ruan Ji, matured into a major literary concern during the Tang. With the emergence of a full-fledged literati class during the Song dynasty, poetry proclaiming deep affection for fellow scholar-officials became the mark of a sensitive gentleman.

Most major poets of the Tang and Song rhapsodized on the theme of friendship, and so to recount all of the works from this genre would be impossible. Instead it is sufficient to concentrate on a single representative example, the masterful poet Bo Juyi (772–846), who eloquently extolled romantic friendship throughout his voluminous oeuvre. He often recounted the happy nights spent together with a dear friend:

> We are fond of the moon, and nights sleep side by side;
> We love the mountains and on clear days view together.[3]

To his friend Qian Hui, a fellow official, the youthful Bo Juyi sent a poem as an imagistic souvenir of a frosty winter night they had shared:

> Night deep—the memorial draft finished;
> mist and moon intense piercing cold.
> About to lie down, I warm the remnant last of the wine;
> we face before the lamp and drink.
> Drawing up the green silk coverlets,
> placing our pillows side by side;
> like spending more than a hundred nights,
> to sleep together with you here.[4]

Another friend named Yu Shunzhi, separated from Bo Juyi by many leagues (*li*) owing to official duties, sent a bolt of patterned purple silk as a small token of remembrance. In return, Bo composed a poem recounting how he agonized over what to do with a beautiful gift made even more precious by the friendship it symbolized. In the end he settled on a way to remind himself of their friendship even as he slept:

> Thousand *li*, friend's heart cordial;
> one strand, fragrant silk purple resplendent.
> Breaking the seal, it glistens
> with a rose hue of the sun at eve—
> The pattern fills in the width
> of a breeze arising on autumnal waters.
> About to cut it to make a mattress,
> pitying the breaking of the leaves;
> about to cut it to make a bag,
> pitying the dividing of the flowers.
> It is better to sew it,
> making a coverlet of joined delight;
> I think of you as if I'm with you,
> day or night.[5]

This theme of separation from friends was not merely a hollow poetic conceit. As fellow bureaucrats, Bo Juyi and his closest companions had no control over where they might be sent to take up local office. He and his friends were transferred away from the glittering delights of life at the cosmopolitan capital and separated in dusty provincial towns across the empire, from the freezing northern wastes of the Gobi Desert to primitive backwaters in the malarial south. Many of his poems decry the pain of leaving friends and familiar comforts for some strange landscape.

Bo Juyi shared greatest affection with his gifted classmate Yuan Zhen. Although they made an agreement they referred to as the "Green Mountain pact" to retire together and live as a pair of Taoist recluses, Yuan Zhen's untimely death prevented their eventual reunion. Throughout their long separation of several decades, they continued to exchange poetry sharing intimate feelings. The melancholy moment of separation of these two emotional and intellectual companions inspired a number of despondent poems.

My body is harassed by closeness to the Throne,
my heart bound by fame and righteousness.
Nights of moons and times of blossoms,
seldom encountering delights of the wine cup.
There was only Gentleman Yuan
who came in leisure and drank with me.
He took my hand and sang drunkenly
in carefree spirits, and at times we laughed and joked.

This year you were appointed Censor;
two months ago you went to Loyang.
Since parting I still have not smiled,
and dust fills my wine cask and ladle.
A scented breeze—night fragrance ended;
cassias and rain—the last blossoms fall.

Autumn's intent, one sighing solitude,
our beings apart, both lonely and forlorn.
How much more so, aging in the bright sun;
we have repudiated our Green Mountain pact.
Who knows my heart as I think of you?
It's a captive falcon and a caged crane.[6]

Bo Juyi even dreamed of his closest friend, and in one instance his
dreams coincided with the delivery of a letter:

Last night the clouds scattered everywhere,
for a thousand *li* the same moon color.
At dawn's coming I saw you in dreams;
it must be you were thinking of me.
In my dream I grasped your hand,
asked you what your thoughts were.
You said you thought of me with pain,
had no one to send a letter through.

When I awoke, I still had not spoken in reply.
A knock-on-the-door sound, rap rap!
Saying, "A messenger from Shangzhou,"
he delivered a letter of yours.
From the pillow I rose sudden and startled,
putting on my clothes topsy-turvy.

I opened the seal, saw the hand-letter,
one sheet, thirteen lines.[7]

In another instance, Bo Juyi awoke expecting to find Yuan Zhen himself instead of merely a letter:

Awakening, I suspected you were at my side,
reached for you but there was nothingness.
The dying lamp's shadow flickered on the wall,
the sloping moon's glow pierced the window.
The heavens bright, I looked to the northwest
ten thousand *li*—were you aware?
Long gone, there's no chance to see you;
indecisive-irresolute, I scratched my white head.[8]

Chinese literature often allows the poet to speak from behind a mask of altered identity and stylized emotions. Deciding which poems express genuine emotions and which act out dramatic roles can be difficult. And yet these friendship poems by Bo Juyi and many other Tang and Song literati convey a sincerity that goes beyond the affected tableaux struck by poets writing on other subjects. At the very least this poetry expresses emotions of a romantic intensity, and much of it even hints at a sexual component to the friendship, a sort of egalitarian homosexuality. But with overt sex banished from occasional poetry as unsuitably vulgar for refined literary discourse, we are left wondering as to the specific nature of many of these friendships.

Despite the general absence of sexual topics from poetry, chance has preserved the manuscript of a long poem by Bo Juyi's younger brother Bo Xingjian (d. 826). This poem, recovered from the caverns of Dunhuang in the barren wilds of far west China, attests the continuation of the homosexual tradition into the Tang. The "Poetical Essay on the Supreme Joy of the Sexual Union of Yin and Yang and Heaven and Earth" ("Tiandi yinyang jiaohuan dale fu") survives in a single manuscript copied by an ignorant Tang scribe who obviously lacked sufficient learning to understand the full meaning of the document. As a result, numerous errors make translation difficult. Moreover, the section on homosexuality has been badly damaged and contains many lacunae.[9] Despite these problems, the "Poetical Essay on the Supreme Joy" provides the earliest surviving manuscript from the Chinese homosexual tradition and as such is invaluable in reconstructing Tang views on sexuality.

The "Poetical Essay" endeavors to set forth the entire possible range of sexual behavior. Just as Dante creates an entire universe from a religious outlook, Bo Xingjian constructs a cosmos of sexuality in which he portrays every face of Eros. Here reside instructions for sexual intercourse, a gallery of famous ugly women, regulations for the imperial boudoir, tales of rape, the joys of the wedding night, and the changes brought by puberty. Toward the end of the poem is included mention of homosexuality, sandwiched between a section on sex in Buddhist monasteries and a final section describing the sex lives of peasants. Unfortunately, the centuries have not been kind to this manuscript: of the section regarding peasants, only a few lines remain. As for the section describing homosexuality, although it is badly mutilated, a translation of the most intelligible portions is still possible.

. . . ravishing[10] retainers and cut sleeves in the imperial palace.
And so there were countenances of linked jade
During years of shining pearls.
Some loved their beautiful refinement;
Others were divided by extreme envy.
. . . .
Otherwise they were like Lord Long[11] Yang
. . . pointing at a flower . . .
Mizi Xia shared a peach with his lord.
In the Former Han, Gaozu favored Jiru,
And Emperor Wu favored Han Yan.
In ancient times, Emperor Hui's retainers wore caps with gaudy feathers,
Sashes of seashells, and painted their faces.[12]

Although choppy owing to the many lacunae, even from this remaining fragment we can see the Tang embodiment of the homosexual tradition. Bo Xingjian opens the section with a mention of the "cut sleeve," thereby harking back to the story of Dong Xian and Emperor Ai in *Records of the Han*. The next line mentions the "linked jade" image found in *A New Account of Tales of the World*. Lord Long Yang and Mizi Xia come from Zhou literature, while the mention of Emperors Gaozu, Wu, Hui are taken from Han historical records. In the space of just a few lines, Bo Xingjian has summed up the high points of the homosexual tradition as known to him. He felt no need to recount in detail the background to each of these references; apparently he thought that the educated reader would be familiar enough with these names and images to fill in the details independently. In this way, as in most great Tang poems, the most important points are left unsaid. Just as the skilled landscape painter leaves a large part of the scroll blank, the good poet talks around his intended message through images rather than coming straight out with his meaning.

Although litterateurs may praise this sort of indirectness as beautifully restrained elegance, the philistine historian wishes for more prosaic detail. From the poem, it seems difficult to derive Bo Xingjian's own attitudes toward homosexuality. It seems significant that he chose to include homosexuality at all in his panorama of sexual life, but relegating it to the end among lewd monks and crude peasants hardly gives it a place of honor. The juxtaposition of monks with homosexuality may, of course, hint at monastic homosexuality. The language itself seems extremely non-judgmental, neither praising nor denigrating the men mentioned. In general, the poem's tone seems quite different from that of earlier poems of the "Jade Terrace" collection. Bo Xingjian writes not out of passion or personal involvement, but out of a desire to make his poem encyclopedic in scope. Thus the poem shows an awareness of the homosexual tradition broad enough that a general audience might be expected to pick up on references such as "cut sleeve," but at the same time it fails to add creatively to the tradition.

Another Tang poet, Li Qi, looked back more selectively on the tradition of homosexuality to ruminate on a single incident: the love of the Jin-dynasty (265–420) general Ji Long, nicknamed the "Stone Tiger," for a singing boy named Zheng Yingtao. Li Qi seemed fascinated by the violence of this love, a violence typical of the chaotic age the Stone Tiger represented. Unsatisfied with sharing his lover with two wives, the boy slandered the women and demanded their death. Li Qi felt moved to immortalize the conflict in stirring verse.

> Yingtao had a beautiful appearance and fragrance
> and was favored [*ze*].
> Resplendently he served in the bedchamber
> and monopolized the private apartments.
> In the rear chamber [*hou ting*] were fine garments
> for thirty thousand women.
> Kingfisher eyebrows cannot be seen
> in the clear mirror.[13]

The tragic tale of ignored wives endangered because of a husband's love for a captivating youth contained sufficient pathos to inspire great literature. But the indirectness of language, so typical of Tang poetry, renders the meaning opaque to Western readers. The rear chamber, or female quarters, are filled with clothing representing the general's numerous neglected concubines. Eyebrows are a synecdoche for the women, while the mirror evokes the general. The author subtly conveys the tragic beauty of the situation in minimal space by effectively employing imagery dense with connotations.

More detailed linguistic analysis of this section of the poem uncovers some significant associations. The word for "favored" (*ze*) employed here originally referred to a marsh or swamp. From that literal denotation it came to mean "to fertilize," and finally "to favor" or "to benefit." Therefore, inherent in the Tang connotations of *ze* was the implication that a man would "enrich" (literally, "fertilize") his beloved. This seems an appropriate way to refer to the systems of patronage and prostitution, which apparently were the main economic support for many socially submissive favorites. The term *hou ting* also appeared, this time in a heterosexual context, whereas later it gradually acquired homosexual connotations, referring to both a private bedroom and the rectal canal. Playing in the *hou ting* thus became a double entendre for anal intercourse. Use of the term in this manner begins to be seen with the rise of vernacular literature.

Prose literature meant for popular consumption made an early appearance in the Tang and continued to gain popularity. The mundane settings and abundance of sexual themes make these stories an excellent source for the study of sexual history, and their direct, colloquial language makes them more valuable for studying the mechanics of sexual relations than do the vague circumlocutions of dynastic histories or the exquisite but irrelevant images of poetry. An excerpt from one early short story demonstrates this openness of content:

> When Wu Sansi saw his beloved's pure whiteness, he was immediately aroused. That night Wu summoned [*jiao*] him so they could sleep together. Wu played in the "rear courtyard" [*hou ting*] until his desire was completely satisfied.[14]

Despite the relative directness of language and theme, classical Chinese in its vagueness still makes the understanding of precise sexual relations difficult. Here, for example, the term *jiao* can be translated as either "to summon" or "to hire." Similar ambiguities permeate the entire range of source materials on Chinese sexuality. Note, too, that in this passage "rear courtyard" has attained homosexual associations.

Another instance from Tang popular literature more clearly involves prostitution, and analysis of this material helps to reveal the social climate prior to the first proscriptions of male prostitution during the Song dynasty. The life of Xue Aocao gives a popularly held stereotype of the prodigal life of a male prostitute. His parents died while he was still young, and he wasted the family fortune on luxuries instead of prudently managing his financial affairs. Every day was spent in fruitless gambling.

Then one day a band of rogues came. Because of his exceptional good looks he was repeatedly sodomized [*jijian*]. He grew accustomed to this "coupling of skins" and at last found his place as a street boy. He indiscriminately associated with Buddhist and Taoist monks, robbers and thieves, and was a beloved to all of them. Day and night men excitedly played in his rear courtyard. One could hang a bushel of grain from his erect penis and it would still not go down! It looked like the shaft of a miller's wheel, and could be used to beat a drum loudly enough to alarm people. Because of this, two of the rogues fought one another over him.[15]

Here the male prostitute is portrayed as a wastrel and gambler who willingly associates with the dregs of society. He enjoys his profession and even has an erection during intercourse. The enormous size of his erect penis, described so vividly by the author, further suggests that, unlike the ancient Greeks, some men of the Tang found a large penis attractive.[16]

This passage shows the emergence of a new term to describe homosexuality. *Jijian*, translated here as "sodomy," has particular significance as the first recorded derogatory term for a homosexual act. The character for the second half of the term, *jian*, features three stylized women seated together. Originally *jian* simply meant "private," though in Chinese this concept has connotations of "secretiveness" and even "illicitness." Gradually more unsavory associations enveloped the word so that it came to denote sexual impropriety. Through this convoluted path, a character picturing three women was eventually used to describe male homosexual acts. This sort of reversal of meanings is not unique. For example, the Latin word *virtus* originally referred to virility, slowly gained the wider meaning of "virtue," and was eventually applied by the Victorians to the ultimate female virtue—chastity. Thus, through a similar process a European word for masculinity came to refer to female chastity, whereas a Chinese word picturing three women came to be used in a term applied to sexual acts that by definition excluded women.

Although *ji* used here in *jijian* means "chicken," the term was not always written this way. The Qing scholar Yuan Mei explains that the original character, also pronounced *ji*, depicted a field above a woman and denoted "a man being like a woman."[17] Clearly this definition implies one man assuming a receptive sexual role. Later it came to be written with the cognate character for "chicken," which soon became the standard usage. Although our staunch Qing philologist doggedly assures us of the incorrectness of "chicken" in this compound, nevertheless, this transposition of characters seems to be more than just a careless error. Literally *jijian* means "chicken lewdness," a reference to a belief that domesticated fowls commonly engage in homosexual intercourse. Along similar lines, the Qing scholar Zhao Yi recorded that during the Song, because ducks were thought to favor homosexual intercourse some people in Zhejiang avoided use of the word "duck" (*ya*).[18]

The incorrect form of *jijian*, which seems to have gained currency in the Tang and Song, makes a similarly unfavorable association between animal sexuality and homosexuality. Western sources would also use comparisons with animals to criticize certain forms of sexuality; even a text as early as the Old Testament compares adulterers to horses and whores to dogs.[19] In Chinese, *jijian* provides a bestial association negative enough to justify rendering it into English as "sodomy." It is the derogation *jijian*, rather than the more poetic and hence favorable terms "cut sleeve" or "half-eaten peach," that appears in Qing laws restricting certain forms of homosexual activity, and in this way functions rhetorically as an implicit condemnation of homosexuality. It seems significant that the chicken form of *jijian* came into use at a time when male favorites played a less prominent role in the official histories of the period. Perhaps this decline in political visibility, together with the rise of a derogatory term for homosexuality, indicates a change in public sentiments. From this paucity of data, however, we can do no more than speculate.

Song–dynasty (960–1279) society reached heights equal in splendor and sophistication to the Tang. Although perennially threatened with pressure from nomadic peoples along the northern frontier, which eventually forced the evacuation of northern

China by a weakened Song government, the society appears in the broad variety of sources surviving from the dynasty as highly urbanized and creative. Inevitably this outward sophistication was accompanied by an appreciation of sensual pleasures. Records from the period describe luxurious restaurants, prosperous casinos, and opulent houses of prostitution. Highly developed expressions of homosexuality accompanied the many other forms of Song sensuality.

Despite a rise in the general visibility of homosexuality, male favorites seem to have experienced a continued decline in their influence on court and government as the mechanics of government shifted increasingly away from political patronage and toward a meritocracy with regularized channels for replacement. More specifically, the increased power of top officials in the civil service, especially the chief councillor, resulted in a decline in the power wielded both directly by the emperor and by his informal surrogates. In other words, the government eclipsed the palace. While the increasing rationality of this system left less room for emperors suddenly to promote illiterate and untrained minions to high office, nevertheless, Song rulers still kept favorites. As *History of the Song (Song shi)* records, "It was unavoidable that there would be favorites at the courts of rulers of mediocre character. Even Taizong had Mi Dechao and Zhao Zan, while Xiaozong had Zeng Di and Long Dayuan, and these rulers definitely cannot be said to have lacked constant enlightenment."[20] The biographies of these favorites show a changing role for rulers' intimates. Significantly, this section is shorter than comparable sections in previous dynastic histories. Of the men who merit inclusion, most came from privileged backgrounds and found favor with rulers only after their entry into the bureaucracy through regular channels.

Song favorites who parlayed their favor into increased power faced enormous opposition from other members of the bureaucracy. In one incident, this resentment exploded into open criticism when floods ravaged the Yangzi River basin. An official blamed the disaster on the emperor's sexual practices, the excesses of which had disrupted the delicate balance of natural forces. As he explained, "Water is extremely yin. It augurs female favorites, male favorites, and inferior people [*xiaoren*]. It simply indicates intimate practices with those at court."[21] By moderating his sexual behavior, it was implied, the emperor would restore cosmic harmony and the floods would cease. In declaring sexual favoritism to have negative cosmic repercussions, officials hoped to preserve their own influence and the orderly hierarchy of their bureaucratic system. Besides revealing the extent of the hostility of these officials toward their rivals, this passage is also noteworthy as an overt association of homosexuality, in the form of political favoritism, with the dark, passive, feminine element, yin.

The Song period marks the last in which favorites received a separate biographical section in official historiography, another sign of declining influence in government. The next major official compendium, the Ming compilation *History of the Yuan* (*Yuan shi*), notes the tendency in Mongol historiography to "minutely record the good while sketchily warning of evil."[22] The Ming historians who made this observation clearly intended it as criticism. Whereas Yuan historians were more empirical than didactic, their Ming counterparts were so preoccupied with stereotypes of good and evil that they often flagrantly disregarded historical fact to construct a moralistic vision of the past. It therefore comes as no surprise that the *History of the Yuan* breaks with tradition by not including a separate section on favorites. Influenced by rising Neo-Confucian puritanism, as well as by a decline in the political power of favorites due to the steady strengthening of the bureaucracy, court historians relegated favorites to an incidental place in their records for the remainder of imperial history.

Song homosexuality was apparently accompanied by the earlier practice of patronage. But whereas the patronage we see from the Han took the form of a benevolent emperor showering a beloved with titles and official emoluments, such methods were inappropriate for the rising classes of merchants and officials during the Song. With urbanization rapidly increasing, the Song elite no longer had to maintain staffs of retainers to provide cultural and sensual amenities. Cities had rich financial bases that could support entertainment and the arts, a context in which sexual favors became more monetized. The system of patronage inherent in class-structured homosexuality thus became systematized for a broader public in the form of prostitution. A less wealthy individual, unable to afford the upkeep of a full-time favorite, would hire a prostitute instead, thereby matching his sexual desires with his financial resources.

The popularity of male prostitution was recorded by Tao Gu in his encyclopedic *Records of the Extraordinary* (*Qing yi lu*), compiled during the early years of the Song:

> Everywhere people single out Nanhai for its "Misty Moon Workshops," a term referring to the custom of esteeming lewdness. Nowadays in the capital those who sell themselves number more than ten thousand. As to the men who offer their own bodies for sale, they enter and leave places shamelessly. And so prostitution extends to the hive of alleys and lanes, not limited to the Misty Moon Workshops themselves.[23]

Another author described the ubiquity of female and male prostitution that characterized the twilight of the Song. "Clothing, drink, and food were all they desired. Boys and girls were all they lived for."[24] Another Song source tells of the common presence of youthful male prostitutes in restaurants, whom the customers would facetiously address as "elder brother."[25] Evidence of widespread male prostitution, so abundant throughout the Song, continues through the rest of imperial history.

Homosexuality was sufficiently widespread that the physiological effects of anal intercourse were noted by medical and legal authorities. An appendix to Song Ci's thirteenth-century treatise *The Washing Away of Wrongs* (*Xi yuan lu*), the world's oldest work on forensic medicine, for example, contains detailed observations regarding the physical signs of anal rape.[26] Under the heading "Extended Periods of Sodomy" it explains, "Examine the anus in question for broadness and looseness. A lack of tightness and constriction is the condition resulting from sodomy over an extended period." Another section states, "Examine the opening of the alimentary canal. If the inside is red and swollen, there has been successful sodomy."

This unique work even records the physical conditions of the anuses of several victims of violent rape. In certain cases legal records would routinely record the physical condition of a cadaver's anus as proof of whether or not anal rape was involved in a crime: "Liang Liubao was engaged in sodomy with [the victim] Xu Yanxian over a long period of time. . . . Although there was not an autopsy, the records clearly state that he had the anus of one who has been sodomized." Such explicit statements from forensic authorities show a growing attention to homosexuality by the law.

Eventually the hordes of male prostitutes who so shocked Tao Gu, together with a rising intolerance of sexually passive men, led authorities to prohibit male prostitution in a law dating from the early twelfth century.

> The biographical records speak of "The Times of Mizi Xia" because of his attractiveness and seductiveness. Up to the present, in the capital and surrounding regions there have been shameless men. They were thus employed because of a desire for clothing and food, and were never corrected or prohibited.
>
> During the Zhenghe reign period [1111–1118] there was first promulgated a law which decreed that men who became prostitutes [*chang*] would receive one hundred strokes of a bamboo rod and pay fifty thousand cash.[27]

Zhu Yu, the twelfth-century author of this account, correctly identified the existence of a homosexual tradition that had evolved from ancient times to the Song, invoking the name of Mizi Xia as a symbol of this tradition. But in a variation on older themes he associated Mizi Xia with male prostitution. Although poetry of the Northern and Southern dynasties had compared the beauty of prostitutes to that of Mizi Xia, Zhu Yu specifically identified Mizi Xia and all passive men with prostitution. Presumably he interpreted the patronage that Mizi Xia received from his aristocratic lover as a form of prostitution. Zhu Yu apparently did not believe that men would willingly become prostitutes; material gain is the only reason he gives for their decision to sell their bodies. Zhu Yu reinforces his contempt for these men by calling them *chang*, a common term usually used for female prostitutes and here implying a receptive sexual role for male *chang*. Shock over free men taking the passive sexual role, perhaps together with a rising number of male prostitutes, seems to have played a role in the rising intolerance of male prostitution generally.

Although the government forbade male prostitution, there is reason to believe that this law became a dead letter. A source published 150 years after that of Zhu Yu records the plight of a flamboyantly effeminate prostitute threatened with prosecution:

> Wu practiced this custom [of prostitution] to an extreme. His lair was in Ximenwai. He applied cosmetics, dressed opulently, had beautiful needle-like fingers, and spoke in a voice like that of a woman. Wu was always imploring others for sex. His nicknames were "Shaman" and "Actor's Costume." Officials accused him of unmanliness and ordered an investigation of his degenerate practices. Nothing could have been more blatant than this, yet still they did not resurrect the old prohibitions.[28]

The final sentence suggests that the laws prohibiting prostitution were not regularly enforced. In any event, Wu's case seems to have been extraordinary. His outrageous wardrobe led others to give him nicknames based on the artificiality of his affectations, while his main offense was excessive "unmanliness." Although this term can denote physical impotence, it can also describe effeminacy. In contradictory developments, many men of Song society admired androgynous male beauty, whereas others despised the social inversion that they believed such beauty represented. Not only were Wu's features delicate, but he accentuated his effeminate traits to an unacceptable degree. Yet even this unusually blatant case of male prostitution did not result in punishment. Although there was a growing disapproval of the effeminacy often associated with male sexual passivity, the previous laissez-faire attitude toward male sexuality generally continued. And significantly, this intolerance was directed not toward the active patrons of these prostitutes, but only toward the passive men themselves. A very clear legal distinction was maintained between different sexual roles.

Given the long history of tolerance for love of the half-eaten peach in China, a change in the character of Chinese thought in general must account for the Song law against male prostitution. In part, the law may have represented a backlash against the rise in prostitution during the Song, a result of increasing prosperity, urbanization, and economic commercialization. The indictment of the effeminate prostitute Wu and his castigation for unmanliness, together with terminological changes in the vocabulary used to describe homosexual acts, further hint at a rising intolerance of the effeminacy associated with the passive role in prostitution.

More nebulous is the possibility of influence from the enormous transformations convulsing Song intellectual life. Part of the impetus for the law against prostitution may be traced to the revival and reinterpretation of Confucianism in the Neo-Confucian movement of the Song. This way of thought should not be confused with the ideas of its namesake. The intervening millennium had wrought enormous changes in intellectual life since the time of Confucius. Important to the movement was a revival of strict sexual propriety as defined in the idealized ancient classics of ritual. Whereas Taoist views on sexual matters tended to be more conducive to individual gratification, Neo-Confucian doctrine stressed familial duty and moral asceticism. Because Neo-Confucians did not specifically discuss homosexuality in their philosophical writings, it is difficult to say exactly what effect Neo-Confucian thought had on attitudes toward the cut sleeve. Yet it seems that Neo-Confucians were responsible for a shift in the entire moral ambiance of this and later periods, a shift with inevitable impact on homosexuality as well as other forms of sensuality.

Han Yu (768–824) began this moralistic revival with statements condemning unbridled passions, such as those implicit in extramarital sexual relationships. He stressed moderation of feelings, saying, "Feelings are inferior when they are directed toward whichever feeling happens to predominate."[29] In regularizing Neo-Confucian ideas, Zhu Xi expanded on Han Yu's demands for emotional restraint by including in his *Reflections on Things at Hand* quotations from earlier philosophers that embodied this theme. He enshrined such statements as "A man with passions has no strength, whereas a man of strength will not yield to passions," and "Generally speaking, if one acts because of pleasure, how can one avoid being incorrect?"[30] The emergence of such views straightforwardly opposed extramarital sexuality and all other sensual pleasures. Nonetheless, we cannot be sure what effect their writings had on the typical patron of prostitutes. It is as difficult to gauge the influence of Neo-Confucians over the average person as it is to measure the influence of any elite philosophic movement over society as a whole. At the very least, in any case, their writings visibly manifested an emerging ideal of temperance in personal conduct.

Buddhist institutions such as temples and monasteries do not seem to have been hostile to homosexuality. Indeed, the Buddhist clergy even developed a reputation, perhaps undeserved, for sensual indulgence of all kinds. And yet lay beliefs and practices, often juxtaposed to institutional Buddhism, in many cases took the concept of sexual sin far more seriously than did some clerical traditions. Considering the profound influence of certain Buddhist ideas on Neo-Confucian thought, the intolerance shown by certain Song officials for specific forms of homosexuality may have had its roots in popular Buddhist tracts. These moral tracts, known as *shan shu*, admonished believers to refrain from what some Buddhists regarded as sin, even though many of these ethical concepts were alien to native Chinese ways and had in fact been imported from Indian sources.

Although these Chinese texts date back as far as the sixth century, they gained widespread use only under the Song and subsequent dynasties.[31] These texts, faithful to their Indian predecessors, are uniformly hostile to homosexuality. This hostility is found already in a sixth-century text, the earliest example of this Chinese genre, which regards homosexuality as a sin.[32] A similar text, composed in 921, goes still further, condemning transvestism in an effort to enforce rigid gender roles.[33] Another tract, written prior to 1694, is more specific in its condemnation of homosexuality. It includes the admonitory tale of a man who sinned against nature deities by burning their statues. In retribution, his life was ruined: he failed the government examinations, became an alcoholic, engaged the services of male and female prostitutes, and had his wife seduced by his friends. He was eventually punished by burning in the deepest regions of hell for eons.[34] In this case, the text uses homosexual prostitution as a symbol of degeneracy and as a cause for divine punishment.[35]

We should not exaggerate the extent of this hostility. Homosexuality maintains a high profile in sources from the Song and subsequent dynasties. Despite the theoretical disapproval of sensuality by Neo-Confucians and Buddhists, and despite the enactment of a law discouraging male prostitution, Song sources uniformly attest the existence of a highly developed system of male prostitution. Always reticent to interfere in sexual matters, the government does not seem to have widely enforced the antiprostitution prohibitions. And the intellectual and political establishment, too diverse to reach a consensus on such sensitive issues, apparently merely accepted the inevitability of discrepancies between ideals and reality. Even in an atmosphere of decreased tolerance, homosexuality continued to be practiced openly enough to attract the occasional attention of writers. A precarious balance between the limited general acceptance of passive homosexuality and the Chinese hesitancy to enforce standards of male sexual conduct allowed male homosexuality to continue openly in the major metropolitan centers of the Song and later dynasties.

5

Popular Indulgence and Bawdy Satire
Homosexuality in Humor

So far this study has dealt almost exclusively with the erotic practices of only a tiny portion of Chinese society. Instead of describing the sexual habits of average people, most ancient records focus only on the lives of a minute privileged elite—rulers, high officials, and literati. Since literacy in Chinese is particularly time consuming and difficult to attain, the average person lacked the luxury of a literary education. As in most societies, full literacy was generally limited to those with money and leisure. Because early Chinese literature was written by the rich for the rich, it is not surprising that it was preoccupied with the sex lives of the rich. In the Chinese context, this orientation meant concern with political affairs to the exclusion of virtually everything else.

Because of this limited view of early sexuality we cannot be sure of the extent of homosexuality in Chinese society as a whole. Although the sexual practices of different classes may often reflect one another, the wide divisions between rich and poor in early China preclude the automatic application of findings from one group to another. But not all of Chinese literature stays completely silent on the sexual lives of the common people. In later imperial history a new literary medium for information about sexual practices began to emerge: anthologies of humor. This genre might seem a less than credible historical source—our first impression is of ingenuous crudity and unsophistication. By necessity a joke is composed of one-dimensional, stereotypical characters and events, often inverted for humorous purposes. But through them we can glimpse the perceptions of the cut sleeve among peasants and laborers.

We must take care to recognize the interpretive limits of these jokes. First, jokes do not necessarily portray people as they would have viewed themselves. Many of these stereotypes may have been imposed by the rest of society. A second caveat regards the ahistoricity of humor. Although we can know approximately when many of these jokes were finally written down, some probably date from earlier eras. Similarly, these jokes created during later dynasties often conform to themes and formulas found in much older anecdotes. Humor in China, as elsewhere, was basically an oral tradition. The few instances of written jokes are usually merely reflections of an original oral form. Their oral nature makes the exact dating of each joke a futile exercise. For this reason I consider them here as a whole, as reflecting the general perceptions of homosexuality in later imperial history.[1]

An important characteristic of these jokes, one deserving full consideration, is the overall negative tone they convey. These jokes often depict bitter relations among the classes, and even among men of the same social class. Some even suggest the specter of homosexual rape, a genuine problem to Qing-dynasty lawmakers. What explains the violence and black humor of many of these jokes? One possibility is that some of these somber jests were circulated in homosexual circles as a means of coping with common problems. Humor functions as an effective way to channel pain and frustration, which explains the countless jokes dealing with death, suffering, and human cruelty. By laughing at their dilemmas, people reduce them to a psychologically manageable scale. Melancholic Chinese jokes about starvation or class violence may have been shared by impoverished male prostitutes or actors to place their seemingly hopeless state in a temporarily humorous light.

Most Chinese homosexual dark humor is not absolutely bleak. Many jokes would have given men a way of dealing with the negative aspects of their condition without impugning the good. This is true of the "stupid in-law" and "wedding night" genres of jokes in which a situation inappropriate for the half-eaten peach creates a humorous effect but does not suggest that male love itself is bad. These jokes may have been a way for men who preferred homosexuality to channel the tensions they felt from their necessary heterosexual obligations. When analyzing Chinese humor we must not ignore this possibility that many seemingly negative jokes first arose among men attracted to homosexuality.

Alternatively, many of these jokes may have been the creation of men prejudiced against passive homosexuality. The days of the Zhou and Han, when little or no stigma was attached to the passive male role, had long passed when these jokes were recorded. Few of the surviving jokes denigrate sexually active men. But the increasing association of passive men with effeminacy and class identity, reflected in Song- and Qing-dynasty legal controls of male prostitution, is seen as well in the viciousness of many of these humorous stories. These jokes may in fact be traces of an embryonic prejudice against certain forms of homosexuality, which culminated in almost universal intolerance by Chinese of the twentieth century.

Most important as an explanation for the negative portrait of homosexuality in these jokes is the negative nature of humor in general. If we were to conclude that because these jokes are negative the Chinese were uniformly hostile toward homosexuality, we would also have to conclude that the Chinese were hostile to all forms of sexuality. Numerous surviving joke books contain thousands of humorous tales mocking every possible aspect of heterosexual experience. Some of these are innocent, as in this example of an oversexed Taoist:

> A Taoist gentleman did the bedroom thing, taking off his clothes, folding his hands, and proclaiming,
> "It's not that I like sex, but I do it to continue my ancestral line." Having done it once, he said, "Yes, it's not that I like it but I do it to increase the population for the Imperial Court." And he did it again. Further he said, "It's not that I like sex, I'm doing it for the expansion and nourishment of Heaven and Earth." And he did it a third time.
> "What will he say the fourth time?" asked an onlooker.
> "He's only good for three times, what else can he say?" answered someone who knew him.[2]

This joke lists some of the arguments that would have been made for men to get married and start a family. Not all heterosexual humor was this innocent. For example, a large number of jokes concerning heterosexuality tell of the exploitation of women. One genre of stories deals with the master of a household forcing the wives of his servants to have sexual intercourse with him.[3] Others deal with incest, adultery, molestation, and rape. The jokes themselves may be funny, but the social conditions that spawned them were extremely serious and often tragic.

> A woman had a swelling on her left nipple so she had a doctor come and look at it. And what he did was to play with her right nipple. The woman got angry and reproved him, whereupon he said,
> "But there's nothing wrong with this nipple (so why can't I play with it?)"[4]

The unflattering portrait of Chinese heterosexual life that these jokes paint does not mean that the Chinese disapproved of heterosexuality, just as the negative jokes about homosexuality do not necessarily indicate censure of homosexual life. The nature of humor simply led the jokesters to dwell on the most negative features of all topics.

Having established some relevant aspects of the basic nature of Chinese humor, we may now progress to the actual content of these jokes. One intriguing area that humor illuminates is the nature of both sexual and social homosexual roles. Most of these jokes describe a homosexual pairing in which an older, higher-status man assumes sexual dominance over his social inferior. These roles are most visible as trans-generational homosexuality, with grown men taking boy lovers.

> A man who liked boys would see a boat laden with shit passing by, summon the breeze with his hands, and smell it. When a customer asked him why, he said it was because it had a "boy's aroma" on it. The boy-lover by his side felt extremely embarrassed by this and he looked downwards, whereupon that man at once exclaimed, "Are you jealous!"[5]

Scatological humor typifies jokes of this genre. The fact that only the older man, and not the boy, associates the smell of excrement with his beloved shows that the boy took the passive role in anal intercourse. Their sexual roles are clearly defined according to age.

A similar joke reinforces the ubiquity of this common theme. This time it takes the form of an encounter between the stereotypical oversexed monk and his young disciple-favorite. Throughout Chinese popular literature men of religion are portrayed as lustful and sexually hyperactive. Even in modern Japan, monks point out jokingly that the Chinese character for hemorrhoid (*zhi*) contains within it the character meaning Buddhist temple (*si*). Of course, this use of the term for hemorrhoid appears in Han medical texts and far predates the introduction of Buddhism into China and Japan.[6] Nevertheless, this joke shows an awareness of a possible side effect of sexual practices linked to Buddhist monks, since clerical hemorrhoids might come either from too much sitting in meditation or from passive anal intercourse. In Chinese humor, although these monks usually direct their inexhaustible libidos toward women, they also find the energy to follow their desires for members of the same sex. But it is always the temple novice, not a priest of the same age, who becomes the passive partner in such a relationship.

> An old priest went into a bamboo garden and he was taking a great shit when his ass got pierced by a bamboo shoot. The novice who was looking on clasped his hands (in reverence) and said, "Amida Buddha, it's Heaven's reward!"[7]

This joke likens anal penetration by a bamboo shoot to anal penetration by a penis. The young novice, a passive sexual partner of the old priest, enjoys the sense of requital in the situation. Although custom forbids the novice to anally enter the priest, heaven requites the injustice by "raping" the priest with a stick of bamboo. This witty instance of karmic retribution would have delighted audiences with its irreverent justice.

A similar joke, this time from the erotic novel *The Golden Lotus* (*Jin Ping Mei*), sexually links Buddhist master and disciple. Once a priest and his disciple went to a benefactor's house with some religious papers. When they reached the door, they found that the disciple's belt had come loose and the papers had fallen out. "It looks as though you had no bottom," said the priest. "If I hadn't," returned the disciple, "you wouldn't be able to exist for a single day."[8]

Many of these jokes do not specify the exact social relation of active and passive partners. But in the case of master and servant, it was apparently expected that the master would take an active sexual role.

> The old man liked boys and could never have enough, no matter how many he used. A dog gave birth to puppies in the office one day, and one of them looked just like the old man. In fact, there

was a startling facial resemblance. Everyone was amazed but nobody could figure out why (this had happened). So they asked a
venerable teacher about it and he pondered the matter for a long
time. Then suddenly he understood why and he said, "I think what
must have happened is this, that every day the bitch was eating up
the shit dropped by (the old man's) attendants!"[9]

According to ancient physiological beliefs this method of oral re-
production was not an impossibility. Even the relatively skeptical
Han philosopher Wang Chong (27–ca. 100) stated, "Hares conceive by licking the pubescence of plants. When the leveret is
born, it issues from the mouth of the hare."[10] If a hare could be
inseminated orally, it does not seem too farfetched for the same to
happen to a dog. But beneath the omnipresent motif of copro-
philia lie sexual roles institutionalized according to social status.
Because he is rich enough to afford servants, the old man can be
assured of a steady supply of compliant passive partners.

Some jokes exploit expected behavioral archetypes for humorous purposes. By reversing the accepted roles of a sexual situation,
an audience could be led to laugh at the strangeness of the inversion. Sometimes these reversals would occur in terms of age:

> A man stopped one night at an eating house. He shared a room
> with a bald old man and thought in the dark that his companion
> was a child. He made advances and since the old man liked doing it
> the buttocks way he was delighted to respond. At the very height
> of their pleasure the first man said, "I'll make a suit of clothes for
> you, I'll buy you clothes! Tell me whatever you want." "I think I'd
> rather have you buy me a coffin," the old man replied.[11]

The mistaken identity, perhaps along with the older man's enjoy-
ment of the passive sexual role, creates amusing confusion. Also
notable is the younger man's offer of patronage, a blending of
money and sex that, as this joke shows, was not limited to the
upper classes.

Another joke demonstrates that role reversals could involve
status as well as age:

The son-in-law greeted the father-in-law and pierced him in the ass, so the father-in-law got very angry. Explained the son-in-law, "It's because I was thinking only about my mother-in-law." After a night had passed the father-in-law reproved him, saying, "You beast, I thought about that all night. Even if it were your mother-in-law, you shouldn't do such a thing!"[12]

Several factors contribute to the ridiculousness of the situation here. First is the son-in-law's violation of stringent incest taboos, making his casual indulgence in incest decidedly offbeat. Second is the sexual role reversal, in which the supposedly submissive son-in-law takes an active role in raping his wife's father. The final punchline results from the father-in-law's unbelievable stupidity. All three major themes are conscious deviations from the accepted social norm.

For many men, sexual roles were not simply a matter of choice. To an indeterminate number of male prostitutes, sexual passivity was a mark of their profession and was often reinforced through conscious effeminacy.

A rich man's son happened to be in the capital at the time of the lantern festival, and he went out in the street to look at the lanterns. Without realizing it (was a whorehouse) he entered a tile building and suddenly a beautiful young man appeared. The youth, all cosmeticked, asked him if he'd like some tea. The rich man's son wasn't acquainted with him so he didn't reply, and he also was ignorant of the youth's profession. The youth repeatedly asked him to come along, saying, "I'm a man who does woman's work."

The rich man's son didn't know what he was talking about so he replied, "Oh, so you're a man who does woman's work! Does that mean you're a tailor?"[13]

Because the prostitute is locked into a passive sexual role, he equates himself with a woman. This innocent joke reinforces the ways in which social roles based on status were often paralleled by sexual activity or passivity.

Despite the shame of becoming a prostitute, economic necessity drove many men and women to sell their bodies. These humiliating circumstances did not deter jokemakers from laughing at the expense of their misery.

> A poor man's wife was beautiful and very exciting (to men) but the husband wouldn't allow them (to make advances). But when the husband left the house to look for food he stayed away all day so his wife had illicit relations and was thereby able to eat her fill.
>
> One day the husband returned home and cried out that he was extremely hungry. Said the wife, "The other day Mr. So-and-so wanted to provide me with the breakfast and dinner meals but because of you I turned him down." The husband felt very sorry and repented over this for a long time.
>
> The wife knew how anxious he was (about food) so she sent him to look in the pot (on the stove). There was white rice and meat, so delightedly he ate to his heart's content. And then he asked where it came from.
>
> "This was given to me by Mr. So-and-so. I was so hungry I couldn't stand it so I merely committed adultery with him."
>
> "Tell me, does he like men too?"[14]

Here a spirited woman is willing to take the initiative to save her family from economic ruin, even at the expense of her sexual integrity. For starving peasants, a life of prostitution provided a chance to break the cycle of poverty. The same lure of upward mobility that led thousands of parents during the Ming to castrate their sons in the hope that they could join the ranks of the eunuchs dominating the court also led men to sell themselves or their children to pimps and troupes of actor-prostitutes. Sexual servitude in one of the glittering "flower gardens" of a cosmopolitan city might have looked more appealing when viewed from the parched fields of a tenant farmer. For this reason we cannot simplistically equate prostitution with downward economic mobility. Although considered socially degrading, prostitution could provide a much higher income than would otherwise have been possible: in this case, then, upward economic mobility accompanied downward social mobility.

Social and economic pressures combined to make some men

conceive of themselves as sexually passive, either for their youth or for a lifetime. This joke, besides showing the potential violence of government authorities toward the poor, illustrates the social position of many passive men:

> An official liked to arrest idlers. A certain man was walking in the fields just when that official came along and, flustered and without a plan, he tried to hide in a hollow tree alongside the road. But there was a man in it already so he was only able to conceal his head. The official came by and ordered his subordinates to arrest him, but the man clung to the tree for dear life and couldn't be pulled away from it so finally they pulled off his robes and beat him on the ass. The man inside the tree asked if the officials had gone, and the man who was being beaten replied, "Don't make a sound, they're now on the outside beating one of the idlers."
> The young man must have been somebody's favorite. How do I know that? Because he thought his own ass belonged to somebody else.[15]

Here these "idlers," known today as the "unemployed," are treated as a social menace whose patent undesirability alone is reason enough to punish them. The "idler" himself is similarly convinced of his own lack of self-worth. According to this joke, by practicing sexual passivity the idler lost control over his own body. In a society that tolerated slavery, the loss of self-possession was not taken lightly. The body was a possession to be bought and sold: by allowing a dominant man to "possess" him sexually, a passive man in later imperial times could experience a tangible reduction in social status.

Simply because a large portion of homosexual activity took place between men of different social backgrounds, we should not simply assume that homosexuality was just a tool for the rich violently to exploit the poor. Homosexuality had a place among the working classes as well. A character in *The Golden Lotus* observes that men "all go in for this sort of thing. Even the beggars in their hovels."[16] These jokes are a notable exception to the general absence of information describing the sex lives of the poor. Already we have read of a sexual encounter taking place at a humble inn at which two strangers must share the same room. The following joke involves men of similarly low social stations:

> A mender of bowls and a messenger were sleeping together in the same inn. The mender noticed the messenger's youth and wanted to play around so he called him over to sleep with him. The messenger figured that the mender was amorously inclined and that he'd better prepare his defenses at once, so he took a knife and inserted it between his buttocks. That way he could ward off danger to his anus.
>
> The mender wanted to plunge courageously straight ahead but because he thought the enemy must have prepared something in advance he covered his turtle head (penis) with the iron he used in mending bowls. That way he could prepare against the unexpected. When the messenger saw the enemy approaching ever closer he shouted aloud, "You'd better hold up your advance, I've brought along a silencer!"
>
> "I'm not afraid," the mender harmoniously responded, "I'm wearing a helmet!"[17]

Both men have very ordinary occupations. The only grounds for dominance and submission are their relative ages—thus the older mender of bowls assumes the active sexual role in his attempted rape of the younger messenger.

Despite this evidence from among the common people, even in humor homosexuality was associated primarily with the rich and privileged. While perhaps merely a stereotype held over from ancient times, this association may have been based on fact. Since many sexual relationships among men seem to have involved favoritism or prostitution, the privileged classes had sufficient social and economic standing to attract submissive men. More generally, wealth provided the leisure to explore varied sexual avenues, as well as the resources to act on sexual fantasies. One joke gives a specific example of patronage by telling of a man who took the passive role in anal intercourse in return for a new suit of clothes:

A favorite appeared wearing new silk clothes and someone saw him and said,

"That silk is really unusual! If it's not from the threads of a silk-worm then it must be from the threads of a spider!"

"Why do you say that?"

"Because thread by thread it must have been dragged out of your asshole!"[18]

A man with money could purchase the sexual services of both men and women. Homosexual desires therefore came to be associated with literati, students, and other upwardly mobile men who had sufficient cash to procure a favorite. The following summary of a joke demonstrates the link made in humor between sexual desires toward men and officialdom:

> An official on an inspection tour was very austere in his behavior but when it came time to go to bed he ordered a subordinate to get into bed with him. The subordinate asked him if he wanted to be fellated or wanted to do it another way. The official asked what the old custom was concerning this and when the subordinate informed him that it was mutual fellation, the official replied again in formal language that they ought to do it in keeping with custom.[19]

The association between scholar-officials and the cut sleeve was so strong that in many of these humorous anecdotes the man who loves other men is facetiously referred to as a "petty official."[20]

Jokes also stereotyped students as enjoying half-eaten peaches. Further insights into this theme come from an early Qing short story, "A Chronicle of True Love" ("Qing zhen ji"), which describes a distinguished Hanlin academician who falls in love with a student he has glimpsed from afar and disguises himself as a fellow student so that the two may attend school together. The bulk of the story describes the scholar's gradual seduction of the boy.[21] Humor handles the same passionate feelings in less subtle ways. One joke tells of a young man who goes to take the official examinations. The length and rigor of these grueling tests made it necessary for candidates to sleep in isolated huts at the site of the examinations. While there, the young man dreams of anal sex:

Every time a young and pretty scholar entered the testing grounds he'd dream that someone was playing with his rear courtyard. But things could never be brought to a successful conclusion. And no matter how often he had this dream it always ended the same way—in failure. He felt especially uncomfortable about this. Later he again entered the testing grounds, and dreamed this dream as before. But this time he felt something stiff entering from the rear, far different from those earlier dreams. He felt overjoyed and said to himself that this time when he took the tests he'd certainly pass them. As he thought about it, he remembered that when he'd felt someone being lewdly intimate with him it hadn't seemed like a dream. And the more he thought about it the surer he became that that was no dream.[22]

The supposedly intelligent student fails even to distinguish dream from reality. This blunder, together with his somnolent association of success at examinations with being successfully anally raped, would have delighted the jealous majority who repeatedly failed these demanding tests.

Another tale of saucy advances reaffirms this link between students and homosexuality:

A young man took a night boat, and a man pressed close to him and pierced his asshole with his penis. Shocked, the young man asked him what he was doing, and someone replied that people usually forced their way in (the way he had). Then the young man asked why that man was only concerned with lewd movements and someone again replied that by nature he loved to shake, where-upon the youth remarked, "I thought the only ones who loved to shake were students!"[23]

While these jokes contain a suprising amount of information on the social circumstances underlying homosexuality, they are equally useful for understanding the physical mechanics of pre-ferred forms of intercourse. Most literary and historiographic sources are too modest to give this sort of intimate description. For humor, however, the crude physical details are often neces-sary for the joke to succeed. These stories speak of a homosexuality devoid of love and emotion. Unlike the early poems that dwell on the romantic content of male love, these jokes reduce all forms of sexuality to the bare essentials.

The vast majority of physically explicit homosexual jokes describe anal intercourse. But there are exceptions. One unusual story mentions mutual fellation between a pair of incestuous elderly brothers:

> When the emperor was visiting (Jiangnan) the old people came to view the procession. There were two brothers among them more than a hundred years old, white-haired but with youthful faces, bursting over with health and good spirits. The emperor asked them what cultivation techniques they'd used to be so vigorous but both men looked down and failed to reply. "I'll absolve you of any crime," said the emperor, "so tell me the truth." They spoke up together and told him they used but one technique, namely that each night they shared the same bed, and held each other's penis in their mouths and then went to sleep. And that's the way they'd preserved such vitality.
>
> Remarked the emperor, "Only you two have a different method, really two old men with seductive penises."[24]

This bizarre story parodies the physiological beliefs of Taoist cultivation, in which it was held that by nourishing the male yang element, a man could extend his life and health. This heavy-handed parody mocks such theories by portraying these practices as incestuous mutual fellatio. It also suggests that fellatio was not a usual homosexual practice, since it appears here as an aberrant habit. The previous joke about the bureaucrat on an inspection tour emphasizes this possibility. The representation of mutual fellatio as a localized custom shows it as a practice outside the mainstream of the Chinese homosexual world.

A second alternative form of homosexual intercourse depicted in old humor involves frottage. Although this technique was favored by many men of ancient Greece,[25] surviving Chinese jokes lack references to intercrural copulation. Occasionally a man is portrayed as rubbing his genitalia against his partner's abdomen.

In one joke this release of sperm onto the stomach of another man is obliquely referred to as a "grease medicine":

A Taoist priest took along his disciple for a religious ceremony at someone's home, and in gratitude they were feasted and they left nothing on the plates. They ate till their stomachs hurt. On the way back the priest's turban fell off and he ordered the disciple to pick it up, but the disciple remarked that if he could pick up the turban he could tie his own shoelaces (which he couldn't because he was so full). Just then they noticed a clump of ox shit and the priest sighed and remarked that if he could shit like that he'd feel relieved in the stomach.

When they got home the priest told the servant to hurry and prepare the rattan bedding for him, that he was going right to sleep. The servant said he'd buy him some medicine to drink for his illness, but the priest replied that he couldn't drink another thing and that instead he'd prefer that a grease medicine be applied to his stomach.[26]

These jokes also depict masturbation. Sometimes it could be furtive, as in this variation on the "stupid in-law" joke:

The father-in-law was taking a nap, completely covered by a quilt, when his son-in-law who was passing by at once put his hand inside the quilt and stealthily removed his father-in-law's pants. The father-in-law was astonished and when he removed the quilt and looked, there was his own son-in-law! Just as he was scolding him the mother-in-law rushed over and said,

"Don't think strangely of him, he did it because he failed to take a good look and thought it was me instead."[27]

Premature ejaculation could also be a subject for humor:

The priest seduced the young disciple and sweet feelings arose, but the young disciple's penis got larger and (semen) oozed out. The priest grasped it from the rear with his hands and sighed, saying: "Oh Amida Buddha, it's pierced through!"[28]

Despite the occasional presence of oral and masturbatory acts in traditional humor, the vast majority describe anal intercourse. At times these jokes can be extremely explicit. Some describe the use of saliva as a sexual lubricant:

> One night the venerable Master spoke to the young priest, saying, "Tonight we ought to do it the vegetarian way."
> "What do you mean by the vegetarian way?"
> "I won't use my tongue (to lubricate the penis)."
> They did it that way but the young priest felt extremely pained so he cried out, "Master, I can't stand it any longer, let's go back to a meat diet!"[29]

Because Buddhist priests are supposed to maintain a vegetarian diet, this priest tries to extend his vegetarianism to sexual intercourse. Of interest is the routine use of saliva as a lubricant during anal sex: to cease using it is shown as an aberration from the usual practice.

Few other literary media allow such a candid look at sexual lubricants. The mid-nineteenth-century novel *Precious Mirror of Ranking Flowers* (*Pinhua baojian*) describes how one character applies a tree fungus soaked in water to the tip of his penis as a way of facilitating anal penetration and protecting himself from exposure to excrement.[30] An even more concrete description of sexual lubricants comes from an extremely rare collection of novelettes entitled *Pleasant Spring and Fragrant Character* (*Yichun xiangzhi*), by an unknown author of the early part of the last century (a handwritten manuscript survives at the Beijing University library). The work contains four separate volumes—*Wind, Flower, Snow,* and *Moon*—each redolent in explicit descriptions of sex between men. One representative incident involves the passionate introduction to anal intercourse of a thirteen-year-old student, Sun Yizhi, by his eighteen-year-old companion, Li Zunxian:

> Li's penis had reached Sun's anus and was fully erect but could not enter. Despite several attempts in different ways, Li still could not succeed in entering Sun. Meanwhile Sun was screaming with pain and begged Li to stop. Li replied to Sun that he did not want to hurt him, but the really great feeling would come later. Li further told Sun that it would help if Sun moved his buttocks. Sun replied that

it hurt everywhere so Li might as well come into him. Li then instructed Sun to hold his own buttocks and press as if to excrete. He would enter Sun at that time. Meanwhile, Li lubricated his penis with saliva, and with a strong push succeeded in entering Sun. Sun's inside was still quite tight and dry. Li used another strong push and reached to the end. Li then pushed up and down, and in and out with force. Gradually, Sun's inside began to feel smooth and slippery. Li was then able to enter and withdraw at ease. Sun at this point began to feel fluid flooding his inside and had a strong sensual feeling. He then began to move his buttocks up and down until he could hardly breathe and indulged himself in this sensuality. Li knew then that Sun was enjoying himself, and pushed his penis with great force while Sun was resting, catching his breath. It was at this point that Sun reached his sexual climax. Sun uttered "dear brother" and turned around and kissed Li on the mouth.[31]

This passage also mentions the use of a lubricant, this time saliva. In addition, the older boy is shown here taking the active sexual role while his junior is the passive recipient of his overtures, in conformity with the active/passive divisions based on social status often seen in humor.

Other jokes reaffirm the prevalence of anal intercourse. One short joke tells of a youth's first experience as a passive partner:

A youth was seduced by a man for the first time, and it was very painful. He ran about wildly a few hundred steps, showing his ass to a passerby and asking,

"Excuse me sir, but look and tell me, please, is the prick still in there?"[32]

Several jokes play off of a side effect of passive anal intercourse, extended periods of which can slowly enlarge the diameter of the rectal canal. According to the propagators of these jokes, this increase could reduce the amount of control a man had over his muscles in the anal region. Accordingly, passive homosexual intercourse is linked with flatulence. This genre of jokes was often connected with Buddhist monks, the perennial target of the most scatological of Chinese humor.

> A priest was afflicted with swollen balls, so he asked a doctor to look at them and the doctor said, "This disease can be cured in others but it's very difficult to cure when priests have it."
> "But why should that be?"
> "Because your large bag is crammed full with the farts of your disciples."[33]

Here "large bag" can be taken to mean the scrotum.

A final topic of interest covered in these anecdotes concerns the prevalence of bisexuality over exclusive homosexuality. As discussed previously, the enormous emphasis on familial obligations made procreation an imperative duty for Chinese men. As a result, men attracted to the cut sleeve almost always participated in heterosexual marriage. Similar circumstances existed in ancient Rome, where the satirist Martial wrote barbed epigrams on the theme of the man experienced in intercourse only with other men trying to apply these skills on his wedding night. Jokes on the same theme amused the Chinese.

> A man got into bed on his wedding night and immediately seized his wife's buttocks and wished to do it (that way).
> "You're wrong," said his wife.
> "I've been doing it that way since I was small—why am I wrong?"
> "Well the way I've been doing it since I was small isn't that way," replied the wife.[34]

The strong-woman figure drolly contrasts her own sexual worldliness with her husband's heterosexual ignorance. In a similar joke the man used to assuming a passive role presents his buttocks to his new wife for her to penetrate:

> On the wedding night a man nestled up to his wife with his buttocks and his wife grabbed them and accused him, saying, "How

come you don't have one?" Whereupon the man also grabbed his wife's [pudendum] and accused her, saying,

"And how come you don't have one?"[35]

This joke even has pictorial confirmation. One old print, probably from the Qing, depicts a confused-looking woman with a false penis strapped to her pudendum standing behind a man who is bent over.[36] Apparently the man, unsatisfied with heterosexual intercourse, had asked this woman to enter his anus with the penis substitute. Just because the situation makes a fanciful subject for humor does not preclude the possibility that it actually occurred.

A second genre of humorous stories dealing with bisexuality and marriage tells of a wife being cheated on by a husband who preferred other men to her. Unable to bear his daily infidelity, she finally ran to her mother and complained:

"I don't want to go along with him as his wife." When her startled mother asked why, she replied,

"Though I'm a woman from a good family, on the contrary I'm being turtled by him!"[37]

The word "turtle" in Chinese described, among other things, a male cuckold. Because her husband took a male lover, the wife unexpectedly expressed her jealousy in terms normally reserved for use by men.

In a comparable situation, an older man provides his passive beloved with a wife. This sort of patronage does not seem to have been unusual. After the marriage, however, the lover continues his sexual relationship with the younger man:

There was someone on very good terms with a favorite, and when he grew up he chose a wife for him.

And having done this he moved freely within the family circle and didn't avoid anyone. One day he was just entering the bedroom when the wife's mother chanced to visit, so she asked her daughter,

"Which relative is he?"

"He's my husband's husband," the wife replied.[38]

She characterizes her husband's love for another man in terms similar to heterosexual marriage: his lover is his "husband." This simile shows an awareness in even the least sophisticated realms of popular consciousness of the potential intensity of love between men. From the Zhou dynasty to the end of imperial history, the relatively erudite media of history, poetry, and novels dealt with homosexuality. But these jokes comically illustrate a detailed knowledge of homosexual life among all levels of society. Homosexual love was not limited simply to the privileged elite, but could be found among the working poor as well.

6

Husbands, Boys, Servants
Yuan and Ming Dynasties (1264 to 1644)

The Tang and Song dynasties produced a dazzling array of cultural and intellectual innovations that mark those centuries as effervescent high points of Chinese civilization. But just as the Song was reaching lofty peaks of artistic and philosophic refinement the military and political situation rapidly deteriorated. Eventually the Mongols, nomads from the plains of Central and East Asia, swept across China and established the alien Yuan dynasty, which lasted eighty-eight years.

Fragmentary information leaves clues as to the native conception of homosexuality among these Mongol conquerors. A law code known as the *Great Yassa*, designed prior to the conquest of China for governing the Mongol tribes, invoked the death penalty for those guilty of adultery and homosexuality.[1] It is possible that this prohibition of homosexuality represents the views of Muslim legalists who were beginning to influence the Mongols, especially given that the only surviving fragments of the *Great Yassa* are preserved in Muslim writings.[2] Contrary evidence attests to the popularity of homosexuality among the Mongols. One Western visitor accused them of being "addicted to Sodomy or Buggerie," while another source notes that homosexuality was almost universal among the Uzbek Khans.[3] Regardless of Mongol attitudes, they do not seem to have had much influence on the situation in China. What remains of the Yuan legal code lacks any mention of homosexuality.[4]

The sources available for studying sexual life during these final centuries grow in variety and richness. In particular, the maturation of prose fiction lends new perspectives to records of sexual life. We are no longer bound to view China from the rarefied isolation of the imperial court, but instead can see sexual life as it was practiced by the majority of people. As a result of this explosion of sources, it would be redundant to focus on the favorites of various Ming rulers. In fact, such a task is difficult during this dynasty because the official Ming history lacks a separate section on favorites. Nevertheless, records describe the favorites of Ming emperors such as Wuzong (r. 1506–1522), the famed "Wanli" Emperor Shenzong (r. 1573–1620), and Xizong (r. 1621–1628).[5] Rather than dwelling on the sexual life-styles of the rich and famous, it is more valuable to examine some of the unique evidence that remains from the Ming regarding more widespread concerns.

The Ming was a time of intense awareness of the long tradition that had accrued to male love by that time. The reading public was dramatically increasing thanks to a population explosion, growing literacy, and refinements in printing technology. These new readers could look back on almost two thousand years of written accounts concerning the cut sleeve. The interested scholar, merchant, bureaucrat, or student with even a basic library could easily read of ancient rulers and their pampered favorites in dynastic histories, romantic love between men of the Six Dynasties period in poetry, the repeated warnings of lacrimose historians against mixing sex and statecraft, and the stylized sadness of the odes of friendship exchanged between Tang literati. The Chinese have always shown particular reverence for the models of antiquity; the long past that had accrued to the shared peach gave later imperial homosexuality an increasing air of self-awareness and tradition. Men of Ming Beijing and Suzhou could proudly point to the remote antiquity of the Zhou and Han as a righteous model for their own sexual practices.

Ming sources allow glimpses of homosexual life from a wide range of classes and regions. Homosexuality may have been known as the "southern custom," but other sources confirm the popularity of the cut sleeve in northern areas as well. One late-Ming source took exception with those who stated that male love was significantly more popular in Fujian and Guangdong than in the rest of the empire, contending that in Zhejiang, Zhili, and the northern provinces love between men was also widespread.[6] Other accounts mention homosexual life in Beijing, where the northern respect for southern elegance led to an influx of male singers, actors, and prostitutes from the south.[7] One source even lists the streets in Beijing noted for male brothels.[8] Taken together, these sources point to a considerable homosexual presence in the major cities.

The mere existence of homosexuality does not necessarily point to tolerance, of course. Fortunately, we find a literary source that provides a moral context for Ming homosexuality in Tang Xianzu's play *The Peony Pavilion* (*Mudan ting*).[9] One comic scene from the work suggests that despite the moral odium heaped upon all forms of homosexuality by Buddhist guides to popular morality, others did not see homosexuality as much different from extramarital heterosexual intercourse. In this scene, the judge of hell must decide on the punishments to be meted out to four recently

deceased men guilty of the sin of sensuality. These include someone who has used fragrant woods in construction of his home (a
violation of sumptuary regulations), another who enjoys singing,
a young frequenter of female prostitutes, and a man who enjoys
homosexuality.

The lightness with which Tang Xianzu viewed male love can be
seen by the context. To equate love of the cut sleeve with singing
and appreciation of fine woods certainly does not indicate moral
outrage. To the contrary, these "sins" were chosen for a comic
scene precisely because of their lack of seriousness. Even during
the judgment, a court officer discloses that the man brought forward for his love of the half-eaten peach has been pursuing a fellow prisoner. The punishments for these sensual indulgences are
equally facetious: all are to be reincarnated as flying creatures.
While the first three prisoners are to be reborn as a butterfly, a
swallow, and an oriole, the lover of men will become a bee. The
judge intones with mock gravity, "And you, bee, a wicked one
you are, with sucking mouth and stinging tail."[10] To Tang Xianzu at least, homosexuality was no more serious than any other
breach of Neo-Confucian asceticism.

For the most interesting and detailed look at Ming homosexuality, we must turn to the works of the eccentric genius Li Yu
(1611–1679/80). His works were widely read in his own lifetime,
partly because of his daringly innovative subject matter, which
was often chosen for didactic purposes.[11] Although many of his
own values did not conform to the standards of established morality, and therefore cannot be seen as representative perceptions
of late-Ming sexual ethics, they are still useful as the unusually
perspicacious insights of a gifted individual into the workings of
his own society.

In his collection *The Twelve Structures* (*Shier lou*) appears one of
Li Yu's most pathetic and unusual tales, entitled "The House of
Gathered Refinements" ("Cuiya lou").[12] This tale concerns two
young men, Jin and Liu, who took a youth from the south named
Quan as a lover. Refusing to participate in the official examina-

tions because of the vulgarity of using learning to pursue a career, they instead decided to open a tasteful boutique as a means of enjoying their carefully chosen wares: books, flowers, incense, and antiques. As for their relationship, "the two friends shared a single Long Yang"—in other words, Quan. Jin and Liu both married women and lived with their families, while Quan remained unmarried and lived at the shop. The older men "each took turns accompanying him for one night. Under the pretense of 'guarding the shop,' in fact they enjoyed the flowers of the rear courtyard."[13]

Their reputation for refined taste and amusing conversation soon made their shop an enormous success among the educated and powerful. And among their customers, "every single one of them had the desires of Long Yang." Unfortunately, Quan's beauty came to the attention of the powerful and corrupt official Yan Shifan. Quan, however, wished only to remain faithful to his two lovers: "He is not a male prostitute [*menzi*] for accompanying officials," his friends declared.[14] Yan summoned Quan and tried to hire him as a favorite. When Quan refused his offer, Yan's passion increased. He locked the youth in his study for several nights. Quan repeatedly refused his advances, and so Yan had no alternative but to release him.

Yan sought revenge for this lowly youth's rejection of him. He convinced a powerful eunuch, named Sha, of Quan's familiarity with books and antiques, suggesting that Sha castrate Quan and take him as a personal servant. Sha served drugged wine to the unsuspecting youth, and after Quan was unconscious Sha laughingly ordered his minions to get to work. "First they undressed him, grasped Quan's penis and scrotum, gently sliced them off, and tossed them on the floor where the dog scampered over to gobble them up." When Quan woke up he discovered his loss, and vowed eventual revenge on Yan for planning his emasculation. In the meantime, Quan had no choice but to become Sha's servant. Soon Sha died and Quan became an imperial retainer. He presented an account of Yan's atrocities to the Wanli Emperor, who beheaded the evil official. Quan achieved ghoulish retribution by using Yan's skull as a urinal while saying, "You cut off my testicles, I got rid of your head—the high is exchanged for the low." Li Yu's moral: "Every evil deed brings its retribution."[15]

This tale describes two different types of sexual relationship based on differences in age and class. First is the ménage of Jin and Liu together with their younger beloved, Quan. This is a voluntary association based on deep affection. The narrator notes with surprise how completely "three people acted as one," leading us to classify this relationship as relatively egalitarian.[16] And yet the three men assumed sexual roles of activity and passivity based on age, which shows the relationship to be trans-generational as well. The older men also maintained heterosexual marriages, which Quan also hoped for before his castration. Thus we see also a complex interplay of heterosexual and homosexual relations. As for Yan's advances on Quan, his threats and violence present an exaggerated example of the sexual intimidation growing out of class tensions. When social pressures, money, and physical coercion failed, Yan could at least spitefully revenge himself on the youth by arranging for his physical mutilation.

A similar tale, also probably from the seventeenth century, appears in the *Hairpins Beneath His Cap (Bian er chai)* collection. In this tale, which survives only in a single badly mutilated version, a young actor becomes the devoted companion of an older man. Their bliss is destroyed by a wealthy villain who kidnaps the youth. Rather than submit to his loathsome kidnapper, the boy actor commits suicide out of loyalty to his lover. Eventually the boy's spirit comes back from the afterlife, visits his former lover, revenges his kidnapping, and finally returns to the spirit world.[17]

The plot of this story parallels in many ways the story by Li Yu, suggesting a common set of conditions in society that may have served as inspiration. The setting and events of these two tales were perhaps embellished for dramatic impact, but the social concerns that underlie them were real. Socially submissive men could find themselves forced by threats or by economic necessity unwillingly to submit their bodies to the sexual pleasure of other men.

Another one of Li Yu's insightful tales is equally violent. The play, whose title can be awkwardly translated as "A Male Men-

cius's Mother Educates His Son and Moves House Three Times"
("Nan Mengmu jiaohe sanqian"), contains a jade mine of detail on
the homosexual customs of Fujian Province.[18] The play begins
with a short poem referring to "those of the southern custom"
(*nanfeng*[b])—a clever neologism that is obviously a play on the
earlier compound "male practice" (*nanfeng*[a]). By substituting the
word "south" for "male" (both pronounced *nan*), Li Yu creates a
homophone that to the listener means both "male practice" and
"south wind." Thus in typical Chinese literary fashion a technical
term is given poetic beauty through association with nature imagery. The term *nanfeng* in the form used by Li Yu thereby in-
geniously combines associations of the act ("male practice") and
the area of its greatest purported prevalence ("southern custom"),
couching it all in a pastoral phrase connoting warm sensual breezes
("south wind").

Having set forth this term, Li Yu states: "Even those of the
southern custom do not know how it began." He consequently
attempts to place male love in an overall moral context, beginning
with a cosmological and utilitarian justification for heterosexual
intercourse:

> People do not know when the southern custom arose or who cre-
> ated it. Nevertheless it has come down to the present age. Actually,
> heaven and earth created the Way of man and woman, which was
> contention for mastery. How could this not be supernaturally in-
> spired? The Way of man and woman is what heaven created and
> earth established.
>
> Just look at the surface of man's body. There is a protrusion. And
> on woman's body? There is a concavity. These are the bodily
> forms. How did this creation come about? Why did heaven and
> earth bestow these physical forms on man and woman? Because
> man takes his excess and fills woman's vacancy so that she will not
> be lacking. As he repairs the vacancy until she is just right, he does
> not perceive the reason for his happiness. It is a tendency arising
> from nature.
>
> What does seductive power bring about? After they meet, a
> man's semen and a woman's blood unite and result in pregnancy.
> After ten lunar months the process is completed and she gives birth
> to a boy or a girl. This is the beneficial result. Why does this

joyous occurrence take place? It is because of accordance with yin
and yang and the desire for intimacy.

The purpose of these laws of masculinity and femininity are
covered by heaven and supported by earth. The benefits of creating
different forms is not false or irrational. The two are naked and
intimate but do not offend propriety. This may be playful dalliance,
but such advances are proper.[19]

According to Li Yu, man and woman originally strove for
dominance. In another line he notes, "Female animals never overcome the males." But Li Yu does not clarify the full implications
of these misogynistic statements; instead he goes on to describe
the necessity for heterosexual intercourse. Perhaps he is implying
that intercourse itself is a manifestation of the struggle between the
sexes. Such a view was certainly quite widespread, with early
handbooks of sexuality sometimes even employing military terminology in their descriptions of the heterosexual act.[20]

Li Yu then argues that nature, in the form of heaven and earth,
mandated heterosexual intercourse as a means for women to fill up
their "lacking" vaginas. In addition to the utility gained from "re-
pairing" women, heterosexual intercourse can also be justified by
its procreative outcome. Despite the morally ambiguous inclusion
of nakedness and unrestrained intimacy within the heterosexual
act, its benefits outweigh its drawbacks. Li Yu then contrasts the
easy justification of heterosexual intercourse with the less evident
advantages of homosexuality:

As for the southern custom, we may discuss forms but there is not
a division between excess and lack. We may discuss desire but there
is no greater result from this mutual happiness and delight. We may
discuss the matter, but there is also no beneficial birth of boys or
girls. How can this be moral?

This practice was created when there was suffering and poverty
among the people. How was this practice useful? Once in ancient
times, as a result of unfortunate circumstances two men happily
began to live together. Why were they happy? Because one suddenly thought up this practice! The other joyfully consented to
doing it.[21]

Li Yu composed this myth to provide a sense of justification to the origins of male love, much as Socrates' myth of the origin of the genders in Plato's *Symposium* attempted a similar etiology for the ancient Greeks. Li Yu's explanation of the original motivations for homosexuality is economic. Because men were poor, they shared living quarters. As a result of this forced proximity, they soon discovered anal intercourse. Li Yu finally concludes that poverty, in antiquity as in his own time, accounted for men becoming favorites: "Due to the fires of lust perhaps some handsome young boys, poor and unable to make a living, because of this could seek clothing and food. These were the extenuating circumstances, as in the present age."[22]

Once again the basis of male homosexual relations is linked to patronage and prostitution, dominance and submission. Another tale from the same period, "Chronicle of Extraordinary Love" ("Qing qi ji"), gives a similar reason for male prostitution. In this story, poverty forces a boy to sell himself to a brothel. Eventually an older man falls in love with him, buys his freedom, and takes him home to live as a concubine. The boy dresses as a woman, using a miraculous liquid that allows him to bind his feet perfectly in only a month. Eventually they are separated by calamity, so the boy takes his husband's son and joins a nunnery where he can raise the boy in safety.[23] Both stories link male prostitution to poverty. Similarly, the only chance for a permanent exclusive homosexual relationship lies in one partner adopting female gender identity.

After giving his utilitarian explanation of homosexuality, Li Yu then goes on to show that the southern custom is "natural" in the sense that it appears in nature as well as among men. He claims that there exists a tree called the "southern custom tree" (*nanfeng shu*).[24] This tree actually consists of two trees, one smaller and the other larger, representing the unequal ages of many men in homosexual relationships in Li Yu's own day. These two trees intertwine to become one. Their coupling is so intense that even if they are chopped down, the two trunks cannot be separated. Here Li Yu is presumably borrowing the famed image of interlocked trees from Han-dynasty literature and pictorial art and interpreting it specifically as an icon of homosexuality.

The story itself is set in Fujian, which Li Yu explains is "the region foremost in passion for men," and concerns two men who become "husband and wife" (*fufu*).[25] First the narrator introduces Jifang, a brilliant and handsome young scholar in his early twenties—in short, the stereotypical romantic ideal. Thoroughly misogynistic, he goes so far as to outline his dislike for women in orderly detail. In this way he resembles an equally ardent woman-hater in the eighteenth-century novel *The Scholars* (*Rulin waishi*) who complained, "They affect me so painfully, I can smell a woman three rooms away!" Instead Jifang has turned to what he describes as the love of the Zhou-dynasty Lord E and the Han Emperor Ai.[26] Unlike the woman-hater in *The Scholars*, though, Jifang bows to social convention and marries a woman. His young wife soon died during childbirth, leaving him to raise his young son by himself.

The other partner in this relationship is Ruiji, a beautiful fourteen-year-old boy from a poor family. Owing to a succession of natural calamities, all men in the prefecture are ordered to attend a special temple festival to appease the deity. Since no women are allowed to go, Ruiji excitedly predicts that during the festivities everyone will be enjoying the southern custom. He is not disappointed. While there, the assembled men hold a beauty contest for handsome youths and post the names of those considered most attractive. Ruiji wins first place.

Jifang falls in love with Ruiji and decides he wants to marry him, expressing his intent using the word *qu*, which usually refers to heterosexual marriage. Apparently Li Yu assumed that the custom of homosexual marriage would be unfamiliar to many of his readers, since he includes an explanation:

> In Fujian the southern custom is the same as that for women. One tries to discern a youth for whom this is the first marriage. If he is a virgin, men are willing to pay a large bride price. They do not skip the three cups of tea or the six wedding rituals—it is just like a proper marriage with a formal wedding.[27]

Accordingly, Jifang goes to Ruiji's father to ask for his son's hand in marriage. The narrator explains that in Fujian bride prices for youths can be quite high: some boys bring up to five hundred pieces of gold. In order to pay for the exceptionally attractive Ruiji, Jifang sells all of his land.

After the marriage, Jifang shows incredible devotion to his young beloved. Yet a cloud remains over this otherwise happy marriage, because both men know that the day of separation will some day come when Ruiji inevitably leaves to marry a woman. In gratitude for all of the love and devotion showered on him by his lover, Ruiji castrates himself so that he can avoid heterosexual marriage and remain with Jifang forever. Remarkably, the scar heals into the shape of a vagina. From this time forward Ruiji binds his feet, dresses as a woman, and remains indoors like a virtuous wife.

To the modern Westerner, this sort of plot development strains credulity. But in the fantastic world of Chinese popular fiction, such events hovered on the cusp of possibility. A sixteenth-century miscellany records what it purports to be the factual case of a man who developed female sexual organs at the age of forty-four and married a close male friend. Though s/he began to menstruate, s/he was never able to bear children.[28] In such a world, the events in Li Yu's tale might have seemed unlikely but certainly not unimaginable.

Popular resentment builds up against the happy couple of Li Yu's fiction, and soon a jealous prefect accuses Jifang of unlawfully castrating a minor. When Ruiji admits that he castrated himself out of gratitude to Jifang, the prefect orders him beaten for self-mutilation, a violation of the Confucian concept of filiality. As he is stripped for beating, a crowd surges forward for a glimpse of his beautiful flesh. Jifang steps forward and asks to be beaten in Ruiji's place. Pent-up jealousies are released in a particularly savage beating that results in Jifang's painful death. On his deathbed, Jifang charges Ruiji with raising and educating his son so that he can pass the imperial examinations. As his husband dies, Ruiji "cries until blood flows from his eyes."[29]

Ruiji sees that Jifang's son, Chengxin, studies diligently, and supports them by working at a relative's shop making shoes.

Ruiji's main worry is that Chengxin will give up his studies because of a frivolous homosexual infatuation. When fellow students and even a teacher try to seduce the attractive young Chengxin, Ruiji finds a new school for him. When Chengxin is fourteen—the age when Ruiji married—a handsome young scholar remarkably similar to Jifang falls in love with Chengxin and attempts to kidnap him. Thinking that in Fujian "boys without fathers esteem the southern custom, whereas in other places they do not," Ruiji takes the boy and they move to Guangdong.[30] Eventually, of course, Chengxin passes the examinations and Ruiji is honored as a "Mencius's mother"—the paragon of widowhood who devotes everything to the education of her son.

Li Yu portrays male marriage in idealistic terms. Despite the jealousy of others, the couple has only the utmost devotion for each other. Even after the death of one husband, the remaining spouse leads a chaste life as a paragon of parental rectitude. This story is one of love, fidelity, and chaste widowhood. The transformation of gender roles is complete, providing one of the few Chinese references to trans-genderal homosexuality. Nevertheless, the bizarre circumstances surrounding Ruiji's castration suggest that the particulars of gender transformation in this case owe more to Li Yu's fertile imagination than to social reality.

Even more important within the story are references to an actual marriage ceremony. This ritual was not simply the product of Li Yu's wild imaginings: men apparently found it desirable to construct homosexual relationships along the lines of heterosexual marriage. The greatest advantage to be gained was the legitimation of the union according to a recognized convention. The efficacy of such legitimizing analogies can be seen as well in cases of prostitution and extramarital heterosexual relations—for instance, in the famous play *The Peach Blossom Fan* (*Tao hua shan*), set in the late Ming dynasty. At that time, among elite courtesans the madam acted as a young prostitute's adoptive mother, and customers of the most desirable courtesans went through a long and expensive "courtship" process prior to sexual intercourse.[31] In this particular drama a matchmaker is introduced into the procedure. Eventually the "husband" and his prostitute "bride" engage in a mock wedding ceremony.[32]

An even earlier work illustrates the analogic use of marital metaphors by those engaged in an extramarital sexual union. In the Tang-dynasty short story The Dwelling of the Playful Goddess (You xian ku), a highly stylized description of an ephemeral sexual encounter between a handsome scholar and a young widow, the widow offers her paramour the role of head of the household at an impromptu feast.[33] By assuming this ritual role of male head of the household, his sexual attachment to her is cloaked in the language of marriage. In this case, as in The Peach Blossom Fan, an important factor in the application of marital forms to extramarital seduction is the presence of a matchmaker.[34] As symbols of the marriage ceremony, and hence of legitimacy, the presence of a matchmaker was considered so important that to legal theorists of the Yuan dynasty it even partially ameliorated sexual impropriety. Although an illicit sexual relationship arranged by a go-between was still censured, the penalties meted out under such circumstances were substantially reduced.[35] The Dwelling of the Playful Goddess follows this way of thinking. In it, the woman's sister-in-law takes on the matchmaker's role, saying, "How can you cut up firewood? Without an axe, it can't be done. How do you take a wife? Without a go-between, she can't be gotten."[36] Here she repeats a line from an ancient poem, appealing to the antiquity of the sentiment to further legitimize this extramarital union.

Similarly, men of certain parts of China also appealed to heterosexual marriage as a model when trying to construct a more stable and respectable type of relationship with one another. As Li Yu acknowledged, the province of Fujian in southeast China was particularly famed for its cut sleeves and half-eaten peaches. The Dutch soldier Hans Putnams, who attacked the Fujian coast in the early seventeenth century, confirmed this fact in calling men of the region "filthy pederasts";[37] and the literatus Shen Defu (1578–1642) stated that men of all social classes in Fujian would take male lovers. Another account confirms the popularity of homosexuality in that province, noting that the Fujianese "look at the young and handsome and remember them. They do not discuss literature and art, but instead notice new patronages." When an official in Fujian would retire from office, it was customary for several hundred "young and handsome" youths to come to his retirement party. One writer described these young men as "like a group of jade bamboo shoots": they would celebrate together for several days, and during this time "favors would be continuous." Rather than being criticized for such behavior, these youths would find themselves recommended for important positions by the recipients of their charms. In this way the end of one career could lead to the start of others.[38]

Shen Defu described the most extreme form these relationships among men could take in Fujian: marriage. Two men were united, the older referred to as "adoptive older brother" (*qixiong*) and the younger as "adoptive younger brother" (*qidi*). Similar terminology was employed among men of seventeenth-century Japan, who referred to participants in a "troth of brotherly love" (*kyōdai keiyaku*) as taking on an "elder brother's role" (*ani-bun*) and a "younger brother's role" (*otōto-bun*).[39] The creation of fictive kinship ties as a means of organizing homosexual relations was not limited to China and Japan. It is also common in groups as different as southern African lesbians and inmates in the U.S. penal system.[40]

In the Chinese case, the term *qi* used in both compounds has many alternate meanings. One early denotation was "a written contract or agreement." It was also used in reference to an exceptionally strong friendship, as in the term "sworn friends" (*qiyou*). And third, it could denote adoption, a much more complicated and diverse social act than its Western equivalent. To Chinese ears, then, the word *qi* would have had connotations of contractuality, deep friendship, and adoption.

We have a description of an actual ceremony for swearing friendship from the works of the invaluable Li Yu. Two men sacrifice a carp, a rooster, and a duck. They then exchange their exact times of birth, smear each other's mouths with the blood of the victims, and swear eternal loyalty to each other. The ceremony concludes with feasting on the sacrificial victims. Afterward they address each other as older brother (*xiong*) and younger brother (*di*).[41] The similarity of this practice to the Fujianese custom of male marriage is obvious, with similar terminology and an important ritual component. Li Yu even suggests erotic overtones to the subsequent encounters of these sworn brothers. And yet the Fujianese marriage ceremony went beyond this earlier custom by abandoning the earlier ritual of brotherhood and adopting the language and ceremonies of heterosexual marriage.

According to the terms of the Fujianese male marriage, the younger *qidi* would move into the *qixiong*'s household. There he would be treated as a son-in-law by his husband's parents. Throughout the marriage, many of which lasted for twenty years, the *qixiong* was completely responsible for his younger husband's upkeep. Wealthy *qixiong* even adopted young boys, whom the couple raised as sons. Usually, these marriages would eventually have to be dissolved because of the familial responsibilities of procreation. As a character in the early-Qing-dynasty short story "Chronicle of Sacrificing Love" ("Qing lie ji") rhetorically asks, "In all history when has there ever been a precedent for two men to live out their lives together?"[42] Similarly, in Langxian's short story "Pan Wenzi" from *Shi dian tou*, two young men who decide to live out their lives together go back on their decision just before their respective fiancées are about to pressure them into heterosexual marriage. To men of the late Ming and early Qing, emotional and sexual relationships with other men could be intense and even enduring, yet they could not exclude heterosexuality.

At the end of a male marriage in Fujian, the older husband paid the necessary price to acquire a suitable bride for his beloved *qidi*. Shen Defu marveled at the heights of devotion reached by these couples. Star-crossed lovers who encountered difficulties even strode together into the sea to drown in each other's arms.

In addition to Shen Defu's account, a separate mention of the Fujianese male marriage is made in a tale called "The Leveret Spirit" ("Tuer shen"). This story, set in Fujian, begins with the furtive love of a common soldier for a higher provincial official.

Eventually the guard is driven to hide in a toilet so that he can surreptitiously observe the official while he is naked. The official becomes suspicious and summons the guard for questioning. Under torture the guard admits his love. The official refuses to be appeased and has the guard killed.

A month later the guard, in the form of a young rabbit, appears in a dream to the local village elder. The leveret spirit declares to the elder his interest in "the affairs of men" and demands that the local men build a temple to him and burn incense in worship. The story concludes with the building of the temple:

> According to the customs of Fujian province, it is acceptable for a
> man and boy to form a bond [*qi*] and to speak to each other as if to
> brothers. Hearing the villager relate the dream, the other villagers
> strove to contribute money to erect the temple. They kept silent
> about this secret vow, which they quickly and eagerly fulfilled.
> Others begged to know their reason for building the temple, but
> did not find out. They all went there to pray.[43]

Male marriage was prevalent enough in Fujian that the men of that region even felt compelled to sacrifice to a patron deity of homosexuality. As with many potentially vengeful spirits in China, this one took the form of an animal. The choice of a rabbit seems more than accidental. During the Qing, male prostitutes were referred to as "rabbits." In northern China, the son of a male prostitute might even be cursed as a "rabbit's fool" (*tu zaizi*).[44] Perhaps this association is attributable to Western influence, since medieval Europeans frequently linked the hare with homosexuality.[45] This anecdote hints that the development of homosexual life in Ming Fujian might have been more highly developed than even the institution of male marriage would indicate. Not only did men form couples, but the male community at large seems to have been involved in organized homosexual cultic activity. Large-scale retirement parties, the all-male festival in Li Yu's tale, and the development of religious rites centered around a cult of male homosexuality all point to involvement of the male community at large.

As Li Yu indicates, the institutionalization of homosexuality as marriage seems to have been the custom of a limited geographic area.[46] Even beyond Fujian, however, men could form very strong bonds of love that lacked an institutional component. The story "Chronicle of Chivalric Love" ("Qing xia ji"), probably written by a contemporary of Li Yu, details a comradely love between two distinguished men, one of them a valorous soldier. Most interesting about this story is the fact that Zhang, the military hero, takes the passive sexual role in their relationship. His lover, Zhong, secretly penetrates Zhang while the soldier sleeps: "In his drunken dream state Zhang felt he was no longer in control of his body. Inside it felt as if some insect were trying to bore into his anus. It felt like a sting but didn't sting. He wanted to take it into himself but wasn't able. . . . So buried in sleep he was that he didn't seem to know whether his body was a man's or a woman's." The two subsequently become devoted lovers. After successfully vanquishing his foes on the field of battle, Zhang returns to his lover for a climactic scene of passionate ecstasy:

> Zhong became slow and gentle, giving tight thrusts and cautious pulls. In a short while waves of passion gushed forth from Zhang's cave of sin and sprayed out like jade mist.
>
> The waves of passion, rich and milky, flowed against the current and, wending past his coccyx, wetted the bamboo mat below.
>
> The waves of passion, frothing and surging, first streamed forth along the length of Zhong's member, then soaked downward along his body.[47]

Most of the information surviving from the period generally concerns less idealized sexual roles. An egalitarian homosexual relationship between social equals might allow for sexual roles to become divested of social connotations. As seen in the Ming masterpiece of erotic fiction *The Golden Lotus* (*Jin Ping Mei*), however, for intercourse between members of different social groups, sexual positions often reinforced social positions. In this novel the insatiable Ximen Qing, not content with the countless encounters of vaginal intercourse with his wife and concubines, turns his sexual appetites to anal intercourse. He convinces his favored concubine to consent to anal sex by promising her a new set of clothes, a promise of patronage not unlike that made by other active men to their male favorites.[48]

Ximen Qing's sexual relations with a handsome youth from Suzhou, nicknamed Shutong, give a detailed look at the place of young male servants in wealthy Ming households. As the boy compliantly says, "I will do your bidding in all things."[49] In return for submitting to his master's sexual appetite, Shutong gains certain influence and privilege. But his passive sexual role also embroils him in the byzantine sexual politics of the household. He eventually runs away when one of his female sexual rivals discovers him in the middle of a tryst with a woman of the household. The novel thus portrays Shutong as bisexual in practice—willing to pander to Ximen Qing for gain, and enjoying sex with women for pleasure.

Another portrayal of the sexual relationship between master and servant comes from Li Yu's brilliant erotic novel *Prayer Mat of Flesh* (*Rou putuan*). In it the protagonist decides to increase the size of his penis by grafting on the penis of a male dog chopped off at the height of copulation. The night before his operation, this ambitious scholar discusses the procedure with a boy servant who "had learned to raise his 'rear chamber' just like a woman and to wriggle his belly muscles in such a way as to facilitate his esteemed visitor's entrance. He was also able to emit cries of pleasure and moans of bliss, which though simulated were just like those of a woman." This encounter comes after a long period in which the scholar had ignored the boy in favor of women.

> "Young gentleman, for a long time now you have been interested only in women and neglected us entirely. May I ask why tonight you are suddenly in a mood to warm up your cooled affections?" The question was uttered in a flutelike, designedly feminine voice.
>
> "In celebration of a leavetaking."
>
> "Leavetaking? Are you planning to discharge me from your service and sell me to another master?"
>
> "How ridiculous! My meaning is not that I intend to part with

you, but rather that this is my ambassador's farewell visit to your rear chamber."

"Why does he wish to say farewell?"

"As you know, I have recently decided to make him a little more stately and imposing by means of a surgical operation. The operation will make him so big and thick that in the future every female 'audience portal,' however spacious, will be too small for him. He will have to force his way in. The tiny gate of your 'rear chamber' will then be quite impracticable. Now do you see why I have spoken of a farewell visit?"

"Your ambassador may be a little on the small side, but he is otherwise in good shape. Why," asked the inexperienced boy, "are you in such a hurry to operate?"

His master explained that in this point women were far from having the same tastes as men, that while men esteem dwarfs, women prefer giants.[50]

The boy then asks the scholar to take him along when he goes to see the many women who will be attracted to his improved penis. That way the boy can enjoy the woman's maids while the master and lady are themselves occupied. The scholar agrees, generously declaring that no general should stuff his belly full while his troops go hungry. In excited gratitude, the boy redoubles his efforts to make their final night pleasurable for his master.

This tale, while not without considerable elements of fantasy, shows the relationship of master and boy servant. The relationship itself is structured according to age and class. Sexual roles of activity and passivity are apportioned based on status, with the socially submissive male accepting the sexually passive role in anal intercourse. Bisexuality mixes freely with homosexuality, showing a fluidity of sexual desires in some individuals. And the boy sees his own sexuality in terms of a sexual life cycle: at present he plays a passive homosexual role because of his youth and beauty; later he expects to experience heterosexual relations. The appearance of male sexual servants in this and other Ming novels shows that not all homosexual relationships were as tied to mutual affection as were those of the male couples of Fujian. The half-eaten peach included exploitation as well as love among its manifestations.

The open place of homosexuality in literature of the period seems to reflect a relative tolerance for the cut sleeve in Ming China. Emigration of Chinese to other places brought with it the export of Chinese homosexual sensibilities. A shortage of women in many of these overseas Chinese enclaves gave added incentive for homosexual practices. The clash between Chinese and European views of homosexuality led to the arrest of men suspected of homosexuality among the Chinese population of Manila. Although the Chinese protested that love between men was an accepted custom in their homeland, the Spanish colonial authorities were intractable. Some offenders were burned at the stake, while others were flogged and condemned to serve as galley slaves.[51] According to the Spanish, Chinese immigrants were causing native Filipinos to take up homosexuality. To prevent the infection of more Filipinos with this damnable vice, Spanish officials posted notices in the Chinese quarters of the city warning them of the fatal penalties for homosexual acts.

The Chinese homosexual tradition found a more welcome reception among the Japanese. The seventeenth-century author Saikaku Ihara traced homosexuality in Japan to the ninth century, when it was supposedly introduced by the famed monk-priest Kūkai following his return from an apprenticeship in China.[52] From the monasteries the practice reputedly spread to the Kyoto aristocracy and thereafter to all strata of society. Although there is evidence to suggest that homosexuality in Japan predated Buddhism, it is significant that the Japanese were aware of the ancient Chinese homosexual tradition. For example, Saikaku apparently had knowledge of contemporary Chinese homosexual slang, asserting that the Chinese called homosexual intercourse *xia zhuan*. Literally this term means "intimacy with a brick," an image of unknown derivation; it may have been a vulgar vernacular term passed on to the Japanese by Chinese traders—commercial contacts between the Japanese and the Fujianese, noted for their open appreciation of homosexuality, make this oral transfer of the term a possibility.

Through such references to Chinese counterparts of Japanese homosexuality, Saikaku relied heavily on the prestige of Chinese culture to justify Japanese homosexual practices. He referred mainly to the most ancient sources of homosexual history in China, such as *Records of the Han* and *Memoirs of the Historian*. One story even centers directly on the love between a Chinese gentleman and a kabuki actor in Osaka—an unexpected setting, since Chinese traders were legally confined to the Chinese quarter of Nagasaki. This brief tale shows a parallelism between the sexual roles of actors in the two countries:

> One spring some years ago, a man from China who had become very devoted to [the actor] Yoshikawa Tamon had to leave and go back to his country. Tamon, weeping bitterly, went as far as the mouth of the river to see him off. The night was cold and it began to rain and storm, soaking him to the skin, but he bore it gladly.[53]

Here we discern the existence of some direct homosexual links between the two cultures, which were sufficient to convey at least rumors of the long and respected Chinese homosexual past. Not only did the tradition of literature regarding the cut sleeve influence all levels of Chinese society, as shown in popular literature of the Ming, but it even extended beyond the borders of China to impress or disgust distant cultures.

孫
嗣
元

7

Reflections at the End of a Tradition
Qing Dynasty (1644 to 1912)

Open sexual expression and erotic literature blossomed under the
Ming. Yet together with this relative lack of inhibitions came
chaos in many areas of life. After the Manchus restored order by
establishing the Qing dynasty in 1644, a period of reaction set in
against what many perceived as Ming libertinism. Literature
generally became more circumspect, shaping our perceptions of
the period. Some scholars have detected a growing social conservatism as well. Vivien Ng has suggested that the Qing dynasty
represents a time when homosexuality was brought under increased regulation as an attempt to firm up the foundations of
society uprooted during the late Ming.[1]

Ming society also contrasts with Qing absolutism in the high degree of individualism expressed by leading Ming intellectual figures. The influential Neo-Confucian philosopher Wang Yang-ming's emphasis on the individual as a repository of truth set off a wave of highly personal and idiosyncratic speculation. This trend in Ming thought culminated in the radical individualism of Li Zhi, who emphasized the shocking originality of his introspective works in their provocative titles, such as *A Book to Burn* (*Fen shu*) and *A Book to Be Hidden Away* (*Cang shu*).[2] While the content of Li Zhi's controversial ideas did not typify their time, in another sense their highly individualistic orientation sums up the pervasive spirit of the age. Ming society has been called an age of great humanism owing to the tolerance shown personal expression. Along with intellectual openness came greater freedom and tolerance in sexual matters as well.

Less philosophically minded officials at the Manchu court had a different view of Ming individualism. Rather than distinctive expression, they saw political and social chaos. Qing rulers kept tighter control over the writings and behavior of their subjects than had their Ming predecessors. And the laws and actions of certain emperors, particularly those most influenced by Manchu customs at the beginning of the dynasty, show a desire to limit other aspects of society that had gone unregulated in the previous age. At the same time, Qing society still shows a high degree of tolerance for some forms of homosexual behavior, as seen in the records major scholarly figures left of their loves.

Qing law expresses this new tendency toward social control through judicial activism. Homosexuality came to be increasingly regulated by the courts, although the actual enforcement of these laws was apparently highly selective. Although legalists of dynasties following the Song did not revive the Song penalties against male prostitution, Qing officials oversaw the promulgation of increasingly sophisticated laws to punish homosexual rape.[3] Perhaps such laws represent one aspect of increasingly conservative tendencies; yet this form of sexual violence was apparently a problem of genuine concern. Several case histories survive describing homosexual rape, and Western moralists, who had long accused Chinese officials of homosexuality, happily seized on these instances as proof of Chinese ethical degeneracy. One British visitor recorded in detail his outrage:

> The commission of this detestable and unnatural act is attended with so little sense of shame, or feelings of delicacy, that many of the first officers of the state seemed to make no hesitation in publicly avowing it. Each of these officers is constantly attended by his pipe-bearer, who is generally a handsome boy, from fourteen to eighteen years of age, and is always well dressed.[4]

When evidence of sexual violence exacerbated the act, Westerners reacted with even greater assurance of their own superiority. An account from a Western journal of 1835 captures the spirit of the West's indictment of Chinese sexual morals:

> [A Chinese gazetteer is] filled with details of a case of this abominable practice, which exists to a great extent, in almost every part of the empire, and particularly in the very officers of the "shepherds of the people," the guardians of the morals of the celestial empire. The sodomite was Woopaou, formerly a soldier under the (Manchu) banners, aged thirty-four years. . . . "Woopaou being in the house of Mrs Wei, where her grandson was at play, seized the lad, and binding him in a blanket (to prevent him from alarming the neighbors), committed violence on his person. The boy then ran home crying, followed by the villain; but his grandmother was enraged, and would listen to no overtures; Woopaou therefore fled, and after an absence of two years returned, was seized, and delivered over to the criminal court for trial." What is to be the result, we have not yet learned. The boy was only eleven years old.[5]

The Western commentary to this early translation of a Chinese legal document links homosexuality with rape. It also states that homosexuality was widespread in China, especially among officials. The implication is that Chinese officials were all similar to rapists. The Chinese returned such insults by charging foreigners with like crimes. The same journal in 1840 reported, "Judging foreigners to be as bad as themselves, (Chinese officials) falsely charge them with the guilt of this sin, and in broad capitals post it up on the factor's own walls, 'where all eyes may see it,' there to remain for months."[6] Whether Westerners were actually guilty of homosexual rape is difficult to determine.[7] Chinese and Europeans slandered one another with mutual accusations of what both agreed to be a reprehensible crime. But whereas Europeans condemned all forms of homosexuality as immoral wickedness, the Chinese concerned themselves mainly with the forceful violation of free men and sex with free minors.

Rape of men seems to have been a concern of jurists as early as the Qin dynasty (221–207 B.C.). A version of the Qin legal code unearthed from the tomb of an ancient official discusses punishment for a servant who "forcibly fornicates with his master or mistress."[8] Yet the Qin code lumps heterosexual and homosexual rape together, and judicial officials of subsequent dynasties do not seem to have departed from the Qin example, probably handling homosexual rape merely through analogy to heterosexual rape.

A specific law for the prosecution of homosexual rape was first suggested in 1679, during the reign of the Kangxi Emperor. Owing to bureaucratic delays, a substatute governing homosexual rape was not finally added to the Qing code until 1740, with minor amendments added in 1819 and 1852.[9] Kangxi personifies the new Manchu morality through his violent hostility to Chinese homosexual customs. Ming rulers either ignored homosexuality or, if inclined, took full advantage of handsome male favorites. The Zhengde Emperor, who lavished loving attention on his Muslim favorite Sayyid Husain, demonstrates the acceptance of homosexuality in Ming court life.[10] Even during the Qing, as the rustic identity of the ruling elite became inexorably cast aside in favor of the splendid sophistication of Chinese civilization, the Manchu emperors became more amenable to Chinese sexual practices as well. The Qianlong Emperor lavished his favorite, Heshen, with honors and high office, and the Xianfeng Emperor found himself attracted to a leading actor, the female impersonator Zhu

Lianfeng. Even the young Tongzhi Emperor scandalized his relatives by publicly wooing a young scholar.

In contrast, Kangxi's more traditional Manchu upbringing seems to have turned him against native Chinese sexual customs, so much so that he even executed three of his son's male favorites when he discovered that they were having sexual relations.[11] It is not surprising that he took the initiative to stop the most exploitive homosexual practices of his own day. First he tried to halt the importation to Beijing of boy actor-prostitutes from the south. He discovered one official who abused his power to force families in southern China to sell their sons into prostitution—one Suzhou servant family had been bullied into selling their son for five hundred taels of silver.[12] In addition to battling the forced procurement of youths for prostitution, Kangxi also fought against more isolated cases of male sexual violence. The result was a comprehensive law code governing the punishment of different varieties of homosexual rape:

I. If a gang abducts a male child of good family and sodomizes [*jijian*] him, whether or not they subsequently murder him, the principals are to be immediately beheaded as in the case of vagabond outlaws.[13] If accomplices joined in the rape, they are to be strangled after assizes. The remaining offenders are to be enslaved and sent to Heilongjiang.

II. If no gang was formed, but there is the rape and murder of a boy, and if the boy sodomized is under ten years old,[14] then likewise [as in the case of vagabond outlaws] there is to be immediate decapitation.

III. If there is the rape of a boy who is ten to twelve years old, there is to be decapitation after assizes. If he consented to rape, then, as in the case of a young woman who consents to rape,[15] there is to be strangulation after assizes.

IV. If a single person commits sodomy, and there is no injury, there is to be strangulation after assizes.

V. [If a single person commits sodomy and injures his victim] but the injured person does not die, there is to be decapitation after assizes.

VI. If there is attempted rape without injury, there is to be punishment of 100 heavy blows and exile to a distance of 3,000 *li*.

VII. If there are injuries short of death, there is to be strangulation after assizes.

VIII. If there is sodomy with consent, then, as in the case of military or civil consensual lewdness, there is to be one month in the cangue and 100 heavy blows.

IX. If there is a false claim of sodomy, the accuser is to be punished in the same degree as the accused person would have been convicted. But in cases that would have called for immediate decapitation, the accuser is to be sent into military exile at a distance of 4,000 *li*.[16]

Most problematic is the eighth article of the code, which prohibits consensual homosexual relations. The legal context for accurately understanding this new and unprecedented judicial hostility to homosexuality has been explained in detail by M. J. Meijer.[17] He notes that the Qing code adopted an unequivocal stand against all forms of extramarital sexuality as a way of strengthening the Confucian ideal of family, perhaps in reaction to Ming chaos. As a consequence, Qing legalists condemned homosexuality in an effort to limit all sexuality to a marital context. Such a rationale accounts for a punishment that, though harsh by modern Western standards, was among the lightest possible under the Qing legal system. And considering the openness of homosexuality throughout the Qing, it is doubtful that the idealistic eighth article of this law was ever systematically enforced.

The portions of the law regarding rape, however, performed a necessary service. European hyperbole aside, there was still a temptation for the strong to sexually abuse the weak. Although rape was usually a heterosexual crime, sometimes men also violated an unwilling male victim. Chinese law dealt with this sort of crime directly, and Qing legal records abound with examples of successful convictions. In one case two men, "perceiving the clear white countenance" of a boy of twelve, decided to "commit successive sodomies upon the boy." Not all such cases made reference to the specific code regarding homosexual rape; some followed the more traditional practice dating from the Qin. In this particular instance, the defendants were sentenced by analogy to a substatute that deals with "successive consummated rapes by more than one man of a respectable woman." Both were executed.[18]

Authorities prosecuted not only successful homosexual rape, but attempted rape as well. A similar case records the deportation to Heilongjiang of a man convicted in 1809 of attempted homosexual rape.[19] Unlike the Song law against male prostitution, homosexual rape law of the Qing was actively enforced. And Qing law treated all rapists comparably, regardless of the gender of their victim. Instead, punishment relied entirely on consideration of the age of the victim and the degree of violence perpetrated.[20]

Even literature deals with the problem of male rape. The works of Li Yu, for example, are filled with examples of sexual violence. This social problem stirred the imaginations of other prose authors as well. One tale tells of an evil spirit who rapes an innocent young man:

> A certain young scholar went to pay a call on a friend. Since it was a summer night he strolled outside the village, losing track of the distance. Suddenly he heard a moaning sound. Following the sound to find its source, he came upon a naked boy lying on the ground. He asked the reason for the boy's pain.
>
> The boy said that earlier in the evening he had passed by a place where he had met a voluptuous woman with flowing hair. She called after him and they struck up a conversation. Desirous of his blossoming beauty, she soon began to flirt and play. Saying that her father was always out, she invited him to her home to sit for a while. She led him to a place where there was a three-pillared cottage. No one was home. The woman closed the door and brought out some fruit, which they ate together. Laughing, she said that since they already got along so well together they should relax on the bed.
>
> She pressed close to him on his pillow. Then the woman suddenly

transformed into a man! His appearance was repulsive! He
viciously used his ruthless strength. Frightened, the boy did not
dare resist. Finally he received the man's pollution. Then he was
beaten with painful malevolence until he fainted. After a long time
he gradually revived, and found himself lying discarded in the
misty underbrush. The cottage had disappeared!

A demon had found the boy attractive and enticed him with the
illusionary form of a woman. After taking advantage of him, the
demon fled. The transformation was successful bait![21]

Of course, examples of homosexuality from this period dwell
on the nonviolent as well. Even during Kang Xi's own lifetime,
a contemporary writer observed that male love was so widespread
that "it is considered in bad taste not to keep elegant manservants
on one's household staff, and undesirable not to have singing boys
around when inviting guests for dinner."[22] Art created during the
Ming and Qing for popular consumption abandoned earlier de-
mureness and began to represent the sexual act. Among surviving
examples of Chinese erotic art are several representations of the
male homosexual act. These pictures often distinguish active and
passive partners through tint—with the skin of the active partner
taking on a darker tone.[23] One painting shows a homosexual encounter between two youths;[24] another depicts a bisexual encounter in which men masturbate each other while one man uses his
other hand to stimulate a woman's vagina.[25] In a variation of this
bisexual theme, another painting shows a man penetrating a
woman's vagina as a second man begins to penetrate the first
man's anus.[26] And a member of an early British embassy described a marble statue, now apparently lost, in the imperial
palace: it depicted two youths engaged in "the vice of the
Greeks."[27] Most of the art of this kind has either been destroyed or
remains inaccessible in private collections. Nevertheless, what
little survives demonstrates the clear existence of a market for
homosexual erotica during the Qing.

In the realm of literature, diffusion of allusions to the homosexual tradition of antiquity was quite widespread by the Qing,

appearing in popular fiction as well as in more scholarly works. The man of letters Zhao Yi showed his own awareness of this heritage by reciting a roll call of famous men from ancient times. "The Three Dynasties [Xia, Shang, and Zhou] already had this practice. Later there were Mizi Xia, Lord E, and Lord Long Yang. And during the Han dynasty there were Jiru, Hongru, Deng Tong, and Han Yan. The 'followers of Dong Xian' went so far as to apply cosmetics and become prostitutes."[28] In a society heavily imbued with a sense of history, awareness of the homosexual tradition was not limited to men most attracted to other men. Even the classical terms for "homosexuality" reflect this sense of history. In the absence of a medical term comparable to the modern word "homosexuality," "homosexuals" were instead referred to as "followers of Dong Xian" or those with the "passions of the cut sleeve." It did not surprise Qing audiences to read an early-nineteenth-century novel set in the Tang, only to have an anachronistic Mizi Xia step into the action.[29] Unlike contemporary gays in China, who exist cut off from this tradition, Qing society was still steeped in an awareness of the ancient icons of the male custom.

Qing popular literature shows male love spanning all social strata. An incident from Cao Xueqin's *Dream of the Red Chamber* (*Honglou meng*), the most famous Chinese novel, points out the diverse backgrounds of men who felt attraction to those of their own sex. In one scene a drunken page mumbles to other young male servants proposing that they should become his passive sexual partners. They ignore this semicoherent proposition. The author contrasts the drunken buffoonery of these servants with an adulterous heterosexual seduction taking place between their employers in the same house.[30]

Another scene explores the Qing perceptions of sexual categories. In this incident, the boorish Xue Pan is severely beaten for making sexual overtures to a dashing young actor.[31] Throughout the novel Xue Pan acts as an oafish comic foil to the talented and sincere young aristocrat Baoyu, his clumsy lewdness serving as a crude contrast to Baoyu's own sexual subtlety. In one instance Xue Pan ogles the amateur actor Liu Xianglian while at a party. Since Liu enjoys acting, Xue Pan naturally assumes that like many young actors Liu is also readily available as a sexual companion. In fact, Liu is from a good family recently come on hard times, and the insecurity of his position makes him ostentatiously masculine. He is egregiously offended by Xue Pan's advances.

Readers unfamiliar with the sexual context of the Qing might assume that Liu is insulted simply because Xue Pan insinuates that he is "gay," as David Hawkes's otherwise admirable translation of the novel implies.[32] Yet the situation is far more complex. Liu takes offense not at the implication that he might enjoy homosexual intercourse per se, but rather at the suggestion that he might be willing to take a passive sexual role. According to conventional hierarchies for actor-prostitutes, sexual passivity to Xue Pan would also have entailed social submission to this oafish boor. This idea enrages Liu to such an extent that he severely beats his admirer and forces Xue Pan to drink foul ooze from a stagnant pool until he vomits. The violence of this incident emphasizes the seriousness with which men of the Qing viewed sexual roles, particularly in such an extreme case as mistaking a free man of good family for a prostitute.

The brilliant complexity of this great novel consists of this continual use of opposition and contrast. Consequently, the author provides a variety of views concerning the many manifestations of homosexuality. For one perspective the author creates characters such as the drunken page and the "Oaf King" Xue Pan. Romanticized views of male love are provided by glimpses of the young aristocrat Baoyu's complex sexual identity. His coy yet ingenuous meeting with a young male actor who specializes in female stage roles is the antithesis of Xue Pan's loutish lust.[33] These differences seem even more directly opposed when Xue Pan's childish jealousy leads him to reveal to Baoyu's father Baoyu's relationship with a commoner of the most despised social order.[34] This news only increases the frustration felt by Baoyu's sternly puritanical father toward his dilettante son.

An even more idealized friendship between Baoyu and another youth is similarly disrupted by the jealous machinations of Xue Pan, again defining polarized viewpoints of homosexuality. A particularly memorable scene takes place in a clan school overrun with what the author terms the "passion of Lord Long Yang."[35] All of these boys are enmeshed in a complex web of conflicting sexual desires. Qin Zhong, the dearest male friend of Baoyu, and Baoyu himself are both entranced by a pair of charmingly affected fellow students. Another boy inflames Qin Zhong by gleefully telling the class that he caught Qin Zhong and his companion "in the rear courtyard, kissing each other and feeling asses as plain as anything." The venue for this act, a "rear courtyard," exemplifies Cao Xueqin's subtle wit. Xue Pan's previous scheming further exacerbates the situation. The boys soon divide into camps based on their sexual loyalties and a general melee ensues. Again the mature sincerity of Qin Zhong's friendship with Baoyu and of the encounter between Qin Zhong and his beloved are both contrasted with the childish raucousness of their less refined schoolmates.[36]

Baoyu and Qin Zhong's relationship is laden with sexual overtones.[37] In addition to the incident at the school, in which other boys assume they are lovers, there is another episode in which they reveal shared eroticism. Just as Qin Zhong begins to consummate his seduction of a novitiate nun, Baoyu rushes in and takes them by surprise: "Suddenly, in less time than it takes to tell, a third person bore down upon them from above and held them fast. The intruder made no sound, and for some moments the other two lay underneath his weight, half dead with fright. Then there was a sputter of suppressed laughter and they knew that it was Baoyu."[38] As the girl rushes off in shame, Qin Zhong begs Baoyu not to tell others about this illicit encounter. Baoyu cryptically replies, "Wait until we are both in bed and I'll settle accounts with you then." The author demurely concludes, "As for the 'settling of accounts' that Baoyu had proposed to Qin Zhong, we have not been able to ascertain exactly what form this took; and as we would not for the world be guilty of fabrication, we must allow the matter to remain a mystery."[39] Baoyu's own sexual designs temporarily thwart Qin Zhong's heterosexual encounter. It comes as no coincidence that Qin Zhong's tragic death occurs simultaneously with the construction of the magnificent garden that is to be the site of Baoyu's growing intimacy with women.[40] As was characteristic of the Qing view of sexuality, the carefree revelry of youth must eventually be supplanted by the responsibilities of procreation implicit in heterosexuality.

Qing fiction also often dealt with the relations of wealthy men and male prostitutes who were not a regular part of the household. We have already touched on one unusually circumspect example of this type of sexual relationship—the encounter between Baoyu and the male actor of female roles in *Dream of the Red Chamber*. The same work also contains a contrasting episode that involves uncouth prostitutes at a gathering of some of Baoyu's more dissolute male relatives. The author sets the scene as an unsavory gambling party attended by Xue Pan and equally debauched associates. "The servants were all pages of fifteen or under. There was also a pair of male prostitutes, powdered, overdressed youths of seventeen or eighteen, whose duty was to ply the guests with drink."[41] The two prostitutes are described as effeminate and affected.

This scene reinforces the double standard of behavior expected from men of the Ming and Qing. Although active men avoided effeminate stereotypes, their passive partners often took on female mannerisms, such as the application of cosmetics, as a complement to their "female" sexual role. To the literatus Zhao Yi's essay on passive men, a commentator appended a discussion of famous men who wore cosmetics. Apparently he considered the two practices to be related. He stated that those who apply cosmetics are favored by men, and singled out actors as universally wearing powder.[42] Thus the signals implicit in wearing white powder changed tremendously over the course of Chinese history: whereas men of the Wei and Jin might have seen powdering the face as a mark of cosmopolitan elegance, to later men it symbolized prostitution and effeminacy.

Cao Xueqin shows the prostitutes themselves as carefree opportunists. As the gambling fortune of one patron declines, they immediately turn their attentions to a more successful participant in the transparent hope of prying away some of his gambling spoils. When a former patron loudly and drunkenly complains that they are being ungrateful to him despite his past favors, they disarm his objections with naive candor:

> "Don't be angry with us, dear old friend. We are only children. We have to do as we are told. Our teacher always tells us, 'It doesn't matter what they are like or what your own feelings are, the person who at any moment has the most money is the one you must be nice to.' Just win a lot of money later on this evening, old friend, and you'll see how nice we shall be to you!"[43]

The scene quickly dissolves into indecorous laughter when a guest crudely counters the boys' rationalizations with the observation, "He's only lost a bit of money, hasn't he? He hasn't lost his prick!"[44] The entire episode presents male prostitution at its most visceral level: as a simple exchange of money for sexual favors.

These older men considered active sexuality to be their rightful privilege, an inevitable outgrowth of their superior social status. They saw young men of lower social position as sexual toys. The witty literatus Yuan Mei exalted the promiscuity of young men in a sardonic epigram:

> The duke of Zhou canonized the rituals.
> How powerful and wonderful these established meanings are!
> There were only shrines to virtuous women,
> But no temples to chaste boys.[45]

The author refers to the legendary establishment of proper rituals and ceremonies by the ancient paragon of rectitude, the duke of Zhou—and thereby justifies his own preference for younger men. Yuan Mei's irrepressible wit led him flippantly to mock the roots of the revered Confucian tradition by humorously linking the duke of Zhou to sex, so enraging the dour historian Zhang Xuecheng with his unrepentant heresy that Zhang angrily denounced Yuan Mei and called for his execution. But the more tolerant majority of officialdom ignored, or perhaps enjoyed, Yuan's audacious joke.[46]

Many of the young men in Qing society referred to in Yuan Mei's controversial epigram were prostitutes, whose sexual skills earned them such ephitets as "little hands."[47] Male prostitutes seem to have catered to different types of clientele, from laborers to scholars. For example, a Western visitor to the port city of Tianjin in 1860 estimated that its thirty-five male brothels contained approximately eight hundred boys "trained for pederastic prostitution."[48] The least fortunate of these youths, about whom almost nothing is known, frequented barber stalls and bathhouses, probably barely surviving on what they could earn by selling themselves.[49] Our knowledge of male prostitution from the Qing concerns almost exclusively the most elite group of male prostitutes: actors.

Acting teachers raised young actors in troupes and were concerned not only with developing a boy's talents but also with enhancing his looks. A winsome appearance could provide additional income, for as one observer noted, if an actor "has a clean, white complexion and is unusually good looking, it is safe to assume that he has other skills unknown to outsiders."[50] Most of the boys in Beijing were brought from southern cities. They were trained to "speak and walk in the most charming manner and to use their eyes with great efficacy." To promote an attractive physique they washed their faces in meat broth, ate a special diet of choice foods, and covered their bodies in ointment at night to soften the skin. "Three or four months after the training program begins, these boys are delicate and genteel as lovely maidens. One glance from them will create hundreds of charms." A nineteenth-century literatus described his personal reaction to a troupe of boy actors: "All of them were about fourteen or fifteen years old. After they finished their singing, they helped me with my drinks. They wore clothes made of light silk, and their sleeves were narrow and tight. They were so delicate and lovely that one could not help but feel a sentiment of endearment."[51] These boys were purchased from their parents on a contract that lasted for a number of years. Their "teachers" acquainted them with thespian skills as well as training in the erotic arts.

> The young boys are always from the south. When they are eight or nine years old their teachers and their parents agree to a contract that lasts for a number of years. They are taken to the capital, where they practice beautiful songs and adorn themselves with captivating clothes. These boys flee the dust of the mortal world to serve wine to guests. And they make a profit at it! Afterward the young men are freed from their contracts. . . . As the poem says,
>
> > Now they come from the south,
> > Aged only thirteen or fourteen.
> > When their youth is gone,
> > They will never again apply vermillion hues.
> > The carriages in front of their doorways will be few.[52]

Although boy actors played a variety of theatrical roles, some specialized in playing the parts of women. Some even went so far as to have their feet bound to complete the effect of feminization.[53] One tale describes a female impersonator named Hu who deserted the theater and disguised his theatrical origins. Beginning as the sexual favorite of an official, he managed to amass enough money to purchase a civil office. As part of a celebration he was hosting, Hu ordered a performance of dramatic entertainments. Unexpectedly, an elderly actor charged from the stage and began to beat Hu with a bamboo rod. The assailant claimed that he had been Hu's acting teacher and that he had been deserted by his pupil and left penniless. As proof of his charge he had Hu's shoes forcibly removed. The crowd of guests was shocked to gaze on the former actor's tiny bound feet.[54]

Most accounts of actors' sexuality do not focus on the macabre or unusual, as in the story of Hu's rise and fall. Yet there is no question that homosexuality was widespread almost to the point of universality among young actors. In reference to their status as actors, and later to their sexual role, they came to be referred to as "officials" (*xianggong*).[55] This term, originally a title of high government ministers, later found use in southern China as a polite term of address for young men. It then became used for young southern male actors brought to the north. And eventually it acquired sexual connotations as a synonym for a passive man.[56] An important source for the history of the Qing theater succinctly states, "The female impersonators of the capital's pear gardens are called 'officials.'"[57] These "pear gardens," a poetic name for theaters, were also centers of male prostitution. Similar poetic descriptions were employed to describe male actors and female prostitutes, both of whom were often referred to as "flowers." And paying a visit to a female brothel or a male actor's house was in both instances called "holding a tea gathering." In fact, similar terms referred to the residences of young actors and to heterosexual brothels. The acting profession was inextricably linked to homosexual prostitution.[58]

Chinese literati saw male actors as potential favorites partly because of the feminine affectations that many actors purposely cultivated. In at least one case, a well-known actor did his best to avoid being looked on as sexually passive. Yet his wealthy admirers consistently perceived him in sexual terms.[59] Another actor stubbornly refused sexual intercourse with his patron, explaining: "Our necks and legs touch and we fondle one another. Although we are both aroused, we have no sexual connection. He has often wondered at my restraint, but I have never changed my behavior."[60] The reason for his restraint is not recorded, though he may have wished to avoid the social disapprobation accompanying sexual submission to another man. The general association of the acting profession with passive homosexuality and hence prostitution contributed to the low social status of actors. Nevertheless, their active patrons included some of the most respected political and intellectual figures of the Qing.

Not all of the homosexual relations of male actors were undertaken purely for financial reasons. Many cases record the deep love felt between actors and their patrons. The famous scholar-official Bi Yuan (1730–1797), known for his turbulent political career as

well as his indefatigable devotion to learning, gained such noto-
riety for his devoted love of the Suzhou actor Li Guiguan that he
inspired the great nineteenth-century homosexual novel *Precious
Mirror of Ranking Flowers* (*Pinhua baojian*).[61] Because Li was tired
of acting, he welcomed Bi Yuan's patronage as a means to escape
from the stage. They exchanged vows of fidelity, and Li Guiguan
lived with Bi Yuan and was addressed by their acquaintances as if
he were Bi's wife.[62]

Yet this sort of intimacy between scholars and actors seems to
have been officially discouraged. When a censor met the actor Wei
Changsheng on his way to the household of his lover, Heshan, a
wealthy and powerful official, the censor ordered Wei beaten.
Qing Chinese generally looked askance at actors as contagions of
immorality. Apparently the defenders of public rectitude considered it unseemly for high officials to befriend men of the most
despised social class. They took even more stringent measures to
deter liaisons between officials and female prostitutes for similar
reasons.[63]

These social and official barriers did not discourage the love felt
by many actors and their patrons, however. Sometimes the actors
themselves would pursue a particularly attractive young literatus.
In one instance, a desirable scholar, Zhu Deshan, simultaneously
patronized two actors. In a curious twist on the usual course of
these affairs, one of the actors presented his "patron" with a large
amount of money in the hope of gaining his lover's full attentions.
The other actor left this jealous ménage, and later blackmailed
Zhu by threatening to reveal this unusual affair to Zhu's father.
Like the relationship of Bi Yuan and Li Guiguan, the friends of
this couple also treated them as man and wife.[64]

Another case of an actor advancing on a patron occurred between Xu Yunting and Yuan Mei. The poet was ecstatic in the
description of his first romantic encounter with the desirable
young actor:

All the Hanlin scholars were crazy about him and clubbed together
to pay for theatricals in which he appeared. I was young and good-

looking, but I was so poorly accoutred that I did not think Yunting could possibly regard me as worth cultivating. But I noticed on one occasion that he often glanced my way and smiled, quite with the air of indicating that he had taken a fancy to me. I hardly dared to believe this and did not try to get into touch with him. However, very early next day I heard a knock at my door. There he was; and we were soon on the most affectionate terms—a state of affairs all the more delightful, because it far exceeded anything I had expected.[65]

This was not simply a case of ordinary prostitution. An actor of Xu Yunting's stature could engage in relationships motivated by desire rather than profit. The earnest candor with which Yuan Mei expressed his love for the youth is eloquent testimony to the esteem in which love of the cut sleeve was held among the scholarly elite of Qing Beijing. As another equally enraptured poet rhapsodized:

> I want to, but do not, send off flower-laden boughs.
> I want to, but do not, think about him.
> My thoughts of him flow forth quickly.
> On spring winds a yellow oriole flies among scattered trees.[66]

This particular poet bemoaned the fact that his beloved "oriole" preferred to fly between various lovers rather than remain permanently with him. Like many of his eloquently brokenhearted contemporaries, he gave vent to thwarted passion in verse.

The pinnacle of literature concerning homosexual themes was reached near the end of the tradition. The name of this monumental work is *Precious Mirror of Ranking Flowers*, published in 1849 by Chen Sen.[67] The "flowers" referred to in the title are actor-prostitutes. This work is important both for its influential place in the history of Qing popular fiction and for its subject matter, which deals with the romances between actors and their scholar-patrons.

The novel is a thematic descendant of Cao Xueqin's masterpiece, *Dream of the Red Chamber*,[68] which saw numerous imitations. Subsequent authors, searching for new settings in which to place panoramic works, turned away from private households, since only a household equal in opulence to that in *Dream of the Red Chamber* could contain such a huge ensemble of characters. Eventually they settled on the brothel as a suitable setting, and several works describe the daily interactions of female prostitutes and their countless customers. Yet in this sort of novel it was difficult to continue the "talented scholar and the beauty" motif central to Chinese romance, since officials were legally prohibited from frequenting the quarters of female prostitutes. As a substitute, the scholars themselves sometimes turned to male actor-prostitutes, with whom they were not forbidden by law to associate. The author Chen Sen was among the literati to enjoy the company of male prostitutes. His firsthand observations formed the foundation of the *Precious Mirror*.

Overall the novel, set in the early Qing, depicts a life of elegance and romance. In this respect it resembles its long line of forebears in romantic fiction, except that in this case both scholars and beauties are men. The novel also contains likenesses to erotic novels such as *The Golden Lotus* in that it is supposedly intended to serve a didactic moral purpose. Chen Sen does not stereotype his characters, but instead depicts a wide range of personalities and emotions that serve as a testing ground for his ethical premises.[69] Only the most central characters are idealized, remaining pure despite the maelstrom of conflicting behavior around them. Chen Sen even enumerates the different types of *qing*, a word meaning "affections," "desires," "passions," or "emotions." Earlier writers had also emphasized this word. To the playwright Tang Xianzu, passion can conquer perceptions of reality, parental authority, and even death. At the beginning of the Qing the author of the collection of homosexual stories *Hairpins Beneath His Cap* (*Bian er chai*) applied this term to love of the cut sleeve. Chen Sen follows their examples. In an outburst of characteristically scholastic taxophilia, he states that actors have ten types of *qing*:

> Extreme passions
> Shrewd passions
> Tasteful passions
> Pure passions
> Virtuous passions
> Impetuous passions
> Straightforward passions
> Drunken passions
> Voluptuous passions
> Seductive passions.[70]

This is how Chen Sen judged the love of the half-eaten peach. He did not prejudge others according to whether they felt affection for men or women, but only by how they manifested their desires. The passions of the cut sleeve were no different from heterosexual passions.

Chen Sen's attitude was representative of the tendency in literature to view sexuality less in terms of a homosexual/heterosexual dichotomy than according to the specific form these emotions took, thereby fulfilling a didactic purpose. The most evident example of this type of juxtaposition occurs in *Dream of the Red Chamber* between the captivating affections of Baoyu and the base lasciviousness of his cousin Xue Pan. Like Baoyu, the protagonist of *Precious Mirror of Ranking Flowers,* named Mei Ziyu, remains superior to many of the less pure sentiments that surround him.[71] Even the "mirror" image in the title is a common metaphor for the use of past precedents as guides to personal conduct. Just as emperors could learn about statecraft by viewing the mirror of history, men of less exalted status could find out about the perplexing world of sexual life by following the adventures of Chen Sen's multitude of characters.

Precious Mirror of Ranking Flowers is both an end and a culmination of the homosexual tradition. In it we can find the reflections of centuries of previous occurrences and concepts. By drawing inspiration for the characters' actions from the romances of the early Qing literatus Bi Yuan, Chen Sen draws the story together with lives and passions of previous times. Having tied the novel to a greater sense of tradition, he makes the action relevant for readers of his own day by having a character wax eloquent on the attractiveness of male favorites in comparison to the stock images of Chinese beauty:

> Across tens of thousands of miles of territory, through five thousand years of history, nothing and nobody is better than a favorite. Those who do not love a favorite should not be taken seriously. . . . Elegant flowers, beautiful women, a shining moon, rare books, grand paintings—these beautiful things are liked by everyone. However, these beautiful things are not all combined. Favorites are like elegant flowers and not grass or trees; they are like beautiful women who do not need make-up; they are like a shining moon or tender cloud, yet can be touched and played with; they are like rare books and grand paintings, and yet they can talk and converse; they are beautiful and playful and yet they also are full of change and surprise. The loss of a favorite cannot be compensated by any beauty in history. The gain of a favorite makes the loss of any beauty of the past a small matter.[72]

The novel gives one of the most eloquent, and final, defenses of homosexuality against what seems to have been a rising chorus of criticism. Whereas Li Yu's writings and early Qing sodomy laws hint at the beginnings of intolerance for homosexuality, the impassioned pleas of one character in Chen Sen's novel shows that by the mid-nineteenth century men of the cut sleeve faced increasing condemnation: "I do not comprehend why it is acceptable for a man to love a woman, but is unacceptable for a man to love a man. Passion is passion whether to a man or a woman. To love a woman but not a man is lust and not passion. To lust is to forget passion. If one treasures passion, he is not lewd."[73]

Precious Mirror reaches a climax during a serious illness of Mei Ziyu. His young friend and favorite, Du Qinyan, visits Mei in an encounter that captures the complex and conflicting emotions of their relationship. Du's uncertainty over his own treatment by

Mei's wife, the deep devotion felt by lover and beloved, the contrast of poetic elegance with disease and decrepitude—all of these interrelated themes are captured in a single brief scene:

> Du went to Mei's house in considerable apprehension, certain that he would be humiliated. But to his surprise Mrs. Mei instead of reproaching him seemed to pity him and urged him to go in and cheer her husband up. With mixed feelings of joy and sorrow, he wondered how serious Ziyu's illness could be and how best to comfort him. But doing as he was told, he went boldly to Mei's room. He found the curtains drawn, the desk covered with dust, and light gauze curtains hanging round a single hardwood bed. The maid parted the curtains and called:
>
> "Here is Mr. Du, sir!"
>
> Mei muttered something in his sleep. Then Du sat on the edge of the bed and saw how lean and haggard his friend had grown. He bent over the pillow and called out in a low voice, his tears falling ceaselessly on the scholar's face.
>
> Then Mei laughed in his sleep and chanted: "On the seventh day of the seventh month in the Palace of Eternal Youth, we spoke in secret at midnight when no one else was near."
>
> After chanting these lines he laughed again deliriously. Du's heart contracted with pain and he shook him gently. He could not speak loudly, however, as Mrs. Mei was outside and he had to address his beloved friend formally. Mei was in fact dreaming of Du in his longing to see him again on the Double Seventh to pour out his heart in Sulan's house. So obsessed was he by this idea that he had chanted these two lines of Tang poetry. It seemed that nothing could wake him. Deep in his dreams, he laughed once more and declaimed: "I thought never to see him again in heaven or in hell. . . ." Still fast asleep, he turned his face to the wall. Du's eyes were brimming with tears but all he could do was to look on helplessly, not daring to call out."[74]

The original readers of this episode were acutely aware that the love of Mei Ziyu and Du Qinyan was not merely an isolated event, but part of a social and cultural tradition stretching back more than two thousand years to the Bronze Age. During that time it had shaped political careers and had inspired sublime literature. Emperors and scholars, monks and prostitutes—a cross-section of society had partaken of the passions of the cut sleeve. Soon this continuity with the past was to come to an end. A growing sexual conservatism exemplified by Qing law, together with a new literary language and influences from Western morality, was soon to sever most links with the homosexual tradition of antiquity. The names of Mizi Xia and Dong Xian would ultimately lose their place as famed icons of male love. From a position of prominence and openness, men involved in homosexual activities would fall to a place of terrified obscurity within their society. This pathetic end to the homosexual tradition had been predicted millennia before by Grand Historian Sima Qian. He saw the destiny of Chinese homosexuality augured by the fateful execution of the most famous symbol of male love: "How violent are the seasons of love and hatred! By observing the fate of Mizi Xia, we can guess what will happen to favorites of later times. 'Even the future a hundred ages hence may be foretold!'"[75]

Epilogue

Because this study has focused on the male homosexual tradition rather than male homosexuality in general, it ends with the twilight of the Qing dynasty. Overall this tradition has portrayed a society in which homosexuality was relatively open and tolerated. Only in the final centuries of dynastic history did intolerance begin to build as the result of a more stringent application of Neo-Confucian rhetoric regarding the family, imported Manchu concepts of sexuality, and a reaction against individualistic Ming permissiveness. This growing antipathy accelerated in the twentieth century to the point where anyone familiar with the situation of homosexuals in modern China finds evidence from earlier centuries almost unbelievable. The homosexual tradition is dead and virtually unknown, even among the educated.

Today, most Chinese see homosexuality as rare or even nonexistent in China. Even psychiatrists in the People's Republic of China (PRC) and Taiwan adhere to this tendency of seeing the world according to moral ideals rather than empirical reality, asserting that Chinese people innately experience a far lower rate of homosexual attraction than Westerners.[1] What little information exists on homosexuality inside the PRC shows lives of fear and loneliness. One study of letters written by gay men to one of the few Chinese physicians who has shown himself sympathetic to their plight reveals many common problems.[2] Filled with frustration at the inability to meet male partners, gay men are eventually forced into unfulfilling false marriages with unsuspecting wives. These marriages often exist as mere facades, with many men in the study complaining about the lack of sexual intercourse or even emotional bonding with their wives.

Beyond these social pressures, gay men in the PRC also fear legal prosecution as well. Although the Chinese criminal code lacks a specific law prohibiting homosexuality, vaguely worded prohibitions against "revolting behavior" and "hooliganism" have been used to prosecute homosexuals. In one case, after the relationship between a respected high school physics teacher and another man was discovered, the teacher lost his job and was sentenced to five years in prison. Although less active in prosecuting homosexuals, Taiwanese law also contains similarly vague provisions that in the past have been used to harass gays. And until very recently, police in Hong Kong have been particularly zealous in infiltrating and exposing gay circles. Although recent liberalizations in all three places have reduced the threat of prosecution, the possibility still exists and so casts a legal stigma on any open expression of homosexuality.

Pai Hsien-yung is one of the few recent authors to confront the predicament of homosexuals in Chinese society. He caused a sensation with his publication of vignettes of 1960s and 1970s gay life in Taipei. Written with an originality and elegance of style that made them impossible to ignore, these stories shocked the Taiwan literary establishment into open discussion of his work. Like that of Yukio Mishima, Pai's language displays a refinement that contrasts sharply with the realistic earthiness of his characters. His descriptions often draw from the ornate artifice of Tang poetry, creating a magical setting for the ordinary and even profane conversations of the seedy male prostitutes, criminals, and unhappy gay men leading double lives who inhabit this beautiful world. Some of the most memorable characters come from Pai's short story "A Sky Full of Bright, Twinkling Stars," a tale that captures the combination of sexual excitement and enervating tropical heat in the cruising grounds of a lush Taipei park. "The Guru" was once a handsome young silent-film star in Shanghai who never made it into talkies. His charisma remains, captivating his youthful audience in the park, but his pathetic memories and present decrepitude symbolize the unhappy state of Chinese gay life.

> He's probably gone through a lot in prison, you know; the police could be very cruel sometimes, especially to people in on morals charges. Once a little Sanshui Street fairy hooked a wrong customer and got arrested; the police really fixed him good. By the time he got out he'd been so scared that he'd lost his voice; when he saw people he could only open his mouth and go *ah, ah*. People said he'd been beat up with a rubber hose. The Guru dragged his feet along heavily, with great dignity, step by step; eventually he made the stone balustrade at the end of the terrace. He stood there by himself against the balustrade, his white, unruly head lifted up high, his tall, gaunt silhouette jagged and erect, ignoring the whispers and snickers buzzing around him. In a moment excitement returned to the terrace. The night was deepening; steps grew more urgent, one by one the shadows went searching, exploring, yearning. The Guru stood there alone. Not until that flesh-ball of a red moon had languidly gone all the way down did he leave the park. When he left he took a Sanshui Street boy along with him. The boy was called Little Jade; he was a pretty-faced little thing, but he was a cripple, so not many people paid him attention. The Guru put his

arm around the boy's shoulder, and the two of them, one tall, one small, supporting each other with their incompleteness, limped together into the dark grove of Green Corals.[3]

Gays in China view their own situation as difficult and uncertain. The rest of society takes a more hostile view of homosexuality. The platitude used most often to condemn homosexuality in contemporary China is that it is a recent importation from the decadent West. A 1983 article in a Hong Kong newspaper summed up Chinese attitudes in reporting the opposition to a proposal to legalize homosexuality between consenting adults. Advocated by liberal British jurists as part of a last-minute effort to rid the Hong Kong legal system of anachronisms before handing the colony over to China in 1997, this proposal encountered strong opposition from Hong Kong Chinese. Ironically, whereas in the last century the British were accusing Chinese of embracing homosexuality, the Chinese have now reversed the charges: those opposing the initiative stated that "besides going against traditional Chinese moral concepts and leading young people astray by luring them to practice it, homosexuality simply constitutes a social perversion."[4]

The Western media have done little to dispel this impression of a traditional China free from homosexuality. Although copious evidence exists to confirm the homosexuality of Puyi, final ruler of the Qing, the creative heterosexual love scenes in the acclaimed film *The Last Emperor* have created a lasting impression in both Asia and the West that Puyi zestfully took full advantage of his female concubines.[5] In both East and West, not only have attitudes toward Chinese homosexuality changed enormously, but the homosexual tradition itself has been forgotten. What could possibly account for such a monumental shift in morality in such a short time?

Much of the new morality seems to have been derived, directly or indirectly, from the West. Following the humiliation of China at the hands of Western and Japanese imperialists, the Chinese developed a love-hate relationship with the West. Spurred on by the

May Fourth Movement, progressives saw Western science and technology as China's salvation. But along with modernization of Chinese science came the desire to adopt "modern" Western ideas in every sphere of existence. Thus in politics, Marxism and democratic liberalism came to be the accepted political ideologies. Even in more mundane areas of daily life, such as dress, Western fashions replaced what were often more beautiful and practical Chinese equivalents. It was during this frenzied casting away of the traditional order that the Chinese finally began to heed missionary criticisms of their sexual morality.

These agonizing transformations have been movingly expressed in the writings of China's greatest authors. Works of the Nobel Prize nominee Ba Jin in particular capture the trauma of a society trapped between conflicting systems of values, with his semiautobiographical masterpiece *Family* (*Jia*) depicting his own thoughts and experiences during the rapid changes undergone by China earlier in this century. Rather than reacting against the stifling straightjacket of traditional values with radical rebellion, as did his contemporary Mao Zedong, Ba Jin decided to write with revulsion of his own compliance and escapism.[6] In one scene, Juehui, the character representing the young and idealistic Ba Jin, looks resentfully on his sleeping grandfather as a symbol of the hypocritical traditions he hates:

> At the moment, his grandfather, lying weakly in the reclining chair, looked very worn-out. Yeye probably wasn't always such an irritable old stick, thought Juehui. He recalled that many of his grandfather's poems had been dedicated to singsong girls, quite a few girls at that. Picturing how the old man probably looked in his youth, Juehui smiled. He must have been a dashing sort then; it was only later he acquired his pious air. . . . Of course that was thirty years ago. As he grew old, he turned into a crusty Confucian moralist. . . .
>
> Yet even now, his grandfather still played around with the young female impersonators in the opera. The old man once invited one of them to the house and had his picture taken with him. The actor had worn his costume for the occasion. Juehui recalled

seeing him putting on his powder and woman's wig in their guest room.

Of course nobody looked askance at that sort of thing in Chengdu. Not long ago, a few old-timers who had been officials under the deposed Qing dynasty—pillars of the Confucian Morals Society, too—made a big splash in the local press, publishing a list they had composed of the "best" female impersonators in the opera. Patronizing these actors was considered a sign of "refinement." Juehui's grandfather, as a well-known gentleman who had several collections of poems published, an epicure of ancient books and paintings, could not go against fashion.

Yet how can you reconcile this "refinement" with the defense of "Confucian Morals"? Young Juehui couldn't figure it out.[7]

The youthful Juehui sees a contradiction between his grandfather's traditional values and his patronage of female impersonators. But those espousing such values saw no such contradiction. In fact, the conflict was between his grandfather's traditional sexual mores and Juehui's Westernized sensibilities. By reacting against his grandfather's values, Juehui hoped to free himself from the insincere constraints of traditional morality. But this mystical faith in the superiority of all things Western caused the rebellious Juehui to reject the suffocating Chinese past, only to embrace an equally restrictive middle-class, missionary morality.

Christian missionaries and other Western moralists had championed a realignment of Chinese sexuality along Western European ideals. Feet were unbound, prostitutes put out of business, and concubinage outlawed. In importing Western sexual morality, however, the Chinese also imported Western intolerance of homosexuality. Stripped of the original religious language, these ideas became accepted by Chinese eager to emulate the West uncritically in every respect. While some observers might want to attribute current official intolerance of homosexuality to Marxism, which has often proven hostile to sexual nonconformity, remarkably similar attitudes exist in each of the "three Chinas"— the PRC, Taiwan, and Hong Kong. In fact, the current views of the Chinese Communist party on homosexuality have nothing to do with the Chinese tradition and seem to have little to do with Marx, but are in fact a secularized version of Leviticus and Thomas Aquinas's *Summa Theologica*.

This new sexual morality was sanctioned by the greatest object of adoration imported to China since Buddhism: Western science. Until the Stonewall rebellion and the gay rights movement in the United States and Europe forced a reevaluation of scientific perceptions of homosexuality, the scientific community had been almost uniformly hostile to what it perceived as a form of sexual pathology. In importing Western science, the Chinese also imported Western scientific misconceptions. The reverential attitude toward science cultivated by Chinese intellectuals made effective criticism of these views impossible. Hu Shih characteristically summed up the spirit of the age: "Ever since the beginning of reformist tendencies in China, there is not a single person who calls himself a modern man and yet dares openly to belittle science."[8] The relative isolation of China from the scientific mainstream has allowed outdated Western ideas about homosexuality to persist. With the connivance of time, the great legitimizer, these archaic notions of human sexuality have gradually risen to the sanctified station of common sense and convention.

Appeal to Chinese traditions as a guide for modern society has also become difficult because of changes initiated within China. The remaking of literary language ranks high among these internal causes. Chinese reformers advocated vernacular (*baihua*) literature as a replacement for the difficult and mannered classical literary language that linked Chinese to their cultural past. With most young people no longer proficient in classical Chinese, they are effectively cut off from the sources of the homosexual tradition. Access to classical works has been made more difficult by the simplification of Chinese characters, so that many young people are now unable to recognize nonsimplified forms. In his novel *1984*, George Orwell described a society in which changes in language give an authoritarian regime the power to rewrite history and make it coincide with the present. In much the same way, China's homosexual tradition has been destroyed. With government officials able to choose what to print in the new characters and language, they have succeeded in expunging all references to homosexuality from even such hallowed classics as *Dream of the Red Chamber*. A government and society imbued with a new form of sexual morality has projected that morality back into the past.

More specifically, changes in language have had two major effects: a Westernization of Chinese sexual categories and a Westernization of the overall terms of discourse about homosexuality. No longer does the average person think of his or her own sexuality in terms of native conceptions emphasizing actions and tendencies rather than essence. The fluid conceptions of sexuality of old, which assumed that an individual was capable of enjoying a range of sexual acts, have been replaced with the ironclad Western dichotomy of heterosexual/homosexual. Instead of "passions of the cut sleeve" or other terms taken from history and literature, Chinese now speak of "homosexuality" (*tongxinglian* or *tongxing-ai*), a direct translation of the Western medical term that defines a small group of pathological individuals according to a concrete sexual essence.

Accompanying this complete shift in sexual categories has come the more general adoption of Western terms of discourse regarding sexuality. Unlike the vast bulk of traditional literature, sexuality is now routinely spoken of as "normal" or "abnormal." An advice column in a Taiwan newspaper exemplifies this new way of speaking about homosexuality: "Although there are psychologists in Europe and America who are gradually coming to view it as normal, I believe that any arguments that homosexuality is rational or normal are shocking and twisted theories."[9] The author of this attack implicitly criticizes homosexuality as being contrary to imported Western-style sexual categories (abnormal) and opposed to Western-style science (irrational). The deviance of homosexuality from these imported norms is so shockingly certain that even contrary arguments from the original source of these categories—Western scientists—cannot refute what has become a dominant Chinese hostility toward homosexuality.

Although the more conservative mainland Chinese media have

generally ignored the subject of homosexuality entirely, the popular press in Taiwan and Hong Kong supply the public with continuing proof of the abnormality of homosexuality by emphasizing the crimes and scandals that sell newspapers. While a few liberal voices in recent years have urged compassion for homosexuals by portraying them as pathetic creatures persecuted by society for an abnormal perversion over which they have no control (the title of a recent book published in Taiwan, *Homosexuality, Suicide, Mental Illness,* sums up this viewpoint),[10] most publications are far less sympathetic. Besides suicide, the news media tend to dwell on raids of gay meeting places, crimes committed by homosexuals, and advice columns filled with anxious letters about homosexuality from parents, wives, and frightened young men.[11] An editorial in a respected Taiwan newspaper sums up popular reaction to these happenings:

> In the past month . . . several major crimes have taken place in gay circles. These have included the cruel murder and dismemberment of a homosexual victim and a homosexual gang's robbery of a Japanese tourist. These together with other evil deeds and malicious incidents amply expose the heart-chilling, violent tendencies that can be set off by abnormal feelings. . . . The police hope that young people with homosexual tendencies can have the courage to seek help from parents, teachers, or specialists to free themselves from abnormal feelings. By all means do not set foot in the same evil circles! Avoid the enticements and slips by which you will sink into crime.[12]

This now-common association of homosexuality with violent crime lacks precedent in native traditions. Convinced of the moral and psychological deviance of homosexuals, society relegates them to its fringes, where homosexuality becomes synonymous with danger, violence, and crime.

Many Chinese now regard the West as a cesspool of sexual and moral decadence. Outstripped by the West in material terms, they take consolation in their own ethical superiority. Chinese moralists often single out the recently imported "fad" of homosexuality as evidence of the spiritual pollution that now infects its place of origin—the United States and Europe. The Western vision of the decadent Orient is now matched with a parallel Chinese view of the exotic and depraved Occident. Yet ironically, the intolerance of homosexuality of which the Chinese are so proud actually originated in the West, while the acceptance of homosexuality that they abhor is more typical of native sexual ideals.

Even so, the basic reasons for intolerance of homosexuality remain different in China and the West. Whereas Westerners generally disparage homosexuality for religious and ethical reasons, to most Chinese homosexuality seems evil because it disrupts the accepted life cycle. They see the self-identified homosexual, who forgoes heterosexual marriage and the raising of children, as a grave enemy of the family structure, which still forms the foundation of Chinese society. And they are correct in asserting that the homosexual who refuses to marry is alien to the Chinese tradition. But this hostility extends beyond the childless Western-style gay to all forms of homosexuality. Even the explosive population problem faced by China, which has forced the government to make excessive procreation a criminal act, has not lessened the social necessity of becoming part of the family structure.

The AIDS crisis has given new visibility to gays in Taiwan and Hong Kong, while in the People's Republic political liberalizations since the death of Mao have allowed the expression of greater individuality in all respects. But this renewed awareness of homosexuality in Chinese society has not resulted in a revival of the homosexual tradition. To the contrary, Chinese gays now conceive of their sexuality according to Western models.[13] Rather than turning to the examples of antiquity to understand Chinese homosexuality and provide justifications of self-worth and models of behavior, they now look to New York and San Francisco for examples to emulate. Not only is the native homosexual tradition unknown among critics of homosexuality, but it has also virtually disappeared among homosexuals themselves.

Appendix

Lesbianism in Imperial China

Since lesbianism remained separate from the male homosexual tradition, it would have been an imposition of Western conceptual categories to have integrated lesbianism into the body of this study. Nevertheless, it is a subject that deserves investigation. I have therefore gathered together what information I could find concerning Chinese lesbianism in dynastic times to produce this separate section.

Unfortunately, references to lesbianism in traditional sources are rare. Partly this lack was due to the relative absence of personal freedom accorded women. Bound to their husbands economically and often forced into seclusion in the home, many women were denied the opportunities to form close bonds with women outside their household. Moreover, the relationships that did form would usually escape notice by men uninterested in women's affairs. Since men also controlled the literary world, this combination of factors meant that few examples of lesbianism were recorded in print. As a result, lesbianism never inspired a sustained literary tradition such as that associated with male homosexuality, and the scattered mentions of lesbianism that remain are unrelated.

In ancient times, some of the relationships between women in the Han court seem to have had sexual overtones. With thousands of women locked in the palace together with only the emperor and eunuchs, it seems inevitable that some should have formed deep attachments to one another. Sometimes these women would form couples, known as *dui shi*. Literally meaning "paired eating," this term may have connoted cunnilingus.[1] Ying Shao (ca. 140–206) noted, "When palace women attach themselves as husband and wife it is called *dui shi*. They are intensely jealous of each other"[2] *Records of the Han* mentions in passing the love of two slave women, Cao Gong and Dao Fang, describing it as *dui shi*.[3] Han records also state how the servant of one empress dressed in male attire, with the context of this transvestism suggesting a possible lesbian relationship.[4]

At times men of the household encouraged lesbianism as a way of adding variety to sexual routine. The seventeenth-century short story "The Pearl-sewn Shirt" includes a scene in which an older woman aids in the seduction of the young beauty San Qiao'er. Using the excuse that her own home is too hot, the older woman asks to sleep with San Qiao'er. She inflames the younger woman with "dirty and obscene local gossip" and tales of her own amorous adventures, then, climbing into San Qiao'er's bed, arouses her with candid talk of sex. Demonstrating how an erotic tool can simulate intercourse, she fans out the lamp flame by pretending to brush away a moth. By this time San Qiao'er has reached a state of ready excitement, and the older woman allows the seducer Chen Dalang, her patron, stealthily to take her place in the bed.[5]

Traditional handbooks on marital intercourse sometimes describe acts combining lesbian and heterosexual elements:

> Lady Precious Yin and Mistress White Jade lay on top of each
> other, their legs entwined so that their jade gates (genitalia) pressed
> together. They then moved in a rubbing and jerking fashion against
> each other like fishes gobbling flies or water plants from the sur-
> face. As they became more excited, the "mouths" widen and
> choosing his position carefully, Great Lord Yang thrusts between
> them with his jade root (penis). They moved in unison until all
> three shared the ultimate simultaneously.[6]

Prints and paintings survive that depict this and similar acts, showing that it was probably considered to be more than just a theoretical possibility.[7]

Of course, most lesbian encounters did not include a male participant. Women utilized a variety of means for self-satisfaction. In addition to the pudendal contact described above (which earned the nickname "grinding bean curd") there was also cunnilingus, manual stimulation of the clitoris, and the use of artificial erotic tools. Some women would even use a tiny bound foot to stimulate their partner's vagina.[8] Olisboi, made from wood or ivory, were often constructed in a double-headed form that offered simultaneous vaginal penetration for both partners. Other olisboi were carved from a plant that swelled on contact with moisture, such as that present in the vagina. Still others were made of silk cloth stuffed with expandable silk threads or bean curd.[9] Women and even some men would sometimes place a hollow ball made from copper or silver in the vagina or anus as a form of stimulus. These various artificial devices are described in surviving literature and are portrayed in erotic art.[10] One surviving print even pictures a limber woman who has strapped a penis-shaped object to her leg next to her foot for the purpose of masturbation.[11]

Prose fiction provides one of the few detailed views of lesbian life, even though the surviving works on this subject were all written by men. Once again the uncanny social insight of Li Yu found fertile subject matter in the world of lesbian love. His first play, *Pitying the Fragrant Companion* (*Lian xiangban*), involves a young married woman's love for a younger unmarried woman.[12] The married woman convinces her husband to take her talented beloved as a concubine. The three then live as a happy ménage à trois free from jealousy. A similar, presumably nonfictional, account in the eighteenth-century literatus Shen Fu's autobiography *Six Chapters of a Floating Life* (*Fusheng liuji*) describes his wife Shen Yun's infatuation with a singing girl. She wanted to procure the girl as Shen Fu's concubine, but his family objected to a union with a girl of such a lowly social background. Instead the girl was forced to marry another man. As a result Shen Yun went into a deep bout of melancholy, fell ill, and died.[13]

A different sort of lesbian love affair is detailed in *Dream of the Red Chamber*. A former actress, Nénuphar, living in the luxurious garden of the Jia family, is discovered by the young master Baoyu as she secretly burns spirit money for the dead. He inquires of Parfumée, another actress, why Nénuphar was doing this.

> "So who *was* she making the offering for?"
> Parfumée's eyes reddened slightly and she sighed.
> "Oh, Nénuphar is crazy."
> "Why?" said Baoyu. "What do you mean?"
> "It was for Pivoine," said Parfumée, "the girl in our troupe who died."
> "There's nothing crazy about that," said Baoyu, "if they were friends."
> "*Friends!*" said Parfumée. "They were more than that. It was Nénuphar's soppy ideas that started it all. You see, Nénuphar is our Principal Boy and Pivoine always played opposite her as Principal Girl. They became so accustomed to acting the part of lovers on the stage, that gradually it came to seem real to them and Nénuphar began carrying on as if they were really lovers. When Pivoine died, Nénuphar cried herself into fits, and even now she still thinks about her. That's why she makes offerings to her on feast-days. When Étamine took over the roles that Pivoine used to play, Nénuphar became just the same towards her. We even teased her about it: 'Have you forgotten your old love then, now that you've got yourself a new one?' But she said, 'No, I haven't forgotten. It's like when a man loses his wife and remarries. He can still be faith-

ful to the first wife, as long as he keeps her memory green.' Did
you ever hear anything so soppy in your life?"

"Soppy" or whatever it was, there was a strain in Baoyu's own
nature which responded to it with a powerful mixture of emotions:
pleasure, sorrow, and an unbounded admiration for the little
actress.[14]

Parfumée herself is on intimate terms with other young women,
and even affects male dress. The original editor of the work notes
that female transvestism was common in that upper-class household.[15] Eventually the actresses take religious vows, a confirmation of suspicions by authors such as the Yuan-dynasty literatus
Tao Zongyi that some nuns engaged in lesbian activities.[16]

Remarkable in the tale of Nénuphar is the resemblance of her
lesbian relationship to marriage. The analogy is not merely coin-
cidental. Other sources document lesbian group marriages. Some
form of heterosexual "group marriage" goes back to at least the
Tang, when it was influenced by non-Chinese customs.[17] A Qing
novel describes an informal group of Shanghai prostitutes who
love one another intensely and are presided over by an iron-fisted
madam. They call their group the "Mirror-polishing Gang."
These women reject contact with men as repugnant, and lavish
money and attention on their female lovers.[18] Even in modern
Taiwan there have been reports of a gang of thirty or so high
school-aged female transvestites who call themselves the "H" (for
"homo") gang. Their leader was arrested and charged with dress-
ing as a man and blackmailing other young women through
threats of physical violence and threats of forcing them into
prostitution.[19] Although hardly typical of modern Chinese lesbianism, this modern version shows a similar tendency for lesbians to form tight groups for mutual support and economic
benefit.

The most carefully documented of the female marriages are the
"Golden Orchid Associations" of southern China. Scholars are
uncertain as to the full implications of the choice of this particular
title.[20] Within the group, a lesbian couple could choose to undergo
a marriage ceremony in which one partner was designated as

"husband" and the other "wife." After an exchange of ritual gifts, the foundation of the Chinese marriage ceremony, a feast attended by female companions served to witness the marriage. These married lesbian couples could even adopt female children, who in turn could inherit family property from the couple's parents.[21] This ritual was not uncommon in the Guangzhou area. One male observer described the marriage ritual and went on to predict dire consequences from the practice:

> Two women dwell together, always existing as if they were one woman. They are as close as a stalk of grain coming through a stone. . . . This infection spreads, to the extent that these [Golden Orchid] associations cannot be escaped within the province. All women who take this oath get to know one another, arranging eventually to unite. They desire and delight in binding together, passing on to a [frivolous] life of music, finally able to end their lives unmarried.[22]

The author of this passage saw these women as remaining unmarried contrary to established morality. They, however, saw themselves as happily married to another woman. Yet there may have been reasons in addition to love that would have made lesbian marriage seem attractive. One reason is religious. Certain Buddhists believe that two people are destined to remarry each other in each successive life. Even if both partners are reincarnated as women, they are still fated to marry.[23] Other factors included admiration of heterosexual chastity, fear of dying in childbirth, and a desire for economic and social independence. That indispensable compendium of Qing social relations, *Dream of the Red Chamber*, describes one woman who takes an oath not to marry, in addition to the actresses who become nuns to escape heterosexual marriage.[24] Like marriages among the men of Fujian, lesbian marriage seems to have been a localized custom found mainly in the Guangdong region. And like its male counterpart, these lesbian marriages were simply the most visible manifestation of a wider range of lesbian practices throughout China.

Notes

Introduction

1. Abbé Renaudot, trans., "An Account of the Travels of Two Mohammedans Through India and China in the Ninth Century" in *A Collection of the Best and Most Interesting Voyages and Travels in All Parts of the World*, ed. John Pinkerton, (London, 1811), 7:195.

2. Galeote Pereira, "Certain Reports of the Province of China" in *South China in the Sixteenth Century*, ed. Charles Boxer (Nendeln, Liecht., 1967), pp. 16–17.

3. Jonathan D. Spence, *The Memory Palace of Matteo Ricci* (New York, 1984), p. 220.

4. Gaspar de Cruz, "Treatise in Which the Things of China Are Related at Great Length, with their Particularities, as Likewise of the Kingdom of Ormuz" in Boxer, *South China*, p. 223.

5. This theme has been artfully explored in detail by Edward Said in *Orientalism* (New York, 1978).

6. The use of homosexuality as justification for hostility toward other cultures has deep roots in the West. The nun Hrosvitha (ca. 935– ca. 1002), for example, condemned the Arabs for homosexuality in her narrative poem *Passio S. Pelagii*; see Sister M. Gonsalva Wiegand, ed., *The Non-Dramatic Works of Hrosvitha* (St. Louis, 1936), pp. 129–158.

7. In addition to the work of Edward Said, who discusses Oriental studies in general, Paul A. Cohen has investigated the particular case of China in *Discovering History in China: American Historical Writing on the Recent Chinese Past* (New York, 1984).

8. Max Weber, *The Protestant Ethic and the Spirit of Capitalism*, trans. Talcott Parsons (New York, 1976), pp. 27–28.

9. Robert Hans Van Gulik, *Sexual Life in Ancient China: A Preliminary Survey of Chinese Sex and Society from ca. 1500 B.C. till 1644 A.D.* (Leiden, 1961), p. 49. Van Gulik employs characteristic modesty by describing sexual acts in the erudite obscurity of Latin. He abandons both Chinese and English to render the terms as *penilincto* and *introitus per anum feminae*.

10. K. J. Dover, *Greek Homosexuality* (New York, 1980), pp. 16, 100–109, 156ff.

11. John Boswell, *Christianity, Social Tolerance, and Homosexuality: Gay People in Western Europe from the Beginning of the Christian Era to the Fourteenth Century* (Chicago, 1980), p. 79.

12. Gilbert Herdt, *The Sambia: Ritual and Gender in New Guinea* (New York, 1987), pp. 161–169; Gilbert Herdt, "Fetish and Fantasy in Sambia Initiation" in *Rituals of Manhood: Male Initiation in Papua New Guinea*, ed. Gilbert Herdt (Berkeley and Los Angeles, 1982), pp. 52–56; Gilbert Herdt, *Guardians of the Flutes: Idioms of Masculinity* (New York, 1981), pp. 277–294.

13. David Greenberg, *The Construction of Homosexuality* (Chicago, 1988), p. 25.

14. On the Mamlukes, see Stephen O. Murray, "The Mamlukes" in *Cultural Diversity and Homosexualities*, ed. Stephen O. Murray (New York, 1987), pp. 213–219; on the chiefs of the Big Namba, see Tom Harrisson, *Savage Civilization* (London, 1937), p. 410.

15. Walter L. Williams, *The Spirit and the Flesh: Sexual Diversity in American Indian Culture* (Boston, 1986).

16. For the Mesopotamian case, see Delbert Hillers, "The Bow of Aqhat: The Meaning of a Mythical Theme," in *Orient and Occident*, ed. Harry A. Hoffman, Jr. (Neukirchen-Vluyn, W. Ger., 1973), pp. 71–80; on Paleo-Siberian shamans, see Charles Ducey, "The Life History and Creative Psychopathology of the Shaman," in *The Psychoanalytic Study of Society*, ed. Werner Nuensterberger, vol. 7 (New Haven, 1956), pp. 173–230.

17. Charles Wagley, *Welcome of Tears: The Tapirape Indians of Central Brazil* (New York, 1977), p. 160.

Chapter One

1. See the example of Zou Yan in Wing-tsit Chan, *A Sourcebook in Chinese Philosophy* (Princeton, 1963), p. 247.

2. Xiaomingxiong, *Zhongguo tongxingai shilu* (History of homosexuality in China) (Hong Kong, 1984), p. 19.

3. Zhao Yi, *Gai yu cong kao* (edition of 1790), 43:5B–6A. Zhao Yi declares, "Among men there are those who are called *mei ren*"; he then quotes examples from ancient texts to prove his statement.

4. *Shi jing* poem no. 94, in Hans H. Frankel, *The Flowering Plum and the Palace Lady: Interpretations of Chinese Poetry* (New Haven, 1976), pp. 52–53.

5. *Shi jing* poems nos. 31, 56, 57, 61, 68, 84, 86, 87, and 116 in Waley's translation are just a few that could easily be interpreted as either heterosexual or homosexual.

6. Arthur Waley, trans., *The Book of Songs* (New York, 1937), p. 292, no. 265.

7. Bernhard Karlgren, trans., *The Book of Odes: Chinese Text, Transcription, and Translation* (Stockholm, 1950), p. 86, no. 133. I have slightly altered Karlgren's capitalization and romanization.

8. [Du Zhengsheng] Tu Cheng-sheng, *Zhoudai chengbang* (Zhou-dynasty city states) (Taipei, 1979), pp. 55–59 and passim.

9. The dramatic shifts in social patterns accompanying the chaos of the Spring and Autumn and Warring States periods are described by Cho-yun Hsu in *Ancient China in Transition: An Analysis of Social Mobility, 722–222 B.C.* (Stanford, 1965).

10. Mizi Xia's biography appears in the *Shuo nan* of Han Fei, the *Shuo yuan* of Liu Xiang, and the collection *Duanxiu pian* (Collection of the cut sleeve), edited by an anonymous scholar who wrote under the nom de plume Wuxia Ameng, which includes information from both earlier versions. A short description of the *Duanxiu pian* appears in Van Gulik, *Sexual Life in Ancient China*, p. 63. The most accessible edition of the *Duanxiu pian* appears in volume 9 of *Xiangyan congshu* (Collected writings on fragrant elegance) (Shanghai, 1909–1911), also described by Van Gulik in the "Abbreviations" to his work mentioned above. For the source of the translation quoted here I return to the original text of Han Fei.

11. Burton Watson, trans., *Han Fei Tzu: Basic Writings* (New York, 1964), pp. 78–79. As throughout this book, I have changed Wade-Giles

romanization to pinyin; I have also corrected Watson's error as to Mizi Xia's surname.

12. *Analects* 6.22.

13. Han Fei used the word *chong* to designate the concept of "favor," a word often applied to a particularly loved female concubine. The ancient dictionary *Shuo wen* defines *chong* literally as "to honor [one with whom one] dwells [*zun ju*]"; *ju* could also have the meaning of someone endowed with special talent (Xu Shen and Duan Yucai, *Shuowen jiezi zhu* [Shanghai, 1981], p. 340).

14. Quoted in Weixingshi guanzhaizhu, *Zhongguo tongxinglian mishi* (The secret history of Chinese homosexuality), vol. 1 (Hong Kong, 1964), p. 13.

15. "Song of the Boatswain of Yüeh," trans. Irving Y. Lo, in *Sunflower Splendor: Three Thousand Years of Chinese Poetry*, ed. Wu-chi Liu and Irving Yucheng Lo (Garden City, N.Y., 1975), p. 26. This poem is preserved in the Western Han dynasty *Shuo yuan* anthology of Liu Xiang.

16. Wuxia Ameng, ed., *Duanxiu pian* 9:1B–2A.

17. Ibid., 9:2A; taken from Lin Zaiqing's *Chengzhai zaji*. This attribution is given in Weixingshi guanzhaizhu, *Zhongguo tongxinglian mishi* 1:30.

18. Dover, *Greek Homosexuality*, p. 16.

19. Doi Yoshiko, *Kodai Chūgoku no gazōseki* (Ancient Chinese stone reliefs) (Kyoto, 1986), pls. 55–58, 60–71, 76; Edouard Chavannes, *La sculpture sur pierre en Chine au temps des deux dynasties Han* (Paris, 1893), pl. 10.

20. T'ung-tsu Ch'ü, *Han Social Structure*, ed. Jack L. Dull (Seattle, 1972), pp. 110, 141, 158, 182, 334; also C. Martin Wilbur, *Slavery in China During the Former Han Dynasty, 206 B.C.–A.D. 25* (Chicago, 1943), pp. 67–68, 85–88.

21. Wuxia Ameng, ed., *Duanxiu pian* 9:1A–B.

22. Ibid., 9:1A.

23. J. I. Crump, trans., *Chan-kuo Ts'e* (Oxford, 1970), pp. 227–228.

24. Ibid., p. 229.

25. This story appears in both *Zuo zhuan* and *Guo yu*; see James Legge, trans., *The Chinese Classics*, vol. 5 (Oxford and Hong Kong, 1868–1893), p. 187; the tale is summarized in Van Gulik, *Sexual Life in Ancient China*, p. 93.

26. Clae Waltham, *Shu Ching, Book of History: A Modernized Edition of the Translations of James Legge* (Chicago, 1971), pp. 74–76.

27. For James Legge's translation and notes, see *The Chinese Classics*, vol. 3: *The Shoo King* (repr. Hong Kong, 1960), pp. 196–197; also Waltham, *Shu Ching.*

28. Identical lists appear in the *Ban fa*, a political text probably dating from the late fourth to early third century B.C., and the *Zhong ling*, a Huanglao text of the third century B.C.; see W. Allyn Rickett, trans., *Guanzi: Political, Economic, and Philosophical Essays from Early China*, vol. 1 (Princeton, 1985), pp. 143, 247.

29. This translation closely follows Burton Watson's in *Mo Tzu: Basic Writings* (New York, 1963). I have made several minor changes to bring Watson's translation of terms of affection in accord with my own.

30. For this practice in Islamic Albania, see Louis Crompton, *Byron and Greek Love: Homophobia in 19th-Century England* (Berkeley and Los Angeles, 1985), p. 135; for Japan, see Donald H. Shively, "Tokugawa Tsunayoshi, the Genroku Shogun," in *Personality in Japanese History*, ed. A. M. Craig and D. H. Shively (Berkeley and Los Angeles, 1970), pp. 97–99.

31. My translation follows Crump, *Chan-kuo Ts'e*, p. 62.

32. Wuxia Ameng, ed., *Duanxiu pian* 9:1B.

33. Ibid., 9:2A.

34. Crump, *Chan-kuo Ts'e*, p. 356.

35. In the gay slang of modern Taiwan, "cruising" is still referred to as "catching fish" (*diao yu*) or, more straightforwardly, "catching people" (*diao ren*). Although this metaphor arose independently of the tale of Lord Long Yang, it still shows some continuity in general perceptions of homosexuality.

Chapter Two

1. Boswell, *Christianity, Social Tolerance, and Homosexuality*, p. 61.

2. See table 1 in Fang-fu Ruan and Yung-mei Tsai, "Male Homosexuality in the Traditional Chinese Literature," *Journal of Homosexuality* 14, nos. 3–4 (1987):23.

3. Sima Qian, *Shi ji*, chap. 125; Ban Gu, *Han shu*, chap. 93.

4. [Sima Qian] Ssu-ma Ch'ien, *Records of the Grand Historian of China*, trans. Burton Watson (New York, 1961), 2:462.

5. Ibid.

6. From Du You's *Tongdian*, as quoted in Wuxia Ameng, ed., *Duanxiu pian* 9:3A.

7. [Sima Qian] Ssu-ma Ch'ien, *Records of the Grand Historian* 2:462–464.

8. I take this term from "The Types of Upward Mobility" in Yungteh Chow, *Social Mobility in China: Status Careers Among the Gentry in a Chinese Community* (New York, 1966), p. 210.

9. Cho-yun Hsu, *Han Agriculture: The Formation of Early Chinese Agrarian Economy (206 B.C.–A.D. 220)*, ed. Jack L. Dull (Seattle, 1980), pp. 78–79.

10. See Song Xuwu, *Xi Han huobi shi chugao* (A preliminary draft of the history of Western Han currency) (Hong Kong, 1971).

11. Donald John Harper, "The 'Wu shih erh ping fang': Translation and Prolegomena" (Ph.D. diss., University of California, Berkeley, 1982), p. 62.

12. Ban Gu, *Han shu* (Beijing, 1974), 46:2203.

13. [Sima Qian] Ssu-ma Ch'ien, *Records of the Grand Historian* 2:466.

14. Wuxia Ameng, ed., *Duanxiu pian* 9:5B–6A. To avoid repetition, this passage is an edited translation of the original. I have deleted ellipses for the sake of readability.

15. Hsu, *Han Agriculture*, pp. 22, 49.

16. Ch'ü, *Han Social Structure*, pp. 168–174.

17. Michael Loewe, "The Former Han Dynasty," in *The Cambridge History of China*, ed. Denis Twitchett and Michael Loewe (Cambridge, 1986), 1:220.

18. Ibid., pp. 227–229.

19. Wuxia Ameng, ed., *Duanxiu pian* 9:8A.

20. [Sima Qian] Ssu-ma Ch'ien, *Records of the Grand Historian* 2:462.

21. Bo Xingjian, "Tiandi yinyang jiaohuan dale fu" (Poetical essay on the sexual union and supreme joy of heaven and earth and yin and yang), in *Shuangmei ying'an congshu* (Collection of the paired plums' shade), ed. Ye Dehui (repr. Hong Kong, n.d.), p. 8A.

22. [Sima Qian] Ssu-ma Ch'ien, *Records of the the Grand Historian* 2:465–466.

23. Wuxia Ameng, ed., *Duanxiu pian* 9:8B–9A.

24. Ibid., 9:4B–5A.

25. See Alfred C. Kinsey et al., *Sexual Behavior in the Human Male* (Philadelphia, 1948); also Paul Gebhard, "Incidence of Overt Homosexuality in the United States and Western Europe," in *National Institute of*

Mental Health Task Force on Homosexuality: Final Report and Background Papers (Washington, 1972), pp. 22–30.

26. Van Gulik, *Sexual Life in Ancient China*, p. 62.

27. Terms such as *chong* and *bi* originally referred to female concubinage.

28. Ch'ü, *Han Social Structure*, p. 22.

29. This custom dates from long before the Han; see He Xiu et al., eds., *Chunqiu Gongyang zhuan zhu shu* (Annotated Gongyang commentary to the Spring and Autumn Annals) (Shanghai, *Sibu beiyao*, n.d.), 8:10A.

30. For the surrounding context of this quotation, see [Ban Gu] Pan Ku, *The History of the Former Han Dynasty*, trans. Homer H. Dubs and P'an Lo-chi, vol. 3 (Baltimore, 1955), pp. 38–39.

31. Wuxia Ameng, ed., *Duanxiu pian* 9:5B.

32. Ibid., 9:8A.

Chapter Three

1. Wang Shunu, *Zhongguo changji shi* (History of Chinese prostitution) (Shanghai, 1935), p. 64.

2. Anne Birrell, trans., *New Songs from a Jade Terrace: An Anthology of Early Chinese Love Poetry* (London, 1982), p. 290.

3. Xiaomingxiong, *Zhongguo tongxing ai shilu*, p. 77.

4. Van Gulik, *Sexual Life in Ancient China*, pp. 159–160. In particular he singles out the Xianning (275–279) and Taikang (280–289) reign periods as being noted for the popularity of homosexuality.

5. For an example, see Li Yanshou, ed., *Bei shi* (History of the North) (Beijing, 1974), 92:3017.

6. Chen Yue, ed., *Song shu* (Records of the Liu Song) (Beijing, 1974), 94:2302.

7. Li Yanshou, *Bei shi* 92:3018.

8. Xiao Zixian, ed., *Nan Qi shu* (Records of the Southern Qi) (Beijing, 1974), 56:971.

9. Chen Yue, *Song shu* 94:2301.

10. Li Yanshou, ed., *Nan shi* (History of the South) (Beijing, 1973), 77:1913.

11. Chen Yue, *Song shu* 94:2301–2302.

12. Li Yanshou, *Bei shi* 92:3017–3018.

13. Ibid., 92:3017.

14. Xiao Zixian, *Nan Qi shu* 56:971–2.

15. Li Yanshou, *Nan shi* 77:1914.

16. Li Baiyao, ed., *Bei Qi shu* (Records of the Northern Qi) (Beijing, 1974), 50:685.

17. Xiao Zixian, *Nan Qi shu* 56:972.

18. Li Yanshou, *Nan shi* 77:1943.

19. Ibid.

20. Shen Yue, *Song shu* 94:2318.

21. Wei Shou, ed., *Wei shu* (Records of the Wei) (Beijing, 1974), 93:1996–1997.

22. Ibid., 93:1988–1996.

23. Li Yanshou, *Nan shi* 77:1935–1936.

24. Ibid., 77:1914–1916.

25. Li Baiyao, *Bei Qi shu* 50:690–692, 694.

26. David George Johnson, "The Medieval Chinese Oligarchy: A Study of the Great Families in Their Social, Political, and Institutional Setting" (Ph. D. diss., University of California, Berkeley, 1970), p. 92.

27. Li Yanshou, *Nan shi* 77:1927.

28. Ibid., 77:1917–1919.

29. Xiao Zixian, *Nan Qi shu* 56:972–975.

30. Wei Shou, *Wei shu* 93:2007–2009.

31. Li Baiyao, *Bei Qi shu* 50:689–690.

32. Wei Shou, *Wei shu* 93:2002; Li Baiyao, *Bei Qi shu* 50:686–689.

33. Wei Shou, *Wei shu* 93:2001–2002.

34. Ibid., 93:1989.

35. Li Baiyao, *Bei Qi shu* 50:687.

36. Ibid., 50:688.

37. Wei Shou, *Wei shu* 93:1990–1996.

38. Li Baiyao, *Bei Qi shu* 50:686.

39. Wei Shou, *Wei shu* 93:1998–2000.

40. For examples, see Li Baiyao, *Bei Qi shu* 50:694; and Li Yanshou, *Bei shi* 92:3029–3030.

41. *Bawang gushi*, written by Lu Lin in the fourth century.

42. [Liu Yiqing] Liu I-ch'ing, *Shih-shuo hsin-yü: A New Account of Tales of the World*, trans. Richard B. Mather (Minneapolis, 1976), p. 310.

43. Ibid., p. 316.

44. According to the *Xu Jin yangqiu* of the fifth-century literatus Tan Daoluan, "The emperor [Sima Yu] was handsome in manner and demeanor, and his movements were dignified and circumspect" (ibid.).

45. Ibid.

46. Hou Lichao, *Zhongguo meinanzi zhuan* (Biographies of beautiful Chinese men) (Taipei, 1986), p. 91.

47. Ying-shih Yü, *Trade and Expansion in Han China: A Study in the Structure of Sino-Barbarian Economic Relations* (Berkeley and Los Angeles, 1967), p. 213. The Han dictionary *Shiming* confirms that "barbarian powder" was used to powder the face.

48. From the third-century *Wei lue* of Hu Huan, in [Liu Yiqing] Liu I-ch'ing, *Shih-shuo hsin-yü*, p. 309.

49. The commentary of Liu Jun (462–521), in ibid.

50. [Liu Yiqing] Liu I-ch'ing, *Shih-shuo hsin-yü*, p. 308.

51. Ibid., p. 314. A less euphemistic translation would substitute "lard" for "congealed ointment."

52. Ibid.

53. Ibid., p. 310.

54. Ibid., p. 311.

55. Ibid., p. 312.

56. Ibid., p. 314. This quotation is preserved in Pei Qi's *Yu lin.*

57. Ibid., p. 315.

58. Ibid., p. 316.

59. Ibid., p. 317.

60. Ibid., p. 315.

61. *Chūgoku no hakubutsukan* (Chinese museums) (Tokyo and Beijing, 1982), vol. 4, pl. 90.

62. [Liu Yiqing] Liu I-ch'ing, *Shih-shuo hsin-yü*, p. 309.

63. Ibid.

64. Ibid., pp. 346–347.

65. Wuxia Ameng, ed., *Duanxiu pian* 9:9B–10A (with deletions).

66. Ibid., 9:2B; originally from Ruan Ji's *Yong huai shi bashier shou.*

67. "Zhou Xiaoshi," from Wuxia Ameng, ed., *Duanxiu pian* 9:9A.

68. "Fanhua shi," from ibid., 9:9B. In my translation I have borrowed heavily from Birrell, *New Songs from a Jade Terrace*, p. 213.

69. This poem has been previously translated. It appears as "His Favoured Boy" in Birrell, *New Songs from a Jade Terrace*, pp. 200–201; and as "The Young Catamite" in John Marney, *Beyond the Mulberries: An Anthology of Palace-Style Poetry by Emperor Chien-wen of the Liang Dynasty (505–551)* (Taipei, 1982), pp. 114–116.

70. Birrell, *New Songs from a Jade Terrace*, p. 292.

71. Ibid., p. 165.

Chapter Four

1. Liu Xu, *Jiu Tang shu* (Old Tang history) (Beijing, 1974), 76:2648.
2. Wuxia Ameng, ed., *Duanxiu pian* 9:12A–B.
3. Howard S. Levy, trans., *Translations from Po Chü-i's Collected Works*, vol. 1 (repr. New York, 1971), p. 104.
4. Ibid., p. 42.
5. Ibid., 2:55.
6. Ibid., 1:90.
7. Ibid., pp. 93–94.
8. Ibid., pp. 97–98.
9. For a textual history of this work, see Van Gulik, *Sexual Life in Ancient China*, pp. 202–203.
10. Reading *lian* for *wan*.
11. Reading *long* for *ling*.
12. Bo Xingjian, "Tiandi yinyang jiaohuan dale fu," pp. 7B–8A.
13. Xiaomingxiong, *Zhonggua tongxingai shilu*, pp. 74–75.
14. Weixingshi guanzhaizhu, *Zhongguo tongxinglian mishi* 1:91.
15. Ibid., pp. 90–91.
16. Dover, *Greek Homosexuality*, pp. 125–127.
17. Yuan Mei, *Sui yuan sui bi* (Suiyuan miscellany) (Shanghai, 1935), 17:7B.
18. This is quoted by Zhao Yi in *Gai yu cong kao* 38.
19. Jeremiah 5:8; Deuteronomy 23:18. For medieval European views, see Boswell, *Christianity, Social Tolerance, and Homosexuality*, passim but esp. pp. 152–156.
20. Tuo Tuo, *Song shi* (History of the Song) (Beijing, 1974), 470:13677.
21. Ibid., 470:13689.
22. Song Lian, ed., *Yuan shi* (History of the Yuan) (Beijing, 1974), 205:4557.
23. Tao Gu, *Qing yi lu* (n.p., Chen shi kangxian zhai kanben, 1875), p. 10B.
24. From *Jinyu lu*, written by Xu Dazhuo circa 1280; in Weixingshi guanzhaizhu, *Zhongguo tongxinglian mishi* 1:95.
25. Meng Yuanlao, *Dongjing menghua lu* (pub. 1147), quoted by Michael Freeman, "Sung," in *Food in Chinese Culture: Anthropological and Historical Perspectives*, ed. K.C. Chang (New Haven, 1977), p. 160.

26. Previous translations of this work are [Song Ci] Sung Tz'u, *The Washing Away of Wrongs: Forensic Medicine in Thirteenth Century China*, trans. Brian E. McKnight (Ann Arbor, 1981); and Herbert Giles, "The 'Hsi yüan lu' or 'Instructions to Coroners,'" *Proceedings of the Royal Society of Medicine* 27 (1924): 59–107. Unfortunately, neither translates the appendix on sodomy. All of my translations of this section are taken from the *Buzhu xiyuan lu jizheng* (The washing away of wrongs, with commentary) (*Beizhi* ed.), pp. 35A–B. These particular cases date from the Qing, though they seem to be continuations of much earlier practices.

27. Zhu Yu, *Pingzhou ketan* (comp. ca. 1119), in Weixingshi guanzhaizhu, *Zhongguo tongxinglian mishi* 1:95.

28. Zhou Mi, *Guixin zazhi* (pub. ca. 1298), in Wang Shunu, *Zhongguo changji shi*, p. 226.

29. Han Yu, *Yuanxing* (An inquiry on human nature), in Chan, *Sourcebook in Chinese Philosophy*, p. 452.

30. Cheng Yi, as quoted in [Zhu Xi] Chu Hsi and [Lu Zuqian] Lu Tsu-ch'ien, *Reflections on Things at Hand: The Neo-Confucian Anthology*, ed. Wing-tsit Chan (New York, 1967), pp. 272–273.

31. For a complete history of this textual tradition, see T. Sakai, *Studies of Chinese Shan-shu: Popular Books on Morality* (Tokyo, 1960).

32. Wolfram Eberhard, *Guilt and Sin in Traditional China* (Berkeley and Los Angeles, 1967), p. 63.

33. Ibid.

34. Ibid., p. 115.

35. Even practitioners of more theologically refined Buddhist practices condemned homosexuality and the mixing of gender roles. The Ming Chan master Rujing (1163–1228) cautioned those who seek enlightenment against being intimate with "eunuchs, hermaphrodites and the like"; see Takashi James Kodera, *Dogen's Formative Years in China: An Historical Study and Annotation of the Hōkyō-ki* (Boulder, Colo., 1980), pp. 120, 174. And the Ming literatus Shen Defu mentioned Buddhism in his moral judgments of homosexuality; see Shen Defu, *Bizhou xian shengyu* (Casual writings from the Worn Brush Studio) (Taipei, 1969), pp. 123–125.

Chapter Five

1. I am indebted to Howard Levy for his careful compilation and lively translation in *Chinese Sex Jokes in Traditional Times* (repr. Taipei,

1974). He has recognized the ahistoricity of this genre of humor, culling jokes from a variety of joke books to represent the range of humorous formulas. His work forms the raw material for this section of my analysis.

2. Levy, *Sex Jokes*, no. 308, p. 226.

3. For example, see ibid., no. 206, p. 178.

4. Ibid., no. 208, p. 179.

5. Ibid., no. 369, p. 257. I have changed "homosexuality" to "boys" to avoid Levy's anachronism.

6. This word is found in the bamboo slip version of *Wushier bing fang* (Fifty-two ailments), which was redacted in the third century B.C. For mentions of hemorrhoids in this early work, see Harper, "The 'Wu shih erh ping fang,'" pp. 409–431.

7. Levy, *Sex Jokes*, no. 326, p. 233.

8. Clement Egerton, trans., *The Golden Lotus*, vol. 2 (London, 1939), p. 124.

9. Levy, *Sex Jokes*, no. 386, p. 264.

10. [Wang Chong] Wang Ch'ung, "*Lun heng*: Selected Essays of the Philosopher Wang Ch'ung," trans. Alfred Forke, *Mitteilungen des Seminars für orientalische Sprachen* 10 (1907): 100.

11. Levy, *Sex Jokes*, no. 364, p. 256. I remove "who liked homosexuality" from Levy's translation; the use of this Western terminology seems anachronistic.

12. Ibid., no. 371, p. 258.

13. Ibid., no. 381, pp. 261–262.

14. Ibid., no. 207, pp. 178–179.

15. Ibid., no. 367, p. 257. I have changed "catamite" to "favorite."

16. Egerton, *Golden Lotus* 4:25.

17. Levy, *Sex Jokes*, no. 382, p. 262.

18. Ibid., no. 373, p. 259.

19. Ibid., no. 374, p. 259.

20. Petty official: *xiao guanren*. For example, see ibid., no. 377, pp. 260–261.

21. Keith McMahon, *Causality and Containment in Seventeenth-Century Chinese Fiction* (Leiden, 1988), pp. 74–75.

22. Levy, *Sex Jokes*, no. 383, pp. 262–263.

23. Ibid., no. 385, p. 263.

24. Ibid., no. 384, p. 263.

25. Dover, *Greek Homosexuality*, pp. 98–100.

26. Levy, *Sex Jokes*, no. 310, p. 227.

27. Ibid., no. 360, p. 254.

28. Ibid., no. 325, p. 233.

29. Ibid., no. 327, p. 234.

30. Chen Sen (Shi Han Shi), *Pinhua baojian* (Precious mirror of ranking flowers) (Taipei, 1984), chap. 23.

31. Since this book was officially banned during the reigns of the Daoguang (1821–1850) and Tongzhi (1862–1874) emperors, it is now almost impossible to obtain. I use a translation from the Beijing University library manuscript made by Ruan and Tsai, "Male Homosexuality in the Traditional Chinese Literature," pp. 31–32, correcting their translation for grammar.

32. Levy, *Sex Jokes*, no. 268, p. 257.

33. Ibid., no. 324, p. 233.

34. Ibid., no. 361, p. 254. I change "homosexual" to "man" so as to avoid Levy's anachronism.

35. Ibid., no. 372, p. 258; again, changing "homosexual" to "man."

36. Abraham N. Franzblau, *Erotic Art of China: A Unique Collection of Chinese Prints and Poems Devoted to the Art of Love* (New York, 1977), print 36.

37. Levy, *Sex Jokes*, no. 370, p. 258; changing "homosexual" to "man."

38. Ibid., no. 380, p. 261; changing "homosexual" to "favorite."

Chapter Six

1. V. A. Riasanovsky, *Customary Law of the Mongol Tribes (Mongols, Buriats, Kalmucks)* (Harbin, 1929), p. 57.

2. Greenberg, *Construction of Homosexuality*, p. 181. I owe a debt to David Greenberg for putting together this information on Mongol homosexuality.

3. Richard Burton, *The Book of the Thousand Nights and a Night*, vol. 10 (New York, 1886), pp. 63–302, touches on many of these issues of Central Asian homosexuality; see also John J. I. Dollinger, *The Gentile and the Jew in the Courts of the Temple of Christ: An Introduction to the History of Christianity*, trans. N. Darnell (London, 1862), p. 238.

4. Paul Heng-chao Ch'en, *Chinese Legal Tradition Under the Mongols: The Code of 1291 as Reconstructed* (Princeton, 1979).

5. Xiaomingxiong, *Zhongguo tongxingai shilu*, pp. 129–137.

6. Xie Zhaozhe, *Wuza zu* (Five miscellaneous dishes) (Shanghai, 1959), 8:209.

7. Northern and southern homosexual life are both mentioned in Shen Defu, *Bizhou xian shengyu*, p. 125. A similar observation was made during the reign of Wanli, as quoted in Albert Chan, "Peking at the Time of the Wanli Emperor (1572–1619)," in *International Association of Historians of Asia Second Biennial Conference Proceedings* (Taipei, 1962), p. 128.

8. Wang Shunu, *Zhongguo changji shi*, p. 323.

9. Tang Xianzu, *The Peony Pavilion* (*Mudan ting*), trans. Cyril Birch (Bloomington, Ind., 1980), pp. 120–135.

10. Ibid., p. 127.

11. For an overview of Li Yu's work, see Patrick Hanan, *The Invention of Li Yu* (Cambridge, Mass., 1988).

12. Unfortunately, Nathan Mao's retelling of this story purposely misrepresents the sexuality of those involved, making his version worthless for scholarly purposes and tarnishing the story's literary merit as well ("The Elegant Eunuch," in Li Yu, *Li Yu's Twelve Towers, Retold by Nathan Mao*, trans. Nathan Kwok-kuen Mao [Hong Kong, 1975] pp. 52–62).

13. Li Yu, *Shier lou* (The twelve structures), vol. 2 (Taipei, 1980), pp. 174, 175.

14. Ibid., pp. 177, 179.

15. Ibid., pp. 193, 204.

16. Ibid., p. 174.

17. McMahon, *Causality and Containment*, pp. 76–77.

18. Li Yu, *Wusheng xi xiaoshuo* (Silent operas), in *Li Yu quanji*, ed. Helmut Martin (Taipei, 1970), pp. 5381–5453.

19. Ibid., pp. 5382–5383.

20. Van Gulik, *Sexual Life in Ancient China*, pp. 76, 157.

21. Li Yu, *Li Yu quanji*, 5383–5384.

22. Ibid., 5384.

23. McMahon, *Causality and Containment*, pp. 77–78.

24. Li Yu, *Li Yu quanji*, p. 5385.

25. Passion for men: *nanse*; ibid., p. 5392. For *fufu*, p. 5387.

26. [Wu Jingzi] Wu Ching-tzu, *The Scholars*, trans. Yang Hsien-yi and Gladys Yang (Beijing, 1957), p. 377.

27. Li Yu, *Li Yu quanji*, p. 5406.

28. Li Yu, *Jiean laoren manbi* (Beijing, 1982), pp. 181–182.

29. Li Yu, *Li Yu quanji*, p. 5441.

30. Ibid., p. 5442.

31. Sue Gronewold, *Beautiful Merchandise: Prostitution in China 1860–1936* (New York, 1982), pp. 8–9.

32. [Kong Shangren] K'ung Shang-jen, *The Peach Blossom Fan* (*T'ao-hua-shan*), trans. Chen Shih-hsiang, Harold Acton, and Cyril Birch (Berkeley and Los Angeles, 1976), pp. 23, 49.

33. [Zhang Wencheng] Chang Wen-ch'eng, *China's First Novelette: The Dwelling of the Playful Goddess*, trans. Howard S. Levy (Tokyo, 1965), pp. 23–24.

34. The matchmaker has long been considered an integral part of Chinese marriage ceremonies. This sentiment appears not only in the *Shi jing* but also in the fourth-century B.C. lyric *Li sao*.

35. [Song Lian] Sung Lien, "The Yüan Code: Illicit Sexual Relations," in *The Essence of Chinese Civilization*, ed. Dun J. Li (New York, 1967), p. 408.

36. [Zhang Wencheng] Chang Wen-ch'eng, *China's First Novelette*, p. 27. This line is taken from the *Shi jing*.

37. Frederic Wakeman, Jr., *The Great Enterprise: The Manchu Reconstruction of Imperial Order in Seventeenth-Century China*, vol. 1 (Berkeley and Los Angeles, 1985), p. 95.

38. Wuxia Ameng, ed., *Duanxiu pian* 9:15B.

39. Paul Gordon Schalow, "'The Great Mirror of Male Love' by Ihara Saikaku" (Ph.D. diss., Harvard University, 1985), 2:90.

40. For southern Africa, see Judith Gay, "'Mummies and Babies' and Friends and Lovers in Lesotho," *Journal of Homosexuality* 11, nos. 3–4 (1985): 97–116; also John Blacking, "Uses of the Kinship Idiom in Friendships at some Venda and Zulu Schools," in *Social System and Tradition in Southern Africa*, ed. J. Argyle and E. Preston-Whyte (Oxford, 1978). For American prisons, see R. Giallombardo, *Society of Women: A Study of a Women's Prison* (London, 1966).

41. Li Yu, *Jou pu tuan* (*The Prayer Mat of Flesh*), trans. Franz Kuhn and Richard Martin (New York, 1963), p. 52.

42. McMahon, *Causality and Containment*, p. 77.

43. From *Zi buyu*, in Weixingshi guanzhaizhu, *Zhongguo tongxinglian mishi* 1:15.

44. Xiaomingxiong, *Zhongguo tongxingai shilu*, p. 179.

45. Boswell, *Christianity, Social Tolerance, and Homosexuality*, pp. 137–138, 253, 306, 356–357.

46. And yet even today the same factors that led men of the Ming to participate in a homosexual marriage ceremony still exist in China. A terse news report in the *Boston Globe* (March 4, 1989, p.6) stated that two men in rural China married on January 10, 1989. Ye Xing, 26, a veteran of the People's Liberation Army, married the farmer Li Linxing, 30, in a traditional ceremony. The former soldier suffered dismissal from his job because of his open homosexuality, and local officials were trying to break up the marriage.

47. McMahon, *Causality and Containment*, pp. 75–76.

48. Egerton, *The Golden Lotus* 2:348–349.

49. Ibid., p. 97.

50. Li Yu, *Jou pu tuan*, pp. 107–108. I have changed "rear audience chamber" to "rear chamber."

51. A summary of the incident appears in Albert Chan, "Chinese-Philippine Relations in the Late Sixteenth Century and to 1603," *Philippine Studies* 26 (1978): 70. For homosexuality among other groups of overseas Chinese, see Persia Crawford Campbell, *Chinese Coolie Emigration to Countries Within the British Empire* (New York, 1923), pp. 110, 211; also J. D. Vaughan, *The Manners and Customs of the Chinese of the Straits Settlements* (Singapore, 1879), pp. 9–10; and Ta Chen, *Chinese Migrations, with Special Reference to Labor Conditions* (Washington, D.C., 1923). Chinese converts to Christianity in China itself were forbidden homosexuality; see P. P. Thoms, trans., "Prohibitions Addressed to Chinese Converts of the Romish Faith" *China Repository* 20 (February 1851): 92–93.

52. Schalow, "'Great Mirror,'" 1:19. For this traditional etiology of Japanese homosexuality, see Aoki Masaru, *Zhongguo jinshi xiqu shi* (History of the modern Chinese opera) (Hong Kong, 1975), p. 447.

53. Schalow, "'Great Mirror,'" 1:280.

Chapter Seven

1. Vivien W. Ng, "Ideology and Sexuality: Rape Laws in Qing China," *Journal of Asian Studies* 46, no. 1 (1987): 57–70. Ng made further remarks on this point at the "Pedagogy and Politics" conference hosted by the Gay Studies Center at Yale and Yale's Whitney Humanities Center, October 1988.

2. William Theodore de Bary, "Individualism and Humanitarianism in Late Ming Thought," in *Self and Society in Ming Thought*, ed. William Theodore de Bary (New York, 1970), pp. 145–248.

3. For a discussion of laws regulating various aspects of homosexuality, see Wang Shunu, *Zhongguo changji shi*, p. 322.

4. Sir John Barrow, *Travels in China* (London, 1806), pp. 100–102.

5. From "Journal of Occurrences," *China Repository* 5 (June 1835): 104.

6. T. H. Bullock, "The Chinese Vindicated," *China Repository* 9 (September 1840): 321.

7. For instances of Europeans being prosecuted in Hong Kong for homosexuality by colonial authorities, see H. J. Lethbridge, "The Quare Fellow: Homosexuality and the Law in Hong Kong," *Hong Kong Law Journal* 4, no.3 (1976): 306–310. Also see J. J. Matignon, *Crime et misère en Chine* (Paris, 1901), pp. 187–209, for an account of European homosexual life in late-imperial Beijing.

8. Katrina C. D. McLeod and Robin D. S. Yates, "Forms of Ch'in Law: An Annotated Translation of the Feng-chen shih," *Harvard Journal of Asiatic Studies* 41, no. 1 (1981): 162–182; also A. F. P. Hulsewé, *Remnants of Ch'in Law* (Leiden, 1985), p. 169.

9. Ng, "Ideology and Sexuality," p. 67.

10. Kwan-wai So, "Chu Hou-chao," in *Dictionary of Ming Biography 1368–1644*, ed. L. Carrington Goodrich, vol. 1 (New York, 1976), pp. 307–315.

11. Jonathan D. Spence, *Emperor of China: Self-Portrait of K'anghsi* (New York, 1975), pp. xxi, 125.

12. Ibid., pp. 126–127.

13. The code here makes a reference to statute no. 273-07.

14. As throughout this book, "years" is used as the translation of *sui*.

15. See statute number 366-00.

16. This section is a translation of statute no. 366-03 in Xue Yunsheng and Huang Jingjia, *Duyi cunyi zhong kanben* (A typeset edition of the *Tu-i ts'un-i* [*Duyi cunyi*]), pt. 5, vols. 41–54 (Taipei, 1970), p. 1082. This section has been previously translated in George Thomas Staunton, *Ta Tsing Leu Lee: Being the Fundamental Laws and a Selection from the Supplementary Statutes of the Penal Code of China* (London, 1810), pp. 569–570; and in *China Repository* 2 (May 1833): 107.

17. M. J. Meijer, "Homosexual Offenses in Ch'ing Law," *T'oung pao* 71 (1985): 109–133.

18. Derk Bodde and Clarence Morris, *Law in Imperial China* (Cambridge, Mass., 1967), p. 428.

19. Ibid., p. 383.

20. Ernest Alabaster, *Notes and Commentaries on Chinese Criminal Law* (London, 1899), p. 368.

21. Wuxia Ameng, ed., *Duanxiu pian* 9:16B–17A.

22. Colin P. Mackerras, *The Rise of the Peking Opera, 1770–1870: Social Aspects of the Theatre in Manchu China* (Oxford, 1972), p. 45.

23. Lawrence E. Gichner, *Erotic Aspects of Chinese Culture* (Washington, D.C., 1957), p. 76.

24. Wu-shan Sheng, *Die Erotik in China: Die Welt des Eros* (Basel, 1967), p. 53.

25. Ibid., p. 102.

26. Ibid., p. 111.

27. Barrow, *Travels in China*, p. 101.

28. Zhao Yi, *Gai yu cong kao* 43:18A.

29. [Li Ruzhen] Li Ju-chen, *Flowers in the Mirror*, trans. Lin Tai-yi (Berkeley and Los Angeles, 1965), pp. 150–154.

30. Cao Xueqin and Gao E, *The Story of the Stone*, trans. David Hawkes and John Minford (Harmondsworth, Eng., and Bloomington, Ind., 1973–1987), 3:279.

31. Ibid., 2:437–445.

32. Hawkes's translation of this incident is misleading. As Xue Pan is being beaten he cries out placatingly, "Wo zhidao ni shi zhengjing ren." Hawkes translates this as "I know you're straight." In fact *zhengjing* has nothing to do with sexual roles. A more accurate translation would be "I know you're respectable." Hawkes's translation leads the Western reader to believe that Liu is offended by Xue Pan's assumption that he is "gay." In fact Liu is affronted by the insinuation that he is a passive actor-prostitute, thereby calling into question his "respectability" (*zhengjing*) or social standing.

33. Cao Xueqin and Gao E, *Story of the Stone* 2:52–53, 61–62. For a detailed analysis of homosexuality in this novel, see [Bai Xianyong] Pai Hsien-yung, "Jia Baoyu de suyuan: Jiang Yuhan yu huaxi ren—jianlun Honglou Meng de jieju yiyi" (The common fate of Jia Baoyu: Jiang Yuhan and the Person with Flower-lined Garments—a discussion of the resulting meaning of *Dream of the Red Chamber*), *Lianhe wenxue* 15 (January 1986): 25–30.

34. Cao Xueqin and Gao E, *Story of the Stone* 2:146–154, 171.

35. "Long Yang zhi xing." David Hawkes mistranslates this phrase as "Lord Long-yang's vice." In fact, *xing* conveys no sense of moral disapproval; on the contrary, it has many favorable connotations. Possible translations include joy, merriment, passion, desire, and appetite.

36. Cao Xueqin and Gao E, *Story of the Stone* 1:206–216.

37. Jonathan Spence has noted the association of food and homosexuality in Qing fiction, with reference to the friendship of Qin Zhong and Baoyu. The Chinese saw food and sexuality as complementary forms of sensuality, as revealed by literary imagery. See Jonathan Spence, "Ch'ing," in Chang, *Food in Chinese Culture*, p. 279. The same sort of imagery appears in the homosexual episodes of *Jin Ping Mei*. For one example, see the line "the boy passed him a sweetmeat and stroked his erect penis," in Egerton, *The Golden Lotus* 2:105. The late-Qing novel *Pinhua baojian* is replete with connections between food and homosexuality.

38. Cao Xueqin and Gao E, *Story of the Stone* 1:299.

39. Ibid., p. 300.

40. Ibid., pp. 321–323.

41. Ibid., 3:493.

42. Zhao Yi, *Gai yu cong kao* 43:18A.

43. Cao Xueqin and Gao E, *Story of the Stone* 3:494.

44. Ibid., p. 496.

45. Yuan Mei, in Weixingshi guanzhaizhu, *Zhongguo tongxinglian mishi* 1:27.

46. David S. Nivison, *The Life and Thought of Chang Hsüeh-ch'eng (1738–1801)* (Stanford, 1966), pp. 263–265.

47. Wang Shunu, *Zhongguo changji shi*, p. 322.

48. Gichner, *Erotic Aspects of Chinese Culture*, p. 76.

49. *Xingan huilan* (Taipei, 1968); see Ng, "Ideology and Sexuality," p. 68.

50. [Caihengzi] Ts'ai-heng-tzu, "Boy Actors in Peking," in Dun J. Li, *Essence of Chinese Civilization*, p. 425.

51. Ibid. A similar description of training can be found in J. J. Matignon, "Deux mots sur la pédérastie en Chine," *Archives d'anthropologie criminelle* 14 (1899): 38.

52. Wang Shunu, *Zhongguo changji shi*, pp. 326–327.

53. Other actors who were unwilling to undergo this painful ordeal

for the sake of their art wore special shoes that imitated bound feet; Mackerras, *Rise of the Peking Opera*, p. 97. Men sometimes had their feet bound for other reasons. At times it was even considered fashionable for ordinary men to bind their feet. See Howard S. Levy, *Chinese Footbinding: The History of a Curious Erotic Custom* (New York, 1966), pp. 192, 195.

54. Levy, *Chinese Footbinding*, pp. 194–195.

55. Zhou Zhifu, *Zhenliu dawen* (Pillow talks) (Hong Kong, 1955), p. 47.

56. See Mackerras, *Rise of the Peking Opera*, p. 149.

57. From *Jintai canli ji*, in Aoki Masaru, *Zhongguo jinshi xiqu shi*, p. 447.

58. Mackerras, *Rise of the Peking Opera*, p. 151. Only the great modern scholar Ch'i Ju-shan has attempted to defend the posthumous reputations of Qing actors by disputing the association between boy actors and prostitution. His main objection is that only close friends were allowed even to visit the home of an actor; for them to spend the night would have required friendship of the greatest intimacy. Ch'i's assessment is faulty on two counts, however. First, he refers to the habits of the best known and most successful actors. Performers who had already achieved a degree of popular success would have been free from the financial necessity of prostitution. Moreover, he neglects to note the murky distinction between outright prostitution and more subtle forms of patronage. The difference between close friends of a higher social status and sexual patrons would have been difficult to completely distinguish. See [Qi Rushan] Ch'i Ju-shan, *Guoqu mantan* (Discussions of the Chinese opera), vol. 1 (Taipei, 1956), pp. 36–37.

59. Mackerras, *Rise of the Peking Opera*, p. 138.

60. Chen Yinguan, as quoted in ibid., p. 100.

61. For an explanation of the pun linking Bi Yuan to this novel, see Ruan and Tsai, "Male Homosexuality in the Traditional Chinese Literature," p. 30.

62. Mackerras, *Rise of the Peking Opera*, pp. 87–88; also see Arthur Waley, *Yuan Mei: Eighteenth Century Chinese Poet* (Stanford, 1970), pp. 98–100. Interestingly, Li Guiguan later knew the literatus Zhao Yi, a major source for understanding Qing homosexuality.

63. Mackerras, *Rise of the Peking Opera*, p. 93. Officials found consorting with female prostitutes could be stripped of their rank; see Bodde

and Morris, *Law in Imperial China*, pp. 435–436. Marriages between female prostitutes and officials were also forbidden; see ibid., p. 259.

64. Mackerras, *Rise of the Peking Opera*, p. 141.

65. Waley, *Yuan Mei*, p. 27. As throughout this book, I have rendered Chinese names according to pinyin romanization.

66. Wuxia Ameng, ed., *Duanxiu pian* 9:15A.

67. The author and date of publication are often incorrectly given as Chen Senshu and 1852. This mistake was even made by Lu Xun. For the publishing history and true authorship, see Liu Ts'un-yan, *Chinese Popular Fiction in Two London Libraries* (Hong Kong, 1967), pp. 131, 134–137; and [Sun Kaidi] Sun K'ai-ti, *Zhongguo tongsu xiaoshuo shumu* (Bibliography of Chinese popular fiction [new edition]), rev. ed. (Taipei, 1983), p. 147.

68. The following observations on *Pinhua baojian* were made in [Lu Xun] Lu Hsun, *A Brief History of Chinese Fiction*, trans. Yang Hsien-yi and Gladys Yang (Beijing, 1959), pp. 319–322, 417.

69. In fact, the novel's alternate title is given as *Qia qing yi shi* (A history of fortune, passion, and indulgence).

70. Chen Sen (Shi Han Shi), *Pinhua baojian*, p. 1.

71. There are many other similarities between Baoyu and Ziyu, the most obvious being the resemblance of names. Both names contain the character *yu* (jade). Like Baoyu's, Ziyu's jade is of supernatural origins. See ibid., p.2.

72. I have used the translation of Ruan and Tsai, "Male Homosexuality in the Traditional Chinese Literature," p. 31, with modifications.

73. Ibid., changing "normal" and "abnormal" to "acceptable" and "unacceptable" to avoid Ruan and Tsai's anachronism.

74. [Lu Xun] Lu Hsün, *Brief History of Chinese Fiction*, pp. 321–322.

75. From [Sima Qian] Ssu-ma Ch'ien, *Records of the Grand Historian* 2:467.

Epilogue

1. Arthur Kleinman and David Mechanic, "Some Observations of Mental Illness and Its Treatment in the People's Republic of China," *Journal of Nervous and Mental Disease* 167, no. 5 (1979): 272. For Taiwan, see Tseng Wen-shing and Hsu Jing, "Chinese Culture, Personality Formation, and Mental Illness," *International Journal of Social Psychiatry* 16, no. 1 (1969): 5–14.

2. Fang-fu Ruan and Yung-mei Tsai, "Male Homosexuality in Contemporary Mainland China," *Archives of Sexual Behavior* 17, no. 2 (1988): 189–199.

3. Pai Hsien-yung [Bai Xianyong], "A Sky Full of Bright, Twinkling Stars," in *Wandering in the Garden, Waking from a Dream: Tales of Taipei Characters*, trans. Pai Hsien-yung and Patia Yasin (Bloomington, Ind., 1982), pp. 143–144.

4. "Tongxinglian hefahua jianyi mingjie renshi qunqi fandui," in *Xingdao ribao* (June 9, 1983).

5. For Puyi's homosexuality, see Jerome Ch'en, "The Last Emperor of China," *Bulletin of the School of Oriental and African Studies* 28, no. 3 (1965): 340–341n. 8; and Henry McAleavy, *A Dream of Tartary* (London, 1963), p. 238; also Pan Jijiong, *Modai huangfei* (The last imperial concubine), vol. 2 (Hong Kong, 1957), p. 22.

6. Ezra F. Vogel, "The Unlikely Heroes: The Social Role of the May Fourth Writers," in *Modern Chinese Literature in the May Fourth Era*, ed. Merle Goldman (Cambridge, Mass., 1977), pp. 145–146.

7. [Ba Jin] Pa Chin, *Family*, trans. Olga Lang (New York, 1972), pp. 64–65.

8. Daniel W. Y. Kwok, *Scientism in Chinese Thought* (New Haven, 1965), p. 12.

9. From the advice column "Yangzi zhuanlan," *Lianhe bao* (April 4, 1982).

10. [Peng Huaizhen] P'eng Huai-chen, *Tongxinglian, zisha, jingshenbing* (Homosexuality, suicide, and mental illness) (Taipei, 1983).

11. For examples of press accounts of the suicide of homosexuals, see "Duanxiu fentao pi wei pangren burong" (Passion of the cut sleeve and half-eaten peach was unendurable), *Xingdao ribao* (November 3, 1980); and "Zhuang Kali Li Guanlong zisha" (Zhuang Kali and Li Guanlong commit suicide), *Zhongguo shibao* (August 20, 1985). For descriptions of one raid on a gay meeting place, the Golden Peacock bar, see "Jin Kongque you nan pei jiu" (The Golden Peacock has men to go with the wine), *Lianhe bao* (April 10, 1983), which includes a list of some patrons; as well as the cleverly titled article "Kongque duo nan fei" (Many men fly from the Peacock), *Shibao zhoukan* (April 17, 1983). A particularly gruesome murder involving homosexuality in 1982 received extremely wide coverage in Taiwan; see "Zheng Mingshan gongcheng sha A Zhong" (Zheng Mingshan confesses to murdering A Zhong), *Lianhe bao* (July 28, 1982). And for examples of anxious letters, see the advice columns in the December 25, 1981, and January 12, 1983, issues of *Lianhe bao*.

12. "'Boli quan' bingtai bianben jiali, 'duanxiu pi' fengqi yingyu ezhi" (The disorder of the "glass circle" alters the fundamentals and becomes more terrible; the "passion of the cut sleeve" should be stopped), *Zhongguo shibao* (April 11, 1983).

13. Information on homosexuality in the contemporary People's Republic is extremely limited; see Ruan and Tsai, "Male Homosexuality in Contemporary Mainland China." Information for Taiwan is more copious, though of low quality. See [Peng Jiaxing] P'eng Chia-hsing, *Tongxinglianzhe de ai yu xing* (Homosexuals' love and sex) (Taipei, 1987); Huang Sha et al., "Bugan shuo chu kou de ai" (The love that dare not speak its name), *Renjian* 7 (May 1986): 20–45 (4 parts); [Er Dong] Ehr Tung, *Bugan shuo chu kou de ai* (The love that dare not speak its name) (Taipei, 1985); [Hu Yiyun] Hu I-yün, *Toushi boli quan mimi* (Exposing the secrets of the glass circle) (Taipei, 1985); [Lin Jiandong] Lin Chien-tung, *Aisi fengbao* (The AIDS controversy) (Taipei, 1985); Peng Huaizhen, *Tongxinglian, zisha, jingshenbing*. Articles on gay life appear regularly in Taiwanese newspapers and magazines, although the tone is usually sensationalistic.

Appendix

1. Barry Chua and S. H. Chua, "A Brief History of Chinese Lesbianism, Part I," *Boston Asian Gay Men and Lesbians Newsletter* (April 1988), p. 9.

2. Wilbur, *Slavery in China*, p. 431.

3. Ibid., pp. 424–425.

4. Xiaomingxiong, *Zhongguo tongxingai shilu*, p. 273.

5. McMahon, *Causality and Containment*, p.46.

6. F. Lieh-Mak, K. M. O'Hoy, and S. L. Luk, "Lesbianism in the Chinese of Hong Kong," *Archives of Sexual Behavior* 12, no. 1 (1983): 22–23.

7. For examples see Franzblau, *Erotic Art of China*, print 28, as well as the prints in Robert Hans Van Gulik, *Erotic Colour Prints of the Ming Period, with an Essay on Chinese Sex Life from the Han to the Ch'ing Dynasty, B.C. 206–A.D. 1644*, 3 vols. (Tokyo, 1951).

8. Levy, *Chinese Footbinding*, p. 143.

9. Marjorie Topley, "Marriage Resistance in Rural Kwangtung," in *Women in Chinese Society*, ed. Margery Wolf and Roxane Witke (Stanford, 1975), pp. 76–77.

10. Van Gulik, *Sexual Life in Ancient China*, pp. 163–166; Van Gulik, *Erotic Colour Prints*.

11. Franzblau, *Erotic Art of China*, print 39.

12. The play is also known as "The Fragrance of Beauties" ("Meiren xiang"); see Nathan K. Mao and Liu Ts'un-yan, *Li Yü* (Boston, 1977), p. 148.

13. Paul S. Ropp, *Dissent in Early Modern China: Ju-lin wai-shih and Ch'ing Social Criticism* (Ann Arbor, Mich., 1981), pp. 146–147.

14. Cao Xueqin and Gao E, *Story of the Stone* 3:132–133.

15. Ibid., p. 237. Transvestism of women and men is a common theme throughout Chinese prose. In most cases it appears independently from homosexuality and consequently has not been dealt with in this study.

16. Xiaomingxiong, *Zhongguo tongxingai shilu*, p. 274.

17. Cui Lingqin, *Jiao fang ji jianding*, annotated by Ren Bantang (Shanghai, 1962), pp. 50–52.

18. *Qingbei leichao*. An epitome of this novel is given in Xiaomingxiong, *Zhongguo tongxingai shilu*, pp. 275–276.

19. "Tongxinglian shaonü zubang guihun" (A gang of young female homosexuals hangs out together), *Shijie ribao* (May 7, 1988).

20. Topley, "Marriage Resistance," p. 76.

21. Lieh-Mak, O'Hoy, and Luk, "Lesbianism," p. 23. The related "hairdressing" ritual of the Guangzhou region seems to have been primarily nonsexual; see Topley, "Marriage Resistance," p. 81. A complete description of this and related practices can be found in Andrea Sankar, "Sisters and Brothers, Lovers and Enemies: Marriage Resistance in Southern Kwangtung," *Journal of Homosexuality* 11, nos. 3–4 (1985): 69–82.

22. Chen Dongyuan, ed., *Zhongguo funü shenghuo shi* (History of Chinese female life) (Shanghai, 1937), p. 300. This section is excerpted from Zhang Xintai's *Yueyou xiaozhi* (Short record of travels in Guangdong). The editor appends his own judgment: "Because homosexual desire leads to non-marriage, it is truly an offense against heaven. It is very harmful to women's health and strength. . . . Women passing time unmarried sink to homosexuality. Since it is extremely widespread, this is truly a great problem."

23. Topley, "Marriage Resistance," p. 76.

24. Cao Xueqin and Gao E, *Story of the Stone* 3: 375, 551–553.

Glossary of Chinese Terms

ai ren 愛人
bi 嬖
chang 娼
chong 寵
di 弟
dui shi 對食
en 恩
fufu 夫婦
hou ting 後庭
ji 婜
jiao 叫
jijian 雞姦
junzi 君子
lian 孌
ling 陵
long 龍
mei 美
mei ren 美人
menzi 門子
nanfeng (a) 男風
nanfeng (b) 南風
nanfeng shu 南風樹
nanse 男色
ning 佞

qi 契
qidi 契弟
qing 情
qixiong 契兄
qiyou 契友
qu 娶
shan shu 善書
si 寺
tongxingai 同性愛
tongxinglian 同性戀
tu saizi 兔崽子
wan 彎
wan tong 頑童
xia zhuan 狎磚
xianggong 相公
xiao guanren 小官人
xiaoren 小人
xie xia 褻狎
xing 倖
xiong 兄
yu 玉
ze 澤
zhengjing 正經
zhi 痔

Bibliography

WORKS IN CHINESE AND JAPANESE

Aoki Masaru. *Zhongguo jinshi xiqu shi.* Hong Kong, 1975.

Ba Jin. *Jia.* Beijing, 1981.

[Bai Xianyong] Pai Hsien-yung. "Jia Baoyu de suyuan: Jiang Yuhan yu huaxi ren—jianlun Honglou meng de jieju yiyi." *Lianhe wenxue* 15 (January 1986): 25–30.

———. *Niezi.* Taipei, 1983.

———. *Taibei ren.* Taipei, 1971.

Ban Gu. *Han shu.* Beijing, 1974.

Bo Xingjian. "Tiandi yinyang jiaohuan dale fu." In *Shuangmei ying'an congshu,* edited by Ye Dehui Repr. Hong Kong, n.d.

Cao Xueqin and Gao E. *Honglou meng jiaozhu.* Edited by Qi Yong et al. Taipei, 1984.

Chen Dongyuan, ed. *Zhongguo funü shenghuo shi.* Shanghai, 1937.

Chen Qitian, ed. *Han Fei Zi jiaoshi.* Taipei, 1958.

Chen Sen (Shi Han Shi). *Pinhua baojian.* Taipei, 1984.

Chūgoku no hakubutsukan. Vol. 4. Tokyo and Beijing, 1982.

Cui Lingqin. *Jiao fang ji jianding.* Shanghai, 1962.

Doi Yoshiko. *Kodai Chūgoku no gazōseki.* Kyoto, 1986.

[Du Zhengsheng] Tu Cheng-sheng. *Zhoudai chengbang.* Taipei, 1979.

[Er Dong] Erh Tung. *Bugan shuo chu kou de ai.* Taipei, 1985.

He Liangjun, ed. *Yu lin.* Taipei, 1972.

He Xiu et al., eds. *Chunqiu Gongyang zhuan zhu shu.* Shanghai, Sibu bei yao, n.d.

Hong Ye, ed. *Maoshi yinde.* Tokyo, 1962.
———. *Mozi yinde.* Beijing, 1948.
———. *Xunzi yinde.* Beijing, 1950.
Hou Lichao. *Zhongguo meinanzi zhuan.* Taipei, 1986.
[Hu Yiyun] Hu I-yün. *Toushi boli quan mimi.* Taipei, 1985.
Huang Sha et al. "Bugan shuo chu kou de ai." *Renjian* 7 (May 1986): 20–45. 4 parts.
Huang Shi, ed. *Huang Shi yishu kao.* 100 vols. 1865.
Lanlingxiaoxiaosheng. *Jin Ping Mei quantu.* N.p., n.d.
Li Baiyao, ed. *Bei Qi shu.* Beijing, 1974.
Li Hengmei. "Woguo yuanshi shehui hunyin xingtai yanjiu." *Lishi yanjiu* 2 (1986): 95–109.
Li Yanshou, ed. *Bei shi.* Beijing, 1974.
———. *Nan shi.* Beijing, 1973.
Li Yu. *Jiean laoren manbi.* Beijing, 1982.
Li Yu. *Shier lou.* Taipei, 1980.
———. *Wusheng xi xiaoshuo.* In *Li Yu quanji,* edited by Helmut Martin, pp. 5381–5453. Taipei, 1970.
[Lin Jiandong] Lin Chien-tung. *Aisi fengbao.* Taipei, 1985.
Lin Zaiqing. *Chengzhai zaji.*
Liu Xi. *Shiming kaoshi.* Taipei, 1978.
Liu Xiang, ed. *Zhanguo ce.* 3 vols. Shanghai, 1978.
Liu Xu. *Jiu Tang shu.* Beijing, 1974.
Liu Yiqing. *Shishuo xinyu.* Edited by [Liu Shengzhai] Liu Sheng-chai. Taipei, 1985.
Lu Lin. *Jin Bawang gushi.* In *Huang Shi yishu kao,* edited by Huang Shi, vol. 79. 1865.
Meng Yuanlao. *Dongjing menghua lu.* Beijing, 1959.
Pan Jijiong. *Modai huangfei.* 2 vols. Hong Kong, 1957.
[Peng Huaizhen] P'eng Huai-chen. *Tongxinglian, zisha, jingshenbing.* Taipei, 1983.
[Peng Jiaxing] P'eng Chia-hsing. *Tongxinglianzhe de ai yu xing.* Taipei, 1987.
[Qi Rushan] Ch'i Ju-shan. *Guoqu mantan.* 2 vols. Taipei, 1956.
Qu Yuan. *Li sao zhengyi.* Edited by Yu Xueman. Hong Kong, 1955.
Ruan Ji. *Ruan Bubing yong huai shi zhu.* Beijing, 1957.
Shen Defu. *Bizhou xian shengyu.* Taipei, 1969.
Shen Yue, ed. *Song shu.* Beijing, 1974.

Sima Qian. *Shi ji.* Beijing, 1974.

Song Ci. *Buzhu xi yuan lu jizheng.* 1904.

Song Lian, ed. *Yuan shi.* Beijing, 1974.

Song Xuwu. *Xi Han huobi shi chugao.* Hong Kong, 1971.

[Sun Kaidi] Sun K'ai-ti. *Zhongguo tongsu xiaoshuo shumu.* Rev. ed. Taipei, 1983.

[Sun Xingyan] Sun Hsing-yen, ed. *Shangshu jinguwen zhushu.* Guangwen shuju edition. N.p., n.d.

Tang Xianzu. *Tang Xianzu mudan ting kao shu.* Taipei, 1969.

Tuo Tuo. *Song shi.* Beijing, 1974.

Wang Chong. *Lun heng jiao shi.* Edited by Huang Hui. Taipei, 1983.

Wang Shunu. *Zhongguo changji shi.* Shanghai, 1935.

Wei Shou, ed. *Wei shu.* Beijing, 1974.

Weixingshi guanzhaizhu. *Zhongguo tongxinglian mishi.* Hong Kong, 1964.

Wu Jingzi. *Rulin waishi.* 4 vols. Beijing, 1975.

Wu Zewu. *Yanzi chunqiu jishi.* 2 vols. Beijing, 1962.

Wuxia Ameng, ed. *Duanxiu pian.* In *Xiangyan congshu,* vol. 9, 2:1A–22A. Shanghai, 1909–1911.

Xiangyan congshu. Shanghai, 1909–1911.

Xiao Zixian, ed. *Nan Qi shu.* Beijing, 1974.

Xiaomingxiong [Ng Siu-ming]. *Zhongguo tongxingai shilu.* Hong Kong, 1984.

Xie Zhaozhe. *Wuza zu.* Shanghai, 1959.

Xingan huilan. Taipei, 1968.

Xu Dazhuo. *Jingyu lu.* In *Guocui congshu,* vol. 54. Shanghai, 1905–1909.

Xu Ling, ed. *Yutai xinyong.* Shanghai, 1936.

Xu Shen and Duan Yucai. *Shuowen jiezi zhu.* Shanghai, 1981.

Xue Yunsheng and Huang Jingjia. *Duyi cunyi zhong kanben.* Pt. 5, vols. 41–54. Taipei, 1970.

Yuan Mei. *Suiyuan sui bi.* Shanghai, 1935.

Zhang Wencheng. *Youxian ku.* Shanghai, 1955.

"Zhuang Kali Li Guanlong zisha." *Zhongguo shibao,* August 20, 1985.

Zhao Yi. *Gai yu cong kao.* 1790.

Zhou Mi. *Guixin zazhi.* In *Xuejin taoyuan,* edited by Zhang Haipeng, vols. 184–186. Shanghai, 1920.

Zhou Zhifu. *Zhenliu dawen.* Hong Kong, 1955.

Zhu Xi and Lu Zuqian. *Jinsi lu.* Shanghai, 1936.

WORKS IN WESTERN LANGUAGES

Alabaster, Ernest. *Notes and Commentaries on Chinese Criminal Law*. London, 1899.

[Ba Jin] Pa Chin. *Family*. Translated by Olga Lang. New York, 1972.

[Ban Gu] Pan Ku. *The History of the Former Han Dynasty*. 3 vols. Translated by Homer H. Dubs and P'an Lo-chi. Baltimore, 1955.

Barrow, Sir John. *Travels in China*. London, 1806.

Birrell, Anne, trans. *New Songs from a Jade Terrace: An Anthology of Early Chinese Love Poetry*. London, 1982.

Blacking, John. "Uses of the Kinship Idiom in Friendships at some Venda and Zulu Schools." In *Social System and Tradition in Southern Africa*, edited by J. Argyle and E. Preston-Whyte. Oxford, 1978.

Bodde, Derk, and Clarence Morris. *Law in Imperial China*. Cambridge, Mass., 1967.

Boswell, John. *Christianity, Social Tolerance, and Homosexuality: Gay People in Western Europe from the Beginning of the Christian Era to the Fourteenth Century*. Chicago, 1980.

Boxer, Charles, ed. *South China in the Sixteenth Century*. Nendeln, Liecht., 1967.

Bullock, T. H. "The Chinese Vindicated." *China Repository* 9 (September 1840).

Burton, Richard. *The Book of the Thousand Nights and a Night*. Vol. 10. New York, 1886.

[Caihengzi] Ts'ai-heng-tzu. "Boy Actors in Peking." In *The Essence of Chinese Civilization*, edited by Dun J. Li. New York, 1967.

Campbell, Persia Crawford. *Chinese Coolie Emigration to Countries Within the British Empire*. New York, 1923.

Cao Xueqin and Gao E. *The Story of the Stone*. 5 vols. Translated by David Hawkes and John Minford. Harmondsworth, Eng., and Bloomington, Ind., 1973–1987.

Chan, Albert. "Chinese-Philippine Relations in the Late Sixteenth Century and to 1603." *Philippine Studies* 26 (1978): 51–82.

———. "Peking at the Time of the Wanli Emperor (1572–1619)." In *International Association of Historians of Asia Second Biennial Conference Proceedings*, pp. 119–147. Taipei, 1962.

Chan, Wing-tsit. *A Sourcebook in Chinese Philosophy*. Princeton, 1963.

Chang, K. C., ed. *Food in Chinese Culture: Anthropological and Historical Perspectives*. New Haven, 1977.

Chavannes, Edouard. *La sculture sur pierre en Chine au temps des deux dynasties Han*. Paris, 1893.

Ch'en, Jerome. "The Last Emperor of China." *Bulletin of the School of Oriental and African Studies* 28, no. 3 (1965): 336–355.

Ch'en, Paul Heng-chao. *Chinese Legal Tradition Under the Mongols: The Code of 1291 as Reconstructed*. Princeton, 1979.

Chen, Ta. *Chinese Migrations, with Special Reference to Labor Conditions*. Washington, D.C., 1923.

Chow, Yung-teh. *Social Mobility in China: Status Careers Among the Gentry in a Chinese Community*. New York, 1966.

Ch'ü, T'ung-tsu. *Han Social Structure*. Edited by Jack L. Dull. Seattle, 1972.

Chua, Barry, and S. H. Chua. "A Brief History of Chinese Lesbianism, Part I." *Boston Asian Gay Men and Lesbians Newsletter*, April 1988.

Cohen, Paul A. *Discovering History in China: American Historical Writing on the Recent Chinese Past*. New York, 1984.

Crompton, Louis. *Byron and Greek Love: Homophobia in 19th-Century England*. Berkeley and Los Angeles, 1985.

Crump, J. I., trans. *Chan-kuo Ts'e*. Oxford, 1970.

de Bary, William Theodore. "Individualism and Humanitarianism in Late Ming Thought." In *Self and Society in Ming Thought*, edited by de Bary, pp. 145–248. New York, 1970.

de Cruz, Gaspar. "Treatise in Which the Things of China Are Related at Great Length, with Their Particularities, as Likewise of the Kingdom of Ormuz." In *South China in the Sixteenth Century*, edited by Charles Boxer, pp. 45–240. Nendeln, Liecht., 1967.

Dollinger, John J. I. *The Gentile and the Jew in the Courts of the Temple of Christ: An Introduction to the History of Christianity*. Translated by N. Darnell. London, 1862.

Dover, K. J. *Greek Homosexuality*. New York, 1980.

Ducey, Charles. "The Life History and Creative Psychopathology of the Shaman." In *The Psychoanalytic Study of Society*, edited by Werner Nuensterberger, 7:173–230. New Haven, 1956.

Eberhard, Wolfram. *Guilt and Sin in Traditional China*. Berkeley and Los Angeles, 1967.

Egerton, Clement, trans. *The Golden Lotus*. 4 vols. London, 1939.

Frankel, Hans H. *The Flowering Plum and the Palace Lady: Interpretations of Chinese Poetry*. New Haven, 1976.

Franzblau, Abraham N. *Erotic Art of China: A Unique Collection of Chinese Prints and Poems Devoted to the Art of Love.* New York, 1977.

Freeman, Michael. "Sung." In *Food in Chinese Culture: Anthropological and Historical Perspectives,* edited by K. C. Chang, pp. 141–192. New Haven, 1977.

Gay, Judith. "'Mummies and Babies' and Friends and Lovers in Lesotho." *Journal of Homosexuality* 11, nos. 3–4 (1985): 97–116.

Gebhard, Paul. "Incidence of Overt Homosexuality in the United States and Western Europe." In *National Institute of Mental Health Task Force on Homosexuality: Final Report and Background Papers,* pp. 22–30. Washington, D.C., 1972.

Giallombardo, R. *Society of Women: A Study of a Women's Prison.* London, 1966.

Gichner, Lawrence E. *Erotic Aspects of Chinese Culture.* Washington, D.C., 1957.

Giles, Herbert. "The 'Hsi yüan lu' or 'Instructions to Coroners.'" *Proceedings of the Royal Society of Medicine* 27 (1924): 59–107.

Goldman, Merle, ed. *Modern Chinese Literature in the May Fourth Era.* Cambridge, Mass., 1977.

Goodrich, L. Carrington, ed. *Dictionary of Ming Biography 1368–1644.* 2 vols. New York, 1976.

Greenberg, David. *The Construction of Homosexuality.* Chicago, 1988.

Gronewold, Sue. *Beautiful Merchandise: Prostitution in China 1860–1936.* New York, 1982.

Hanan, Patrick. *The Invention of Li Yu.* Cambridge, Mass., 1988.

Harper, Donald John. "The 'Wu shih erh ping fang': Translation and Prolegomena." Ph.D. diss., University of California, Berkeley, 1982.

Harrisson, Tom. *Savage Civilization.* London, 1937.

Herdt, Gilbert. "Fetish and Fantasy in Sambia Initiation." In *Rituals of Manhood: Male Initiation in Papua New Guinea,* edited by Herdt, pp. 44–98. Berkeley and Los Angeles, 1982.

———. *Guardians of the Flutes: Idioms of Masculinity.* New York, 1981.

———. *The Sambia: Ritual and Gender in New Guinea.* New York, 1987.

Hillers, Delbert. "The Bow of Aqhat: The Meaning of a Mythical Theme." In *Orient and Occident,* edited by Harry A. Hoffman, Jr., pp. 71–80. Neukirchen-Vluyn, W. Ger., 1973.

Hsu, Cho-yun. *Ancient China in Transition: An Analysis of Social Mobility, 722–222 B.C.* Stanford, 1965.

———. *Han Agriculture: The Formation of Early Chinese Agrarian Economy*

(*206 B.C.–A.D. 220*). Edited by Jack L. Dull. Seattle, 1980.

Hulsewé, A. F. P. *Remnants of Ch'in Law.* Leiden, 1985.

Johnson, David George. "The Medieval Chinese Oligarchy: A Study of the Great Families in Their Social, Political, and Institutional Setting." Ph.D. diss., University of California, Berkeley, 1970.

"Journal of Occurrences." *China Repository* 5 (June 1835): 104.

Karlgren, Bernhard, trans. *The Book of Odes: Chinese Text, Transcription, and Translation.* Stockholm, 1950.

Kinsey, Alfred C., et al. *Sexual Behavior in the Human Male.* Philadelphia, 1948.

Kleinman, Arthur, and David Mechanic. "Some Observations of Mental Illness and Its Treatment in the People's Republic of China." *Journal of Nervous and Mental Disease* 167, no. 5 (1979): 267–274.

Kodera, Takashi James. *Dogen's Formative Years in China: An Historical Study and Annotation of the Hōkyō-ki.* Boulder, Colo., 1980.

[Kong Shangren] K'ung Shang-jen. *The Peach Blossom Fan* (*T'ao-hua-shan*). Translated by Chen Shih-hsiang, Harold Acton, and Cyril Birch. Berkeley and Los Angeles, 1976.

Kwok, Daniel W. Y. *Scientism in Chinese Thought.* New Haven, 1965.

Legge, James, trans. *The Chinese Classics.* 5 vols. Oxford and Hong Kong, 1868–1893.

Lethbridge, H. J. "The Quare Fellow: Homosexuality and the Law in Hong Kong." *Hong Kong Law Journal* 4, no. 3 (1976): 292–326.

Levy, Howard S. *Chinese Footbinding: The History of a Curious Erotic Custom.* New York, 1966.

———. *Chinese Sex Jokes in Traditional Times.* Repr. Taipei, 1974.

———, trans. *Translations from Po Chü-i's Collected Works.* 4 vols. Repr. New York, 1971.

[Li Ruzhen] Li Ju-chen. *Flowers in the Mirror.* Translated by Lin Tai-yi. Berkeley and Los Angeles, 1965.

Li Yu. "The Elegant Eunuch." In *Twelve Towers: Short Stories by Li Yü Retold by Nathan Mao.* Hong Kong, 1975.

———. *Jou pu tuan* (*The Prayer Mat of Flesh*). Translated by Franz Kuhn and Richard Martin. New York, 1963.

Lieh-Mak, F., K. M. O'Hoy, and S. L. Luk. "Lesbianism in the Chinese of Hong Kong." *Archives of Sexual Behavior* 12, no. 1 (1983): 21–30.

Liu Ts'un-yan. *Chinese Popular Fiction in Two London Libraries.* Hong Kong, 1967.

Liu, Wen-chi, and Irving Yucheng Lo, eds. *Sunflower Splendor: Three*

Thousand Years of Chinese Poetry. Garden City, N.Y., 1975.

[Liu Yiqing] Liu I-ch'ing. *Shih-shuo hsin-yü: A New Account of Tales of the World.* Translated by Richard B. Mather. Minneapolis, 1976.

[Lu Xun] Lu Hsün. *A Brief History of Chinese Fiction.* Translated by Yang Hsien-yi and Gladys Yang. Beijing, 1959.

McAleavy, Henry. *A Dream of Tartary.* London, 1963.

Mackerras, Colin P. *The Rise of the Peking Opera, 1770–1870: Social Aspects of the Theatre in Manchu China.* Oxford, 1972.

McLeod, Katrina C. D., and Robin D. S. Yates. "Forms of Ch'in Law: An Annotated Translation of the Feng-chen shih." *Harvard Journal of Asiatic Studies* 41, no. 1 (1981): 111–163.

McMahon, Keith. *Causality and Containment in Seventeenth-Century Chinese Fiction.* Leiden, 1988.

Mao, Nathan K., and Ts'un-yan Liu. *Li Yü.* Boston, 1977.

Marney, John. *Beyond the Mulberries: An Anthology of Palace-Style Poetry by Emperor Chien-wen of the Liang Dynasty (505–551).* Taipei, 1982.

Matignon, J. J. *Crime et misère en Chine.* Paris, 1901.

———. "Deux mots sur la pédérastie en Chine." *Archives d'anthropologie criminelle* 14 (1899): 38–53.

Meijer, M. J. "Homosexual Offenses in Ch'ing Law." *T'oung pao* 71 (1985): 109–133.

Murray, Stephen O. "The Mamlukes." In *Cultural Diversity and Homosexualities,* edited by Murray. New York, 1987.

Ng, Vivien W. "Ideology and Sexuality: Rape Laws in Qing China." *Journal of Asian Studies* 46, no. 1 (1987): 57–70.

Nivison, David S. *The Life and Thought of Chang Hsüeh-ch'eng (1738–1801).* Stanford, 1966.

Pai Hsien-yung [Bai Xianyong]. *Wandering in the Garden, Waking from a Dream: Tales of Taipei Characters.* Translated by Pai Hsien-yung and Patia Yasin. Bloomington, Ind., 1982.

Pereira, Galeote. "Certain Reports of the Province of China." In *South China in the Sixteenth Century,* edited by Charles Boxer, pp. 3–44. Nendeln, Liecht., 1967.

Renaudot, Abbé, trans. "An Account of the Travels of Two Mohammedans Through India and China in the Ninth Century." In *A Collection of the Best and Most Interesting Voyages and Travels in All Parts of the World,* edited by John Pinkerton, 7:179–230. London, 1811.

Riasanovsky, V. A. *Customary Law of the Mongol Tribes (Mongols, Buriats, Kalmucks).* Harbin, 1929.

Rickett, W. Allyn, trans. *Guanzi: Political, Economic, and Philosophical Essays from Early China.* Vol. 1. Princeton, 1985.

Ropp, Paul S. *Dissent in Early Modern China: Ju-lin wai-shih and Ch'ing Social Criticism.* Ann Arbor, Mich., 1981.

Ruan, Fang-fu, and Yung-mei Tsai. "Male Homosexuality in Contemporary Mainland China." *Archives of Sexual Behavior* 17, no. 2 (1988): 189–199.

———. "Male Homosexuality in the Traditional Chinese Literature." *Journal of Homosexuality* 14, nos. 3–4 (1987): 21–33.

Said, Edward. *Orientalism.* New York, 1978.

Sakai, T. *Studies of Chinese Shan-shu: Popular Books on Morality.* Tokyo, 1960.

Sankar, Andrea. "Sisters and Brothers, Lovers and Enemies: Marriage Resistance in Southern Kwangtung." *Journal of Homosexuality* 11, nos. 3–4 (1985): 69–82.

Schalow, Paul Gordon. "'The Great Mirror of Male Love' by Ihara Saikaku." 2 vols. Ph.D. diss., Harvard University, 1985.

Sheng, Wu-shan. *Die Erotik in China: Die Welt des Eros.* Basel, 1967.

Shively, Donald H. "Tokugawa Tsunayoshi, the Genroku Shogun." In *Personality in Japanese History*, edited by A. M. Craig and D. H. Shively, pp. 85–126. Berkeley and Los Angeles, 1970.

[Sima Qian] Ssu-ma Ch'ien. *Records of the Grand Historian of China.* Translated by Burton Watson. 2 vols. New York, 1961.

So, Kwan-wai. "Chu Hou-chao." In *Dictionary of Ming Biography 1368–1644*, edited by L. Carrington Goodrich, vol. 1. New York, 1976.

[Song Ci] Sung Tz'u. *The Washing Away of Wrongs: Forensic Medicine in Thirteenth-Century China.* Translated by Brian E. McKnight. Ann Arbor, Mich., 1981.

[Song Lian] Sung Lien. "The Yüan Code: Illicit Sexual Relations." In *The Essence of Chinese Civilization*, edited by Dun J. Li, pp. 408–413. New York, 1967.

Spence, Jonathan D. *Emperor of China: Self-Portrait of K'anghsi.* New York, 1975.

———. *The Memory Palace of Matteo Ricci.* New York, 1984.

Staunton, George Thomas. *Ta Tsing Leu Lee: Being the Fundamental Laws and a Selection from the Supplementary Statutes of the Penal Code of China.* London, 1810.

Tang Xianzu. *The Peony Pavilion (Mudan ting).* Translated by Cyril Birch. Bloomington, Ind., 1980.

Thoms, P. P., trans. "Prohibitions Addressed to Chinese Converts of the Romish Faith." *China Repository* 20 (February 1851): 85–94.

Topley, Marjorie. "Marriage Resistance in Rural Kwangtung." In *Women in Chinese Society*, edited by Margery Wolf and Roxane Witke. Stanford, 1975.

Tseng Wen-shing and Hsu Jing. "Chinese Culture, Personality Formation, and Mental Illness." *International Journal of Social Psychiatry* 16, no. 1 (1969): 5–14.

Van Gulik, Robert Hans. *Erotic Colour Prints of the Ming Period, with an Essay on Chinese Sex Life from the Han to the Ch'ing Dynasty, B.C. 206– A.D. 1644.* 3 vols. Tokyo, 1951.

——. *Sexual Life in Ancient China: A Preliminary Survey of Chinese Sex and Society from ca. 1500 B.C. till 1644 A.D.* Leiden, 1961.

Vaughan, J. D. *The Manners and Customs of the Chinese of the Straits Settlements.* Singapore, 1879.

Vogel, Ezra F. "The Unlikely Heroes: The Social Role of the May Fourth Writers." In *Modern Chinese Literature in the May Fourth Era*, edited by Merle Goldman, pp. 145–159. Cambridge, Mass., 1977.

Wagley, Charles. *Welcome of Tears: The Tapirape Indians of Central Brazil.* New York, 1977.

Wakeman, Frederic, Jr. *The Great Enterprise: The Manchu Reconstruction of Imperial Order in Seventeenth-Century China.* 2 vols. Berkeley and Los Angeles, 1985.

Waley, Arthur. *Yuan Mei: Eighteenth Century Chinese Poet.* Stanford, 1970.

——, trans. *The Book of Songs.* New York, 1937.

Waltham, Clae. *Shu Ching, Book of History: A Modernized Edition of the Translations of James Legge.* Chicago, 1971.

[Wang Chong] Wang Ch'ung. "*Lun heng*: Selected Essays of the Philosopher Wang Ch'ung." Translated by Alfred Forke. *Mitteilungen des Seminars für orientalische Sprachen* 10 (1907).

Watson, Burton, trans. *Han Fei Tzu: Basic Writings.* New York, 1964.

——. *Hsün Tzu: Basic Writings.* New York, 1963.

——. *Mo Tzu: Basic Writings.* New York, 1963.

Weber, Max. *The Protestant Ethic and the Spirit of Capitalism.* Translated by Talcott Parsons. New York, 1976.

Wiegand, Sister M. Gonsalva, ed. *The Non-Dramatic Works of Hrosvitha.* St. Louis, 1936.

Wilbur, C. Martin. *Slavery in China During the Former Han Dynasty, 206 B.C.–A.D. 25.* Chicago, 1943.

Williams, Walter L. *The Spirit and the Flesh: Sexual Diversity in American Indian Culture.* Boston, 1986.

Wolf, Margery, and Roxane Witke, eds. *Women in Chinese Society.* Stanford, 1975.

[Wu Jingzi] Wu Ching-tzu. *The Scholars.* Translated by Yang Hsien-yi and Gladys Yang. Beijing, 1957.

Yü, Ying-shih. *Trade and Expansion in Han China: A Study in the Structure of Sino-Barbarian Economic Relations.* Berkeley and Los Angeles, 1967.

[Zhang Wencheng] Chang Wen-ch'eng. *China's First Novelette: The Dwelling of the Playful Goddess.* Translated by Howard S. Levy. Tokyo, 1965.

[Zhu Xi] Chu Hsi and [Lu Zuqian] Lu Tsu-ch'ien. *Reflections on Things at Hand: The Neo-Confucian Anthology.* Edited by Wing-tsit Chan. New York, 1967.

Index

Compositor: Asco Trade Typesetting Ltd.
Text: Bembo
Display: Bembo
Printer: Maple-Vail Book Mfg. Group
Binder: Maple-Vail Book Mfg. Group